This particular set of notes is for a campaign speech made in Milwaukee, Wisconsin, on September 29, 1928, during the Presidential campaign.

THE HAPPY WARRIOR

F.D.R. Col.

The Happy Warrior

A biography of my Father
ALFRED E. SMITH

EMILY SMITH WARNER
with
HAWTHORNE DANIEL

DOUBLEDAY & COMPANY, INC.

GARDEN CITY NEW YORK 1956

LIBRARY OF CONGRESS CATALOG CARD NUMBER 56–9408

To my daughters,
Mary and Emily

Contents

ILLUSTRATIONS

Between pages 96–97

Mr. and Mrs. Alfred E. Smith at the time of their marriage

Alfred E. Smith when he was Speaker of the New York State Assembly

Catherine Mulvehill Smith, the Governor's mother

Between pages 192–193

The President of New York City's Board of Aldermen and his family

Alfred E. Smith in 1930

Governor Smith meets his daughter and son-in-law, Mr. and Mrs. John A. Warner

Governor Smith and his two younger sons

The Executive Mansion as it appeared during the years of Governor Smith's incumbency

Fishing continued to be one of the Governor's favorite sports

Campaigning for the Presidency in North Carolina during 1928

Boating on Peconic Bay in 1930

Between pages 288–289

Major Bowes' "Amateur Hour" in the 1930s

Governor and Mrs. Smith, accompanied by Bishop Ralph L. Hayes and Monsignor Fulton J. Sheen in 1937, when the Governor and his wife were received by His Holiness, Pope Pius XI

Governor Smith boards Wendell Willkie's campaign train during the 1940 Presidential campaign

Governor and Mrs. Smith take part in the Easter parade on Fifth Avenue in New York City on April 13, 1941

THE HAPPY WARRIOR

Oliver Street and the Lower East Side

NEW YORK is a city of neighborhoods. All the way from Coney Island to the Bronx that fact is evident. Flatbush differs as sharply from Morningside Heights as Albany from Omaha. Gramercy Park, Beekman Place, and Harlem are in many ways as individual and separate as Boston, Toledo, and Seattle. Even today these differences are obvious, but the neighborhoods of yesterday were even more distinct.

My earliest recollections are of one of these neighborhoods on the Lower East Side, where, on December 23, 1901, I was born not far from Brooklyn Bridge. I was the second of five children, all of whom were born in this area, though no two of us arrived at the same address. Each new member of the family necessitated a little more space, and that resulted in frequent moves, which ultimately brought us to Oliver Street, where we lived for more than twenty years. We were not the first of our family, however, to be born in that neighborhood. Our father had been born only five or six blocks away on South Street, and his father had actually been born on Oliver Street itself. More than a hundred years ago—long before the Civil War—the very neighborhood I knew as a child was home for earlier members of our family.

Our neighborhood was very sincerely religious. Largely Catholic, for many people of Irish and Italian extraction have long lived in the vicinity, the area forms a part of the parish of St. James, which, I have been told, included some eighteen thousand people in the early nineteen hundreds. And St. James' Church, only one short block from where we lived, occupied much the same position in James Street that the house in which we lived occupied in the corresponding block in Oliver Street.

The church naturally formed, as it still does, the heart and center of the parish, and in that compact neighborhood it was an intimate part of our daily lives. The rectory, standing back to back in relation to the church, is at 23 Oliver Street, and there has always been constant contact between the residents of the neighborhood, the priests who have occupied the rectory, and the church itself. Besides the church, however, another influence also serves to bind the neighborhood together. This is the parochial school at the corner of James Street and New Bowery and across James Street from the church itself. Associated with the church, it has taught boys and girls of the parish for generations. This school to which my brothers, my sister, and I all went was the one Father also attended.

It was in 1908 that we moved across Oliver Street to No. 25. Our old quarters had been a five-room, third-floor, walk-up apartment of the kind long known to New Yorkers as a "railroad" flat, with the rooms opening from one to the next in a row from the front of the building to the back. At our new address, however, we had a house all to ourselves. It was a structure of three stories and a basement, as the houses on both sides of it were, and with all of it except the third floor assigned to us we had much more room than we had ever had before. We rented the house from the church, and Father Curry, the pastor of St. James', who lived with several other priests in the rectory next door, reserved the top floor for the use of the rectory.

Though the neighborhood was heavily Catholic, it was not exclusively so. Other roots were deeply imbedded all about us. A small Spanish and Portuguese Jewish cemetery, which dates from 1656, still looks out through its sturdy iron fence onto New Bowery within a stone's throw of St. James' Church. And on Oliver Street, hardly farther from the Jewish cemetery in the other direction, stands a heavily columned Protestant church long known as the Mariners' Temple. Founded as a Baptist church late in the seventeen hundreds, it gained its nautical name because so many sailors from the sailing ships that formerly lay at the South Street piers attended services there.

Children were numerous in this neighborhood, and large families were common. When my brother Walter was born in 1909, he brought the number in our house to five, but that was not exceptional. Up the street a few doors Mr. and Mrs. Michael Rofrano also had five—all girls, whose ages more or less matched ours—while the Driscolls, who lived next door to them, had nine. The Mulligans, who lived next door to the Rofranos on the other side, had five of their own, and the Mannings, who lived three doors nearer us, also were the parents of five. These five families alone, all of whom lived on one side of the street within a stone's throw of each other, had twenty-nine children, and though the total number in the block was subject to much fluctuation as families came and went and as children were born and grew up, there were usually at least that many more, while endless numbers of others lived in nearby streets.

Among so many there were always plenty of any given age, and each of us formed our own friendships. My closest friends were Marion Riordan, Marie Nolan, and Edith and Olga Manning, whose fathers were important Oliver Street residents. Daniel Riordan first repre- sented our district in the state Assembly and then in Congress. Judge Nolan was a city magistrate, and Dr. Joseph Manning was a physician.

Others, writing of the Lower East Side of half a century ago, have spent much time describing ramshackle tenements, neighborhoods filled with poverty and crime, and streets lined with saloons and houses of very ill repute. Far be it from me to say that no such conditions ever existed there. But I cannot say too strongly that nothing of this nature existed in our neighborhood, and we children were never permitted to wander to other vicinities where we might come upon them. Except when the weather interfered, and when our attendance at school and church occupied our time, we played in the street as city children have always done. Once suppertime had come, however, we were called home, and home we stayed. To go out in the evening was a great event for us, and we seldom did so.

There was no wealth in our neighborhood, but neither was there any grinding poverty. Incomes were very much less than they are today, and commonly enough, I suppose, this family or that ran short of funds, but destitution was rare for the people were energetic and self- reliant.

This was the neighborhood in which every member of our family had been born, and Father himself was very intimately a part of it. His roots were deep in these surroundings, and because it is my purpose to tell what I can of him, I should begin by pointing out that it was here he absorbed a large part of what formed his character.

Even before we moved to Oliver Street, Father had been elected to the New York State Assembly, where he served from 1903 to 1915. Thus when the Assembly was in session—usually from January to

April—he spent most of his time in Albany. During the rest of the year, however, he had many political duties to perform, and much of the time, including almost every weekday evening, he was likely to be found in the office he maintained in the local Democratic club in Madison Street. Widely known as the "Downtown Tammany Club," this political organization occupied a two-story structure between Oliver and Catherine streets, and it was a local influence of exceptional importance.

Politics in the city of New York—Tammany Hall politics, that is—has always been an activity closely related to the lives, the problems, and the needs of those upon whose support Tammany depends, and the local Tammany clubs have usually been very human institutions. Each club has always known its neighborhood intimately, and the Downtown Tammany Club was an especially successful example.

As a child I knew merely that the club existed, and that in some way it was important. When we lived at 28 Oliver Street, it was possible to look out of our kitchen window into the second-story windows of the club, which stood just around the corner. The second floor of the clubhouse contained the "ballroom," and we often watched while dances and other parties were given there, but just why Father had to spend almost every evening at the club I did not know, though I understand it now. He went there so that anyone in the district who cared to see him could do so, and because most of the men were employed, they could come only in the evenings.

They came for a variety of reasons—economic, political, and personal. A man might come, for instance, because he was sick or out of a job. Another might come in the hope that his son—a policeman, possibly, or a fireman—could be transferred or put in line for promotion, and others, with endless problems, were forever wishful of seeing Tom Foley, the leader of the club, or John Mulligan, the Tammany captain of the district, or Father, who, now that he was an Assemblyman, was also a person of influence.

Tom Foley was the Tammany leader of the district—a warm and friendly person to whom, more than any other, Father owed his early political success. Originally a blacksmith, he had opened a saloon in 1872 at the corner of Oliver and Water streets, and for many years he lived at 15 Oliver Street.

"He was in politics practically all the time," Father said on one occasion, "but he was never very desirous of being in the front ... The force of circumstances drove him into the leadership . . . Nobody had the grip on the people Foley had."

Even when I was a child I knew him—a genial, smooth-shaven, moonfaced man—and every other child in the neighborhood knew him. Every year, when the Downtown Tammany Club held its outing at Sulzer's Harlem River Park on 126th Street and Second Avenue, a good nine miles uptown from Chatham Square, we all felt that Tom Foley was personally responsible for the affair. That was very largely true, just as it was that "Tom Foley's picnic" was not an outing merely for the voters of the district. He, personally, was responsible for the idea that included in these outings every family and all the children of the district. It was his idea, too, that, in addition to the usual supplies of food and the usual arrangements for the streetcars that took us uptown and back, there should be such huge supplies—wagonloads, in fact—of candy, toys, ice cream, and cake for the scores of chattering, perspiring, excited young people of the Second Assembly District of New York's Fourth Ward.

Children are apt to accept the normal activities of their elders without much question, and certainly that was true of me. I was much more conscious of my own little problems and affairs than I was of the remote and little understood activities that concerned my father. Thus our games, and our church and school activities, remain much more prominently in my mind than the explanations I overheard as Father told Mother of his activities in Albany.

Few people today will find it easy to understand how our family of seven was able to live in reasonable comfort on the salary Father received as a member of the Assembly, for it was only $125 a month. Yet we did, and we occasionally had a modest luxury or two. In 1905, when I was three, we rented a little cottage for the summer in Connecticut. We took a steamboat from Peck Slip all the way to Bridgeport, and from there went by trolley to Walnut Beach, where, I remember, the rooms of our cottage were divided from each other merely by partitions that did not go up to the rafters overhead.

I recall the events of those years only in bits and pieces, and small happenings are often clearer than larger and more important ones. When I was nine, for example, I had to have two teeth pulled. I have forgotten what the trouble was, but the coming ordeal seemed very great to me, and I remember how concerned I was when Father took me by trolley up to Fourteenth Street, where the dentist's office was.

But when I was given gas the teeth came out painlessly, and Father then took me down the street a way—perhaps it was to Hearn's—and, to my delight, bought me a parasol.

This, he told me, was "for one tooth," and for the other I had lost he bought me a pocketbook. Then, instead of taking me back to Chatham Square by trolley, he hailed a black and shiny hansom cab, and the two of us, together with the parasol and the pocketbook, rode all the way to Oliver Street in most unusual style.

In 1910, and for several years thereafter, we spent our summers in a house at Far Rockaway, where we children came to be intimately familiar with sand, sunburn, and salt water. During our very first summer there Father obtained a goat for us, which we named Jim. There was a set of harness for him, too, and a little blue wagon with the single word PATROL painted in gold on each side. Later we were given a second goat named Billy and a little two-wheeled sulky for him to pull. The goats and their harness, as well as the two small vehicles, were somehow transported to Oliver Street. Adjoining our back yard was the stable of a Madison Street undertaker, and it was here, in a stall not in use, that Jim and Billy were housed. Billy was an intractable creature, and the sulky he drew could carry only one small passenger at a time, but Jim was patient and amenable, and the "patrol wagon" was a roomy little vehicle. Thus, at one time or another, most of the children in Oliver Street rode behind Jim, though he was never permitted to haul the patrol wagon out of our immediate neighborhood. I am not sure how long we kept the goats. After a time they were replaced by Shetland ponies, though these much more desirable pets always remained at Far Rockaway, where we saw them only during the summer.

When the Legislature was in session, Father always went to Albany on Monday afternoon, returning each Friday afternoon, and ultimately —I cannot say just when—Mother, my brother Alfred, and I regularly met him, on his return, at the Knickerbocker Hotel, which then stood at Forty-Second Street and Broadway. The three youngest members of the family, too small as yet for such adventures, were left with Sophie, our maid of all work—or later with Nellie—at home, but Mother, Alfred, and I, meeting Father at six or six-thirty, had dinner with him at the Knickerbocker and then went to the Palace Theatre in Times Square which presented for many years the very best that vaudeville had to offer.

For Alfred and me, and for Mother and Father, these were most enjoyable occasions, and I have never forgotten my feeling of importance as the waiters in the ornate old dining room of the Knickerbocker served us. The only trouble was that these dinners always came on Friday, and both Alfred and I, like many other Catholics, have little taste for fish. Thus week after week we studied all the delectable items on the menu, but ended up by ordering eggs prepared in one way or another. Even yet I remember how much I wanted some of the other and more wonderful dishes with which the Knickerbocker's menus always seemed to be so generously filled.

Since Father was in Albany all week long, or busy at the Downtown Tammany Club when the Legislature was not in session, he was seldom at home except on Sunday. Then, however, our house was a busy, entertaining place—especially on Sunday evenings.

On Sunday mornings we always went to church at ten o'clock. When church let out at eleven, we walked to Brooklyn Bridge, five blocks away, and across the bridge to where, not far from its Brooklyn end, our grandmother—Father's mother—lived with Aunt Mamie and her eight boys at 9 Middagh Street.

Almost invariably Father took some of his friends with him on that long Sunday-morning walk, and I almost always went, as well. Often, too, Alfred and Catherine joined us, and later Arthur and Walter. Sometimes friends of mine went too—Marion Riordan, Marie Nolan, and Edith and Olga Manning, perhaps—all eagerly talking about dresses, parties, boys, and anything else that popped into our heads.

With eight boy cousins of various ages we found 9 Middagh Street a sprightly, enjoyable place, though we usually stayed only half an hour or so. We entertained ourselves by playing the Victrola in the parlor while Father and the friends who had come with him were talking politics with Grandmother—a pastime at which she was adept and which she never failed to enjoy.

Coming back, we sometimes walked and sometimes rode the trolley, and Sunday afternoons had no regular pattern. Sunday evenings, however, usually saw any number of people gathered at our house. Judge and Mrs. Nolan, and Marie, were almost sure to be there, and both Jimmy Walker, who was then in the Assembly with Father, and his wife often came as well. It was not until much later that Jimmy Walker became Mayor of New York City.

Mrs. Walker had been on the stage before their marriage, and she sang very well, while Jimmy played the piano for her. Always an entertaining person, and the liveliest company, he had already written several songs, including the then well-known, "Will You Love Me in December as You Do in May?"

On one of those Sunday evenings when he was at the piano he began to play a piece that we had never heard before. He was forever improvising, so it was not surprising that he should bring forth a previously unheard tune. But now, to my unbounded delight, for I was only twelve, he gaily announced that the words and music of this selection had been written for and were especially dedicated to me. Whereupon Mrs. Walker, to her husband's accompaniment, began to sing the song.

I don't remember the air, and even the words escape me except for a single fragment. The title of the song was "Meet Me after School," and though I learned the words that very evening, I can recall only a single couplet:

> Meet me after school
> Down by the swimming pool.

I wish that I remembered more of that song. It was not great music, I know. And Jimmy Walker, though he had much innate ability, was in no sense a great man. Both he and that little song, however, had something bright and attractive about them, and I have never forgotten the schoolgirl thrill I felt that evening because of Jimmy Walker's generous and thoughtful gesture.

By now, of course, I was beginning to have a little more understanding of life in our section of the city. I looked askance at the tenements that lay beyond Madison Street, which we so seldom crossed, and I began to feel some trepidation as I passed certain doubtful addresses. White's Bakery and the Union Candy Shop were still familiar places to me, and I was quite at home in the Catherine Street grocery at which we dealt. Our Oliver Street block had no shops or stores except a laundry at one corner of Madison Street and a little grocery on the corner opposite. But I knew the drugstore on our side of Chatham Square as well as several places of business on Catherine and James streets, and some on Madison Street. There was a pickle factory directly across Madison Street from the Downtown Tammany Club, and I still remember the pungent aroma that emanated from it when the weather was warm and its doors were open.

Father was deeply immersed in politics during all these years, but I knew nothing at all about such matters and thought I cared less, though I knew that a certain kind of excitement got into the atmosphere of Oliver Street whenever Election Day arrived. But then came the election of 1913, which followed the unexpected death of Mayor Gaynor and the short incumbency of Ardolph L. Kline.

The campaign was an exciting one, with John Purroy Mitchel running on the Fusion ticket against McCall, the Tammany-supported Democratic candidate, and even I knew that something unusually important was under way. On the evening of Election Day I remember watching while Mother tied two brooms boldly upright on the iron railings that led down beside the six steps from our doorway to the sidewalk. The election returns were not yet in, but we good Tammany Democrats were confident of victory, and those two brooms, tied prominently there before our doorway, signified the "clean sweep" we were so sure to make. Later, however, the telephone bell rang. It was Father, calling from the Downtown Tammany Club.

"Take in the brooms," was his message to Mother. "We didn't make a clean sweep after all. Mitchel has won."

Such a defeat was of immense significance in our solidly Democratic and wholeheartedly Tammany district, and more than I realized, I suppose, it formed the topic of discouraged conversation. Once the election was over I gave the matter little attention. But sometime thereafter when, one Sunday noon, we were on our way back from Brooklyn and Father and two friends were talking politics ahead of where Marie Nolan and I were following, I overheard a remark that opened up an entirely new line of thought.

Up to now Father had been just my father—a kindly, thoughtful, generous person, firm, when firmness was needed, but, it seems to me, seldom lacking in understanding where youthful problems and shortcomings were concerned. Earlier that year he had been elected Speaker of the state Assembly and the whole family had gone to Albany to be present on the day he first presided. I had been deeply impressed by his obvious importance in those surroundings, but though I had begun to see him in a new light I gave the matter no special consideration. He was my father and I had not learned to look at him in any other way.

I loved him, but the love of children, real though it is, is more subconscious, I suppose, than conscious. Or at least that is the way I believe it was with me.

But now, while Marie and I were chattering, I saw that one of two men who had just passed Father paused and turned about to stare. I never knew who he was. I had never seen him before, and I doubt if I ever saw him again. But as he stood there with his companion, staring back at Father, Marie and I passed close beside him.

His obvious interest in Father had attracted my attention. Certainly I was alert when I heard him speak to his companion, and I have never forgotten what he said.

"There," he declared, "goes the next Mayor of New York."

That remark came as a great surprise to me. It told me Father was a public figure of much more than ordinary importance—something that had never before made so great an impression on me. I had realized when I had seen him mount the rostrum as Speaker of the Assembly that he was a person of real consequence, but in the light of this unexpected revelation, Father's familiar figure almost seemed to take on new characteristics. There was no change in his appearance, and yet, somehow, a change had come. Perhaps it was at that moment that my interest in politics began, for from then on I followed Father's career with ever growing interest.

CHAPTER TWO

Boyhood, Youth, Politics, and Marriage

AS I GREW OLDER I came to be very close to Father in his political activities, and ultimately, each time he was called upon to enter some new campaign, I was seldom very far from his elbow. During my youth and early teens, however, his campaigns, so far as I was concerned, were of little moment. He had first been elected a member of the New York State Assembly shortly before my second birthday, so I have no recollection of the event, but he was forced to run for re-election every year so long as he remained an Assemblyman, and I came to accept his campaigns as a regular part of life. Year after year the returns in our Assembly district showed so little variation that we children were never in doubt about the outcome, and were consequently little excited over these contests. It was not until much later that we learned—somewhat to our surprise—that political defeat for Father was a possibility after all.

Much has been written about Father's youth and early manhood. Still, I am sure that I can add at least a little to what has already been recorded of those years. My knowledge is, of course, secondhand. Father was always willing to tell about his early experiences, and I loved to listen. Therefore what I know of his formative years finds its source for the most part in what he himself told me. However, many facts are traceable to what others have had to say or have written about him, though I think it necessary to add that some of those accounts have been either inaccurate or actually imaginary.

I have already referred in some detail to our old Oliver Street neighborhood, but I feel the fact should be stressed that even when Father was born on South Street on December 30, 1873, the Smith family was not new to the area. Grandfather Smith—Alfred Emanuel Smith, Sr., that is—himself had been born on Oliver Street. I have been told that this event took place in 1840, but that may not be accurate. It certainly does not agree with the statement I also recall that he was fifteen years older than Grandmother Smith, who, we know, was born in 1850. But whatever the date of Grandfather Smith's birth—and 1840 cannot be so very far wrong—he was as much a part of this portion of the city as his son and his grandchildren were later. It was from here that he enlisted in a Civil War regiment that was sometimes referred to as the "Bowery Boys." I have no knowledge of any battles or campaigns in which he took part. His most notable action, so far as I know, had to do with a fire that took place in the Willard Hotel in Washington. Even in this connection I know no details except that he is said to have hung down from one of the upper windows in order to pull an endangered person up from the next floor below. But it is not surprising that we as children knew little about him, for he died when Father was only twelve, so that even Father felt impelled to say in his autobiography, "I do not remember ever hearing him tell where his parents came from."

Grandmother Smith, however, was a very real person in our lives, and one who impressed everyone who knew her. As I first remember her, she was only in her fifties though, childlike, I thought of her as being very old. She had carried many burdens, and may have appeared older than her years. My clearest recollection of her has to do not with her gray hair or her age, but with the keenness of her interest in politics and the eagerness Father always displayed in keeping her informed on all his activities.

Her own mother and father—Father's grandparents—were Thomas and Maria Mulvehill, both of whom were born in Westmeath, an inland Irish county which lies to the west of Dublin. It was Father's recollection that they came to America in 1841 on a packet ship of the Black Ball Line. These were sailing ships, and westward passages across the Atlantic in those days were usually slow. Father always said that in their case the crossing took sixty days. However, in view of the fact that the Black Ball Line prided itself on the "speed" of its ships, that voyage was either of exceptional slowness or has been inaccurately reported. Still, whatever the time of that crossing, it seems reasonably clear that their ship docked at the foot of Beekman Street, from which—so the family story goes—the young Irish immigrants, who had one infant son with them, walked only about three blocks before they saw, at the corner of Dover and Water streets, a sign which read "Rooms to Let."

Father told us that it was on the second floor of the building occupying that corner that his mother's parents established their first home in America, and it was there, above a grocery store on the first floor, that their daughter Catherine was born some nine years later—in 1850. The family still lived in those same second-floor rooms when Catherine Mulvehill attended St. James' School, which, in her girlhood, was located on Roosevelt Street, and while living in this house she also became acquainted with Alfred Emanuel Smith, the Civil War veteran, now a boss truckman, whose horses were kept in a nearby stable.

Grandfather himself had been born no more than three or four blocks away, and he was a widower with one small daughter when he married Catherine Mulvehill. This was in September 1872, and they went to live at 174 South Street, only some three blocks from the bride's birthplace and only one block farther from the bridegroom's. It was here, at the very end of the following year, that Father—Alfred Emanuel Smith, Jr.—was born.

The changes that have taken place in this part of New York in the years since Father's childhood are not easy to visualize. Where, for example, not a sailing ship is now to be seen at any commercial pier in the enormous port of New York, then the busy South Street piers, which formed the very center of the city's nautical affairs, were visited by little else. Here and there some tall-funneled paddle-wheel ferry nosed into its slip after each round trip to Brooklyn, but steamships, which in those days still usually carried auxiliary sails, only rarely crept in to take their places at the piers that more commonly accommodated tall-sparred sailing ships.

For the lack of any other playground the boys of the vicinity often congregated in South Street or on its piers. I remember hearing Father tell how he and his companions performed their boyish gymnastics on the long, thin bowsprits that thrust themselves out over the cobblestones and busy trucks of South Street: the bowsprits of clipper ships just in, perhaps, from around Cape Horn—of smaller, slower ships and barks and brigantines from the Mediterranean and North Sea ports—of coasting schooners from Maine or Massachusetts or Nova Scotia, some of which, no doubt, were on their way to or from the West Indies—and of fishing schooners that crowded in together in the redolent atmosphere of the big fish market at the foot of Fulton Street. And high above all this hung the slender, curving cables of the huge and slowly evolving Brooklyn Bridge, which plainly made a much greater impression on this growing South Street boy than all the ships that came and went from the many busy piers.

Father often said that he and Brooklyn Bridge "grew up together," and certainly no picture of that portion of the city in his boyhood would be complete without the still to be completed bridge standing in the background. In fact, it provided more than a mere background, for though the giant stone structure which supports the New York end of the cables was erected not far from where he lived, Brooklyn Bridge itself, arching high across the river, was being created cable by cable and bit by bit directly overhead. Work on the bridge had begun in 1870, the year before Father was born, but it was not opened for use until 1883, so it is no wonder that he felt that he and this great structure had "grown up" together. From the time of his earliest remembrance he had seen the work progress, and long before the enormous span was completed, his father, eager to cross the bridge before it was open to the public, took the boy on what must have been a real adventure in his young life, for the two of them, making their way from New York to Brooklyn along the board runways used by the workmen, were among the very early few who first crossed the river by that new route.

Working days were long and work was heavy in the 1870s. Sundays offered almost the only opportunity for relaxation. Thus Sundays were used to the full. At every opportunity throughout each summer the family went to Coney Island or Staten Island. In those days, too, for that was long before the port had so thoroughly contaminated its surrounding waters, Grandfather and many others often swam in the East River beneath the slowly growing bridge. So usual was this pastime that rows of bathhouses had been built near the ponderous base of the New York tower of the bridge, and it was here, with a rope about him to keep him from being swept away by the strong East River currents, that Father learned to swim.

By odd coincidence Father's only sister was born on his own second birthday—December 30, 1875—in the South Street house, and for the next nine years the family continued to live there. In 1884, however— the year after Brooklyn Bridge was opened—the house changed hands and the family moved to 316 Pearl Street, three blocks back from the waterfront. Ultimately, too—the year was 1885—the long hours and the heavy work that were a necessary part of the trucking business began to tell on Grandfather's health, and he had to find lighter employment.

He obtained a job as a watchman while trying to keep the trucking business going as well. It was not long, however, before his health broke entirely.

In the spring of 1886 the family moved again, this time to 12 Dover Street, which brought them once more almost directly beneath Brooklyn Bridge, and it was there, after a long illness, that Grandfather died the following November.

The family finances were at low ebb. The trucking business had been continued, but by degrees all but one horse and one truck had been disposed of in order to pay for medical expenses and keep the family going. When Grandmother and her children returned to the little flat in Dover Street after the funeral, she was, understandably, discouraged and downcast.

As Aunt Mamie, who was ten at the time, recalls that cold November day, there was no fire in the flat when they reached home from the cemetery, and they built one in the kitchen stove. Grandmother began to prepare their very simple supper, but her mind was elsewhere.

"I don't know where to turn," she said, more to herself, perhaps, than to her children. And Aunt Mamie remembers that it was Father who replied.

"I'm here," he said. "I can take care of you."

There was more to the problem, of course, than the boy understood, which is not surprising for he was only twelve. So pressing were the family's economic problems that on that very evening Grandmother, who had learned the trade of umbrella making before her marriage, took her young son with her and went to see the forelady of the umbrella factory in which she had formerly worked. Luckily the woman lived in nearby Madison Street, and luckily, too, a position was open. Working in the factory all day and adding to her earnings by taking "homework" with her each evening, she kept the family going for the ensuing year. The strain was too great, however. She could not keep it up. Now, assisted by her landlady, she rented a little shop that had long been vacant in the basement of the Dover Street house and purchased such supplies as were necessary for opening a small candy and grocery store. It was a miniature enterprise, yet it enabled Father and Aunt Mamie to attend school for the next two years. Grandmother tended the place when the two children were in school, but both of them took their turns at other times, and Father sold papers in the afternoons as well.

It is sometimes hard to understand how he found time for all he did, even as a boy. By his own account, for example, he was a Fire Department "buff." When he was a boy, these young enthusiasts were called "buffaloes," and at every opportunity he was at the enginehouse of Engine Company No. 32 in John Street, where he performed the usual duties assigned to such young volunteers. He frequently visited the Fulton Street firehouse, where his mother's brother, Peter Mulvehill, was for many years the driver of No. 10 truck. But this was not all. In addition to attending school, working behind the counter in the little store, and selling newspapers every afternoon, he was a member of the Altar Boys' Association of St. James' Church for five years, beginning when he was ten. He served regularly on the altar, and once when the boys drew lots to see who would serve at the early Masses during the winter, he was assigned to the six-o'clock Mass throughout the month of January.

Father was always interested in animal pets, and even under the limitations that surrounded him in his boyhood, he found opportunities to collect them. One wonders how he ever managed it, for he never explained in much detail. However, I often heard him refer to a strange assortment of boyhood pets, and in his autobiography he wrote that at one time he had "a West Indian goat, four dogs, a parrot and a monkey, all living in peace and harmony in the garret of the South Street house." Just how all these came into his possession at the same time I never learned, but sailors often had such pets, and from time to time no doubt some were willing to give them to the boys who played about the piers. And in those days before dog catchers and dog tags unattached dogs were numerous and easy to adopt.

One of the outstanding events of Father's boyhood was the great blizzard of 1888. It descended on the city on March 12, and, along with more impressive places of business, the little Dover Street candy and grocery store was buried beneath the snow. Father himself had put up the shutters the preceding evening, but after the storm the snow lay so deep that the little store was lost to sight. Because there was no way to enter the place from within the building, it was impossible to reopen it until noon on the day after the blizzard had ended. But Father, by his own admission, was not especially concerned about the inconvenience that any potential customers might experience, or even by any possible damage the merchandise might suffer. He was really troubled because the family's little Scotch terrier and her four puppies had been left without food in the room behind the store. They were in no danger except that the room was without heat, but Father was not content until the place was finally opened and the dogs were fed some twenty-four hours after the blizzard had ended. Once that had been accomplished, Father, along with many others, was attracted to the East River, which, for the first time in living memory, was solidly frozen from shore to shore. Groups of men and boys were on the ice, and some had already walked across to Brooklyn and back. Along with a number of other boys, Father naturally followed, but not long after he and his companions had returned, the ice broke up, one large floe carrying a score or more of people down the river toward the bay before they were finally rescued by river craft and set ashore again.

These details of life on the Lower East Side in the seventies and eighties are small but they may serve to give some inkling of Father's boyhood. The family had little of this world's goods, and during the years that immediately followed Grandfather's death, the margin between actual need and what it was possible for them to earn was very narrow indeed. Even at the lowest ebb of their fortunes, however, they were never destitute. They were self-reliant and resourceful, and always managed, though now and then with little or nothing to spare, to make their way in the world. By the spring of 1888, when Father was fourteen, the income from the store, though it was eked out by the sale of newspapers and by other minor earnings, proved too small to supply even the family's most modest needs. Consequently, about a month before he would have graduated from the eighth grade, Father left school and got a job as a "truck chaser." Working for a certain William J. Redmond, and being paid at the rate of three dollars a week, it was his task, in those days before the advent of the telephone, to hurry about the waterfront on a constant outlook for the trucks of his employer. This was necessary so that the drivers might be given any new instructions that current developments necessitated. Otherwise they would have lost valuable time in returning to the company's office or stable for new assignments.

Three dollars a week, of course, was important in the family's scheme of things. It was about now, however, that the little store had to be closed, and more income was urgently needed. Father began looking for other work, and he found it shortly as an assistant shipping clerk and "general all-round handy boy" for the oil firm of Clarkson & Ford in Front Street near Peck Slip.

On this new job he was paid the very acceptable sum of eight dollars a week, but even with this increase the family's needs were such that he found it necessary to earn additional money in the evenings. These evening tasks followed no set pattern. He accepted any job that came his way. One that was so out of the ordinary that he later occasionally mentioned it occupied him during the evening of September 7, 1892. This was when John L. Sullivan, the then reigning heavyweight champion, fought James J. Corbett for twenty-one rounds in New Orleans before going down in defeat, and Father, who was eighteen, was hired because he had "a good, loud voice" to read to an eager Lower East Side gathering the telegraphic reports of the contest as they came off the wire.

Not long after this, economic pressure forced another change, and Father deliberately set about finding a better paying job. It was in the Fulton Fish Market that he finally secured a place that paid all of twelve dollars a week—"a very good salary," he once wrote in telling of those days, and one that was augmented by the six dollars and a half a week that Aunt Mamie was now earning by addressing envelopes for a firm in Vesey Street.

Father's new position was with the wholesale commission house of John Feeney & Company, and when he wrote his autobiography more than thirty years later he explained that his position "had the lofty title of assistant bookkeeper." Despite the title, however, he was called upon to do anything that had to be done about the market. Happily, his "very good salary" was not all he received, for he and the firm's other employees were permitted to take home as much fish as they wanted for the use of their families and themselves. Father naturally took advantage of this opportunity, as all the others did. In fact, he took fish home so regularly that he may not have been entirely conscious that he was exaggerating when he later wrote about "the complete fish diet" upon which he and his mother and sister subsisted at this time.

Much has been written about Father's connection with the Fulton Fish Market, but he was employed there for less than two years. "Assistant bookkeeper" though he was called, he helped handle endless barrels of fish and large quantities of cracked ice. He also attended to certain record-keeping tasks, though these took little of his time, despite his title. And the task to which he most frequently referred in later years was the one that armed him with a strong pair of marine glasses and took him up to the roof of the market, from which he watched for those returning fishing craft with which the company dealt.

As they made their way back to New York Harbor and up the East River to the Fulton Fish Market, these fishing smacks often came by way of Buttermilk Channel, which lies between Governor's Island and Brooklyn, and from the roof of the market they could usually be seen and recognized as they rounded the island's easternmost tip a mile and a half away, perhaps, or a little more. It was important that they be seen and recognized at the very earliest moment, for by watching carefully to see whether the incoming craft rode high in the water or low, one could make a useful guess as to the size of the catch. The advance notice thus gained was usually not very great, and even the sharpest eye could not estimate the catch with much accuracy. Nevertheless, in the hands of a competent commission merchant even the fragmentary and approximate information sometimes proved useful. It might, for instance, give a slight advance warning of the arrival of a glut or might foretell a scarcity. When wind and tide speeded the arrival of the incoming craft, this information proved of very little help, but sometimes adverse winds and currents in Buttermilk Channel and the East River held them up for some time after they had been sighted, and the market price of whatever kind of fish the incoming craft was known to be carrying shifted up or down depending upon the apparent size of the slowly arriving catch.

Watching from the roof, however, occupied little of Father's time. More often than not he was busy at heavier tasks. He worked from four o'clock each morning—except on Fridays, when he arrived at three—to four in the afternoon, when the market closed, but though his pay was well above the average of that being earned by boys who had not quite reached manhood, it was not as much as the family really needed, even when it was supplemented by Aunt Mamie's earnings. It was on that account, as well as because the work was heavy and the hours not to his liking, that Father looked farther afield and found a job with the Davison Steam Pump Works, which then was located on Wythe Avenue, Brooklyn. He was hired as a shipping clerk, but this title, like the one he had been given at the Fulton Fish Market, did not accurately suggest his duties. "Clerk" he may have been when, at times, he had to record something about the steam pumps and pipes and

fittings in which the firm dealt. But he had to handle those heavy
supplies too, and it is fortunate that he had by now grown to be a
sturdy young man who, though of only medium height, was strong
enough for even this heavy work. He actually did not have to be at
work until seven. Still, it was a long way to the Davison plant in
Brooklyn.

Outside of the increase in pay that this new job brought, there was
little else about it that attracted Father. Certainly his later references
to it were much less frequent than the comments he made about the
Fulton Fish Market, though that may have been due, in part at least,
to his sense of humor, which probably detected something colorful
and diverting in the fish market that was lacking in the steam pump
works in Williamsburg. Father seldom spoke of the place, and though
he took the job because the pay was better, I never heard him say just
what the salary was. I am sorry that I know so little about this particular job, for it was the last one he held before his political career actually
began, and it is quite possible—though I recall nothing he ever said that
bears me out—that this apparent lack of interest in his work in the
steam pump plant was what made him turn elsewhere, thereby causing
him, at last, to enter the field that occupied him for the remainder of
his life.

Perhaps no greater change has taken place on the Lower East Side
since the 1880s and 1890s than that which has to do with politics. It
was Father's belief that this change came about largely because of the
disappearance of the neighborhood spirit. When he was a boy, and even
when my brothers, my sister, and I were children in Oliver Street, the
city's various localities were integrated communities. Everyone was
widely acquainted with his neighbors, and this acquaintance amounted
to very much more than the halfhearted nodding acknowledgment of
each other's presence that sometimes passes for neighborliness today.
There was something sincere and meaningful in the friendships of
those days, and whole neighborhoods were bound together thereby.
Every birth or wedding or death was a significant event, and not to
know one's neighbors was as unlikely then as it is common now.

Every neighborhood had its meeting place. The policeman on the
beat knew everyone by name, and was equally well known by everyone.
And just as each person knew his own address, so he also knew the
number of his Assembly district, and even of his precinct. The police

captain of each precinct was known and recognized and spoken to by everyone even when he was out of uniform, and few people failed to know their Alderman, their Assemblyman, and the leader of the local political club. In every section of the city widespread interest was always evident in matters relating to neighborhood welfare. This interest was constant, too, and meetings at which such matters were discussed were both frequent and well attended.

It is not unlikely, of course, that the comparative lack of diversions and the inadequacy of transport played an important part in increasing community interests. There were no motion picture theaters, no subways, and no automobiles. There were elevated lines, but transportation about the city was nevertheless slow, and for that reason alone each neighborhood tended to become more unified and integrated. Incomes were limited, luxuries were few, and the people of those days were apt to look to each other for diversion.

Under these conditions it was natural that practically all the men, and even many of the older boys, should interest themselves in politics. There was an aura about every sort of public employment that has been lost in these later days. As Father once pointed out, few bank clerks of the eighties and nineties earned as much as a policeman or a fireman, and because most appointments to the police force and the Fire Department were made as a result of neighborhood politics, those who obtained them were usually well and favorably known. And that was also true of other city employees.

To a greater extent than may have been apparent, this natural and widespread interest in politics was directed into practical political channels by the political clubs. Each club took a prominent part in the annual elections, but in addition to that it also played an important part in all sorts of charitable and social activities. Then, too, anyone in the neighborhood could go to the club at any time for almost any kind of advice, and the club was always there when a person found himself in trouble.

Tammany was the dominant political force in New York in those days, and the various local Tammany clubs were widely known for their interest in the personal affairs not only of their members, but also of everyone else in the area. Collectively they were a powerful influence in city politics, but to the local resident the neighborhood club he knew was usually a very human and a very helpful institution. Many a ton of coal was delivered in those days by order of the local club when some family would otherwise have been without fuel. Generous baskets of food and packages of clothing were frequently provided for orphaned families or families stricken by serious illness. Hospital and other medical care were frequently provided and many a boy—many a girl, too— found work as a result of help that was given. Christmas parties, as well as summer picnics, were regular events, and whole neighborhoods were usually included at such times. These clubs were immensely important in neighborhood affairs, and young men hoping for appointment to almost any city job, or intent on making their way up the political ladder, found it advisable to visit them in the evenings.

Success in politics—even success in neighborhood political club politics—has always required more than merely a willingness to hang around the club. An objective observer of politicians as a group is apt to agree that, with very rare exceptions, they are likable as individuals. For the most part, and regardless of party affiliation, they find it easy to be friendly. They are almost always interested in people, and often they are inclined by their very natures to be helpful to those about them. There are exceptions to every rule, of course, in politics as elsewhere. Nevertheless, in this field especially, the ability to make friends and to hold them is of great importance. And Father, even as a boy, seems to have been fortunate in this regard.

His education was limited. He attended St. James' Parochial School only from the autumn of 1880 to the early spring of 1888, and had no other formal education. So far as I know, his scholastic record was not outstanding. On the other hand, the school he attended was an especially good one. In this connection it is interesting to note, in view of the many changes that have taken place on the Lower East Side since then, that in the 1880s St. James' was one of the leading Catholic parishes in New York. A parish census then showed sixteen thousand communicants who looked to this one church, thus placing it, in membership, ahead of the cathedral itself. And St. James' Parochial School was not only the largest of its kind in the city, but also one of the best.

In the years during which Father attended this school, there was considerable rivalry among the city's parochial schools in the field of elocution, a gold medal being awarded annually for the outstanding "senior" elocutionist, and a silver medal for the outstanding "junior" contestant. When Father was eleven, he was chosen as the junior contestant to represent St. James' School in the city-wide contest, while Daniel Donovan, an older boy, was chosen as the St. James' senior. The contest was held that year in the auditorium of the De La Salle Institute, which stood on Second Street near Second Avenue.

"I remember being dressed in my Sunday suit," Father wrote many years later, "and with my sister being taken to the Hall by my mother, who would not let me go so far uptown alone."

Father's "oration" that evening dealt with the death of Robespierre —not an ideal subject for an eleven-year-old boy. Still, both he and his fellow contestant, Daniel Donovan, must have done very well, for Daniel was awarded the senior medal as a result of his efforts that evening, and Father the junior one—a double victory of which the school was naturally very proud.

Obviously their teachers had more than a little to do with that double victory, but it seems fair to suggest that both boys had some natural aptitude for public speaking, and this aptitude, which was later a subject of frequent comment so far as Father was concerned, certainly came to play an important part in his political career.

The instruction in elocution St. James' School offered formed only a part of the training for public speaking that Father was given in the parish. The church was very active, and among the various organizations it encouraged there was one in particular—the St. James' Dramatic Society—that was locally influential. This society seems to have been very energetic, and the plays it gave were both numerous and well presented. Those who took part in these presentations no doubt enjoyed the work, but there was a serious reason behind these activities, too. A home for orphaned girls was being supported by St. James' Church, and each year the dramatic society gave two plays, the proceeds from which were assigned for the use of the home. These plays were staged with so much ability and care that the basement auditorium of the church was filled, even crowded, every night for the two-week run.

Those were the days when amateur theatricals were much commoner than they are now, and amateur dramatic societies were numerous. There is little doubt, however, that the St. James' group was more competent than most. This seems to have been recognized even by the city's theatrical producers, who were often very liberal in the help they gave.

Father was always interested in the theater. Long before he was old enough to become a member of the dramatic society, he and Aunt Mamie, together with other children of the neighborhood, went through the motions of producing plays in the attic of the South Street house. But it was not until he was seventeen, and was beginning to think of himself as a young man, that he became a member of the St. James' Dramatic Society and was given a minor part in *May Blossom,* a play which had then only recently achieved success at the Madison Square Theatre.

I know nothing of his performance in this first part, but the fact that he was given more important roles in many succeeding plays suggests that he had some acting ability. In fact, it was not long before he was accepted as one of the society's most useful members. In a Civil War play called *The Confederate Spy,* he played the lead. In *The Mighty Dollar,* by William J. Florence, Father played the part of the Honorable Bardwell Slote, a Congressman, and among other plays in which he was given prominent parts were *A Kettle of Fish,* by Augustin Daly; *Incog,* by Charles Dickson; and *All the Comforts of Home,* by William Gillette. Some of these were so well handled that the dramatic society was asked to repeat them elsewhere.

Of all the productions in which Father appeared, quite the most successful was Dion Boucicault's then famous play, *The Shaughraun.* First produced at the Drury Lane Theatre in London in 1875, this play had earned for Boucicault his reputation as the best Irish actor and playwright of his time. And even in the hands of the St. James' amateurs the play was so successful that it was given on three different occasions in the basement of the church, and ran for two weeks each time. The same group also gave it on two succeeding nights at the London Theatre in the Bowery, and twenty years or so later, when Father was Sheriff and the parish was in need of funds, it was again produced for a one-week run in the basement of the church, with some of the original cast—Father among them—taking part.

I cannot speak from firsthand knowledge of any of these plays except *The Shaughraun,* for that was the only one I ever saw in which Father appeared. And because I was only fifteen when it was revived, it is likely that my judgment of it was not entirely objective. Certainly I found it impossible not to see that it was really Father, and not Corry Kinchela, each time that villain appeared upon the stage. And the villain's henchman, Harvey Duff, despite his make-up, was just as plainly Judge Nolan, the father of my friend, Marie. Even Robert F. Folliott, the handsome hero, was much more plainly our good friend James J. Walker, who had not been in the original cast.

There was much neighborhood intimacy in the basement of the church, where these plays were given, and this sometimes created problems for those on the stage. Father often told of playing the part of Jem Dalton, the villain, in *The Ticket-of-Leave Man,* in which Dalton, in a struggle with Hawkshaw, the detective, had his pistol knocked from his hand by that representative of law and order. Under the circumstances Dalton was obviously helpless and about to reap the wages of sin, for he was down on one knee near the footlights with his pistol plainly visible on the stage just out of reach. But a small boy, breathless with excitement and keenly alive to the "danger" that had arisen, found it impossible to control himself. Rising from his seat in the first row, he leaned over the footlights, picked up the pistol, and tried to thrust it into Father's unwilling hand.

"Here you are, Al," he eagerly remarked in a stage whisper that could be heard throughout the hall.

The audience naturally roared with laughter, and Father, the defeated villain, did his best to keep his face straight as he ignored the proffered aid.

These were all amateur performances, but Father's appearances on the stage did not end there. Stories have been told of opportunities he had to appear on Broadway, but I am sure nothing of the kind ever occurred. Father never mentioned them, though now and then he referred to the many times he appeared among the "supes"—the supernumeraries—who were occasionally required in some of the more spectacular productions at the old Windsor Theatre on the Bowery. He had a friend whose task it was to round up extras when they were needed, and consequently from time to time Father appeared on the Windsor stage, though only in mob scenes or background groups. One of these plays was *In Siberia,* and another was *The Fall of Rome,* but the best known one of all was *The Last Days of Pompeii.*

In view of the fact that throughout this period he worked at his job for twelve hours a day, six days a week, it seems remarkable that he had the inclination and the energy required for these additional tasks. Undoubtedly these activities aided him in developing an appealing public manner and a good speaking voice. Whether or not he would have made his mark had he turned his attention seriously to the stage I have no way of knowing. But his youthful experience before the footlights was to prove helpful when he began to make his way in politics. Certainly he was later at ease before every audience, and he was always able, throughout his political life, to think clearly and effectively on his feet.

Because politics played so important a part throughout the Lower East Side during Father's boyhood, he must have been conscious of the political activities that went on about him even when he was very small. The influence of the local political clubs was too obvious to be missed, and the excitement of the campaigns—the torchlight parades, the marching songs and chants, the bonfires that blazed in the streets on every election night—could not have failed to attract the attention of such a boy as he. By his own admission, however, we know that the first political meeting he ever attended was at the Oriental Club in Grand Street in 1894, a few months before his twenty-first birthday.

Despite his youth Father already counted among his very good friends a number of men older than himself, the most important of whom, at this particular time—and for some time to come—was a wholesale and retail grocer, Henry Campbell by name, who had a large and successful business in Vesey Street on the other side of the lower tip of Manhattan from where Father lived, but who owned a good deal of real estate in the Lower East Side, where he was well known and politically influential. He was a bachelor, and the home he maintained was on Madison Street, no more than a few minutes' walk from where Father, Grandmother, and Aunt Mamie were still living on Dover Street.

I am sorry that I do not know the origin of this friendship, for it had an important bearing on Father's career. It is possible that the two had first met in connection with some of the activities that centered about St. James' Church—even, conceivably, some activity of the dramatic society. What I do know is that despite the disparity in their ages Henry Campbell, the successful older businessman, and Alfred E. Smith, the twenty-year-old amateur thespian and employee of a firm that dealt in steam pumps, were very particular friends. It seems, in fact, that the middle-aged bachelor, living alone as he did in his Madison Street house, took a kind of fatherly interest in his young friend. "Practically every Sunday," Father once told me, "I went to his house to dinner."

This relationship was already well established when, in the summer or early fall of 1894, Richard Croker, who was then the leader of Tammany and, as such, the greatest single political force in the city of New

York, made a move which set off a kind of minor revolution among the voters of the Lower East Side.

The Honorable Timothy J. Campbell—a Democrat, naturally, but not related to Father's friend, Henry Campbell—was then the Representative in Congress of what was sometimes known as the "Oriental district," which was composed of the lower part of Manhattan Island and Staten Island. A person by the name of Miner, however, who owned Miner's Bowery Theatre and who had ambitions to go to Washington, succeeded in obtaining Croker's backing for the nomination that year. The theater he owned was within the Congressional district he hoped to represent. His actual residence, however, was on Madison Avenue, far uptown and outside the district, and on this account Croker's support of the man resulted in many protests. The Honorable Timothy Campbell was popular in the Lower East Side, and it was in his behalf that the meeting at the Oriental Club in Grand Street was held—the first political meeting that Father ever attended.

Representative Campbell's friends were numerous at the meeting, and when one of them took the platform and told those in the audience that Croker himself had sent word to "Big Tim" Sullivan, the most important Tammany leader of lower Manhattan, that Miner was to supplant Tim Campbell, it became plain that many who were present were entirely willing to oppose Croker's action. It is true that the revolt failed to keep Miner from getting the nomination, and Tim Campbell, because of that, could enter the contest only by becoming a candidate on an Independent ticket. When he did this, his supporters not only did all they could in his behalf, but also enthusiastically joined with the anti-Tammany forces which were supporting William L. Strong for Mayor of New York City.

Father, though he was not yet twenty-one, and therefore was unable to vote, nevertheless threw himself energetically into the campaign. Primarily he was a supporter of Tim Campbell, but in the political speeches he made—and he made a good many—he spoke not only in Campbell's favor, but also in favor of the anti-Tammany ticket as a whole.

In view of later developments it is interesting to point out these details about Father's anti-Tammany beginnings. It is impossible to say how much or how little his activities in that election of 1894 affected the outcome. It is likely that the final result was little affected, and we know that Tim Campbell was defeated. Still, the anti-Tammany forces elected William L. Strong as Mayor, and when he was inducted into office early in January 1895, Henry Campbell, who had also supported the anti-Tammany ticket, was able to obtain for Father an appointment as process server in the office of the Commissioner of Jurors.

This new position paid only sixty dollars a month, which was little more than Father had been earning at the steam pump plant. But the work was much more to his liking, for now in his daily round he was able, as he once said, to meet "all kinds of people, from the small store-keeper in Fordham to the broker and banker in Wall Street."

It was natural for Father to throw himself wholeheartedly into any work he was called upon to do, and he did just that in this instance. The result was that before long he was made an investigator, with an increase in pay, and was assigned to the task of checking all applications for exemption from jury duty.

Still living with Grandmother Smith and Aunt Mamie in the Dover Street flat, to which Grandmother's sister had also come, Father now entered upon a new phase in his career. What had gone before might, in a way, be likened to the tuning of a musician's instrument. Now, though probably with no clear understanding of the fact on Father's part, the prelude had begun, and in the years that followed, the theme that was to dominate five busy decades of his life slowly developed.

It was less than a year before he joined the staff of the Commissioner of Jurors that Father first met Catherine Dunn, the girl he was to marry. She herself had been born in the Oliver Street neighborhood, though he hadn't known her there, for her family had long since moved far uptown, and lived, in 1894, on Third Avenue near the corner of 170th Street. Her father had formerly operated a sailors' supply store on the Lower East Side and the family still had relatives in this old part of the city. It was through one of these—John Heaviside, a school-mate of Father and a cousin of Katie Dunn—that Father met this uptown family. John was the son of a policeman who was assigned to the Oak Street precinct, and having been sent by his family on an errand to the Dunns' somewhat distant home, he asked Father to go along.

It was on this occasion that Father and Katie Dunn first met, but because 170th Street was then so very remote from Dover Street, they did not meet again for months. Father frequently saw John Heaviside, however, and often inquired about John's uptown relatives. The reason for Father's interest in the Dunns was fairly obvious, and ultimately John took his friend to 170th Street on another visit. Other visits followed, and because the young lady occasionally visited her downtown relatives, Father found it possible to see her there as well.

As often happens, Father made a better impression on the young lady than on either of her parents. He was a likable person even in the eyes of Grandfather and Grandmother Dunn, and he gave them the impression that he was willing to work hard at his job. Then, too, he was obviously a good Catholic, as the Dunns were, and his friends and acquaintances spoke well of him. Still, he seemed to have too much interest in the stage. It was this that most troubled Mr. and Mrs. Dunn. The stage had its place in the world, but what if young Alfred Smith should wish to go on the stage professionally? He might succeed, and yet they were troubled by the possibility of having their daughter marry an actor.

It was some time before Father got wind of this feeling. When he learned of it he promptly made it plain that he had no stage ambitions whatever. His interest in politics had clearly begun to develop, and though there were doubts about the adequacy of his income, it was clear that he was doing reasonably well. Aunt Mamie, Father's sister, was married by now—had been married in 1895 to John Glynn, a policeman. The two had moved to the Bronx for a time, and then, after returning to the Lower East Side, where their first son was born, had moved to Brooklyn, where Grandmother later went to live with them.

It was on May 6, 1900, that Father and Mother were married in the Church of St. Augustine on 167th Street, the Bronx, and Father Kean, who had been pastor of St. James' Church for twenty years, actually officiated. Catholic priests are not inclined to leave their parishes for such reasons. In this case, however, Father Kean was glad to do it because of his regard for the bridegroom, who, in his turn, always held the pastor of St. James' in the most reverent regard.

There was no wedding trip for the newly married couple. Instead they went directly to Bath Beach, Brooklyn, where they spent the summer. Then they moved to a flat at 83 Madison Street, only two or three blocks from St. James' Church. It was at this Madison Street address that my brother Alfred was born, his arrival necessitating the move to 79 Madison Street, where I was born. Next, the family moved to 9 Peck Slip, where my sister Catherine was born, and where we lived until we moved to Oliver Street. And it was while we still lived at the

Peck Slip address that Father took the second significant step in his political career.

Probably up to this period in his life, had he been an introspective person, he would have thought of himself as part and parcel of the Lower East Side. In a way he never lost his love for and understanding of this portion of the city. Now, however, he was about to step onto a broader stage, where, as the years passed, he came to be so masterful an actor.

CHAPTER THREE

The Downtown Tammany Club and the Legislature

THOUGH AT THIS TIME Father was a political appointee, it was several years before he began to take much interest in organization politics. This may have been at least partly due to the fact that his duties constantly took him all over New York County, which then included not only the whole of Manhattan, but also the extensive though still sparsely settled area of the Bronx. In fact, he was so frequently compelled to serve subpoenas in remote sections of the Bronx, where the city's transportation system was very sketchy, that he found it advisable to keep his bicycle at what he once called "my Bronx headquarters"—the home of Grandmother's brother, Peter Mulvehill, who then lived on a little farm not far from where the Bronx Zoo is today. On the Lower East Side developments were under way which ultimately changed the political picture there and opened up new opportunities that greatly widened Father's political horizons.

Throughout the nineties Patrick Divver was the Tammany leader in the district in which Father lived. The anti-Tammany revolt of 1894 had shaken his power somewhat, but he had retained his position as leader and had not forgotten those who had rebelled. Father had been only a minor figure in that fight, but nevertheless he was down in Divver's black book as a result. However, a good deal of opposition to Divver had developed in the district, and by 1901 his leadership was plainly in danger.

The term "anti-Tammany" has frequently been used in connection with the political developments that took place in our old neighborhood at this time, but the opposition which developed was aimed at Divver personally, and not at Tammany. Earlier, when Father had been one of those who had supported Tim Campbell against Croker's chosen candidate for Congress, it had been Croker's insistence on nominating another candidate which had caused the revolt, and the support the district gave the anti-Tammany ticket in the field was hardly more than incidental.

During the 1890s the political situation in New York had undergone much change. The city of "Greater New York" had come into existence on January 1, 1898, and as a result Tammany found itself confronted with problems of a kind that had never troubled it before. So far as the Second Assembly District—Father's old neighborhood—was concerned, however, these city-wide problems were largely lost to sight because of the local leadership fight in which Thomas F. Foley had entered the field against Divver.

Foley, a long-time local resident, was a remarkable character and an admirable one. He had come to New York from Ireland at the age of twenty-two and, having originally been a blacksmith, as I have said, was a big, broad-shouldered man. Friendly and with an inborn liking for people, he had opened a saloon on Water Street at the corner of Oliver in 1872, and had continued to operate it. He and his wife lived on Thirty-Fourth Street, which is a long way from the Lower East Side, but he seemed to be more at home at 15 Oliver Street, where, for many years, he lived on one floor of a three-story house. In fact, he was always more clearly a part of the Lower East Side than of his 34th Street neighborhood, and for more than fifty years he regularly attended St. James' Church.

Because of his ownership of the Water Street saloon he has been referred to as a saloonkeeper. That term, however, has certain connotations that are misleading in this instance. Saloon *owner* he certainly was, but his interests were much more clearly centered in the people of the neighborhood, than in the saloon he owned. He was a friendly man with a sincere love of children, though he had none of his own. He was extremely generous, and in many ways was an outstanding character in the Lower East Side of his day. When I came to know him, he was well along in years and I was only a child, but I nevertheless felt the genuineness of his friendship, which was obvious to everyone.

There were very few people living in the Second Assembly District he did not know, and he had known many of them all their lives.

Father, even as a boy, had known him well, and for years, despite the difference in their ages, the two had been good friends. Consequently, though Father had played no part in district politics since his appointment to the staff of the Commissioner of Jurors, he became an enthusiastic supporter of Tom Foley in the 1901 fight for the district leadership. Because he had a natural flair for such work, he was made one of Foley's lieutenants—and an election district leader—at this time and thus also became an active member of Tammany.

Throughout the time of Patrick Divver's leadership nominations to the Board of Aldermen and to the New York State Assembly usually went to candidates who were in a position to control important blocks of votes, and more often than not, apparently, these candidates were saloonkeepers. While the Foley-Divver fight was under way, Tom Foley—himself the owner of a saloon—made a public statement to the effect that if he were successful in his bid for the district leadership he would see that younger men were given a chance at these offices. How much this promise affected the outcome I do not know, but when Foley won—and that was the result of this very hot contest—one of his first important moves as leader was to support Joseph P. Bourke for nomination as a member of the Assembly from the old Second Assembly District. And Bourke was certainly one of the younger men. He and Father were the same age, and had attended St. James' School together.

As Tom Foley played the game of politics, it was a full-time job. It had always been perfectly natural for him to have a wide acquaintance, and a large proportion of those who knew him considered him their friend. But now, with so many new responsibilities the Tammany district leadership had thrust upon him, he was especially careful to keep in close touch with the people of the district. And because it was impossible even for a man of Foley's instincts to perform all the political tasks and attend to all the endless requests that the people of the district were able to think up, he saw to it that his political lieutenants were also available whenever possible so that they could attend to their share of these political chores.

A district leader, as such, holds no political office. Neither has he any political authority. His political influence, however, is often greater than that of many who are actually in office. And party leaders are apt to be especially important in the matter of nominations. In fact, they often control such matters, which was the case in the old Second Assembly District.

By now, Father was recognized by a great many people of the neighborhood as an up-and-coming young man. He never went in very heavily for scrapbooks, so it is rather difficult to trace his progress. About this time, however, he began to keep a few clippings, for he had become Secretary of the Seymour Club of the Second Assembly District, an organization of which his friend, Henry Campbell, was president, and the newspapers now and then mentioned him. One clipping he kept said in reference to him that "he is ambitious to become a member of the Legislature and is looking for the nomination from his district."

It goes without saying that if the newspapers knew of this ambition Father's friend Henry Campbell also did. And because Tom Foley missed very little that was going on in the district, it is safe to assume that he did too. However, it was not until two years after Foley had become district leader that Father's opportunity came.

In 1901 Foley had chosen Joseph P. Bourke for nomination as Assemblyman. He was a likable young man, and seemed to have a good deal of political promise. He was elected not only in 1901, but also in 1902, for he was personally popular in the district. Unfortunately for his political future he began to let his personal popularity interfere with the work Foley expected him to do at the Downtown Tammany Club in Madison Street, where the leader himself and his political lieutenants maintained their contacts with the people of the district. Even when the time approached for his renomination in 1903, Bourke spent much less time at the club than Foley thought he should, and the result was that the leader decided to replace him with some more co-operative candidate.

At first Foley turned to Pat Whalen, a young man of the district who was a clerk in the office of William Travers Jerome, the well-known District Attorney of that day. Whalen, not unnaturally, talked over Foley's suggestion with Jerome and, being advised not to accept, told Mr. Foley that this was his decision. Foley did not press him, for that was not his way, but he permitted word to get out that Bourke was not to be renominated, and Henry Campbell no sooner got that news than he went to see Foley about it. He asked if it was true that Bourke was to be replaced, and when Foley admitted it was, Campbell suggested Father.

Various stories—some of them so detailed as to be unconvincing—have been written about the meeting between Foley and Campbell. I know nothing of what took place, and Father knew nothing of it at the time. The newspaper clipping to which I have referred makes it plain that he had been hoping for some time to be elected to the Assembly, but in later years he often said that he was surprised when Henry Campbell came to see him one afternoon at the office of the Commissioner of Jurors and told him that Foley planned to have him nominated that very evening.

It was obvious that Foley's recommendation was enough to assure the nomination, and any Democratic nomination in the old Second Assembly District left the election in no doubt. The minute Henry Campbell imparted his news Father realized he was on his way to the Assembly. On the other hand, the news had come most unexpectedly, and it is easy to imagine how excited he was. Some of his friends were excited too, though there was at least one who was unimpressed.

Judge Thomas Allison—a Republican, incidentally—who was Commissioner of Jurors at the time, seems to have had an especial fondness for Father, and when he was told the news Campbell had brought, he advised against accepting the nomination, contending that election to the Assembly would lead nowhere. Henry Campbell, however, took the opposite view, and Father himself, eager and enthusiastic, had no doubt as to the course he wished to pursue. He welcomed the opportunity, and because we had no telephone in our Peck Slip flat, he hurried home to tell Mother the news, sending a friend to Brooklyn meanwhile so that Grandmother might also be informed.

From all accounts Father's wardrobe in those days was very limited. So far as really presentable clothes were concerned, he had only the blue serge suit he was wearing when he got the news and a winter suit that had been carefully folded away the previous spring. Of the two the winter suit was preferable, but Mother, in putting it away, had protected it with mothballs, the odor of which could not quickly be eliminated. Within a very few hours, Father knew, the convention would be ready to notify him "officially" of his nomination, and when that time came, he would have to appear before the assembled delegates. It was unthinkable that he should enter the hall and express his thanks while surrounded by the unmistakable and penetrating odor of camphor, so the winter suit could not be used. The blue serge suit he had worn to the office that morning would have to do, but unfortunately it was none too new. It might even have been more than a little shiny, and certainly it was out of press. Consequently, as I heard him say in later years, he happily "contemplated" his coming nomination in the kitchen of the Peck Slip flat while wearing one of Mother's voluminous aprons and carefully pressing that only available suit.

In the practice of politics not a few pretenses have evolved into important customs, and one of these has to do with "notifying" each successful candidate of his nomination. Usually candidates keep themselves intimately informed about the developments that lead to their nominations, and word of their success reaches them on the wings of the wind. Even in Father's case it is likely that he knew before some of the convention delegates did that they were about to "choose" him. And yet, such things being ordered as they are, it was plain that the convention would play its predetermined part, and then would solemnly appoint a committee to "find" the candidate, notify him of the action the convention had taken, and invite him to appear before it. Advance arrangements were carefully made for Father to be "found" and notified at the St. James' Union, the parish club in Oliver Street, which was just around the corner from the Madison Street convention hall.

"All the delegates were men I had known for years," Father said many years later, "and I was received in the convention hall with loud acclaim."

On more than one occasion I have heard him say that during the campaign which followed, when he saw his picture in so many shop windows throughout the district, he thought he had reached the very zenith of his political fortunes.

"It was then," Father once remarked, "that I began to see the real significance of the expression 'Politics makes strange bedfellows.' Two years before these had been my political 'enemies,' but now they were supporting me."

Apropos of "strange bedfellows," one of Father's was a bookmaker, although, as everyone knew, Father had little interest in the sporting world. But a zealous supporter persuaded him to go to the races one day on the theory that he would see a great many people from the district. No sooner had he arrived than his bookmaker acquaintance rushed up to him and asked him to place a bet. When he seemed reluctant, the bookmaker became insistent and said, "What's the matter, Al? Aren't you a good sport?"

Thus challenged, Father placed a ten-dollar bet, though he purposely selected a very "long shot." To his surprise—and no doubt to the bookmaker's chagrin—the horse won, but Father never asked for his winnings.

"Give me back my ten dollars," he told the bookmaker. "You can forget the rest of it. But never call me a poor sport again." It is true that the area was still beset by the remnants of the rivalry that had originated during the Foley-Divver fight, though Patrick Divver had died in the meantime. Now, however, Divver's former followers, hoping to appear as "regular" once again, placed Father's name prominently on their political banner when they hung it across Madison Street.

Because I was within two months of my second birthday when the election of 1903 was held, it may be that I was at least vaguely conscious that something exciting was happening. I have often heard about it, however, and it surely resembled later elections that I actually recall.

In the absence of any adequate meeting hall in the district the campaign was carried on entirely in the streets, the campaigners usually speaking from the tail ends of horse-drawn trucks. Under the conditions that usually prevailed, they were compelled to make themselves heard above the rattle of the Madison Street horsecars and of the steel-tired wagon wheels that rumbled up and down the streets over the cobblestones. Furthermore, the periodic roar of the elevated trains that ran up and down New Bowery and the somewhat more distant but more constant noise of the traffic that moved back and forth across Brooklyn Bridge all had to be considered by the political orators.

Father was opposed by Paul M. Kaminsky on the Republican ticket, and by a Socialist, a Prohibitionist, and an Independent. Our whole family was naturally very excited, and I have been told that Grandmother and Aunt Mamie came over from Brooklyn on Election Day, remaining until the polls had closed and the returns came in. The very first returns clearly forecast Father's victory, and the final tabulation gave the Prohibitionist 5 votes, the Socialist 106, and the Republican 1,472. I do not know what support the Independent candidate was given, but it had no great bearing on the final outcome, for Father's supporters rolled up a total of 4,942, a 3-to-1 lead over all his opponents combined.

Now that Father had been elected, the Commissioner of Jurors, Judge Allison, looked up the statutes and decided that there was nothing in the law that called upon a county official to resign prior to his actual assumption of any new office to which he had been elected. Therefore Father remained a member of the staff of the Commissioner of Jurors until the end of the year—a fortunate thing, for the family really needed the salary that was involved. And this was not the only help he received. I have often heard him tell how Henry Campbell, shortly after that election, took him up to Brooks Brothers, then at the corner of Astor Place and Fourth Avenue, and bought him his first cutaway and his first dress suit.

"The old neighborhood," Mr. Campbell remarked, "should have as well dressed an Assemblyman as the uptown people have."

Father obtained his introductory glimpse of Albany on the evening of Tuesday, January 5, 1904. Some five years earlier he had passed through the city on his way to Cliff Haven on Lake Champlain, where he had taken part in an amateur theatrical production given for the benefit of a Catholic summer school, but now, as a newly elected member of the state Assembly, he had his first opportunity to look about the capital of the Empire State. The weather was not conducive to sightseeing for a cold wave had moved down out of Canada, and when Father entered Keeler's Hotel at the corner of Maiden Lane and Broadway, a thermometer outside registered 15 below zero.

With Tom Caughlan, the Assemblyman from the First Assembly District, which lay at the southernmost tip of Manhattan, Father had taken a room at Keeler's for that first night in Albany. Later they moved to a furnished room, which they occupied throughout the session, but on that first evening, when they had reached their hotel room, Father recalled a newspaper story he had read a day or two before of a hotel fire in Chicago in which several lives had been lost. And remembering the account, he thought of the big fireplace downstairs in the lobby of Keeler's—a fireplace in which, as he and Mr. Caughlan had entered, a roaring fire was burning while someone was feeding still more wood to the flames in an effort to combat the cold.

Away from home for the first time in five years, unfamiliar with his new surroundings, and vividly conscious of the details of the Chicago tragedy, he went to the window to see where the fire escape was. To his alarm the window opened merely onto a court and no escape route was visible. Tom Caughlan's reaction to this was apparently little different from Father's, for the two of them played pinochle until five o'clock in the morning, and even then they took turns sleeping until breakfast time.

In 1904, when Father first went to Albany, New York State was being governed under its fourth constitution. The first of these had been adopted in 1777 and had provided for comparatively few changes in the provincial system that had existed up to then. Under it the state government was established on a popular basis, and the powers of the Governor were curtailed, but no provision was made by which amendment or revision was possible. The succeeding constitutions took this weakness into account, and when the fourth constitution went into effect in 1894, it continued a provision that had first appeared in the third—a provision under which the Legislature was directed to call a constitutional convention at least once in twenty years to revise the constitution if the people requested it. Under this constitution the legislative power was vested in a Senate of fifty members elected biennially, and an Assembly of 150 members elected annually. A member of the New York State Assembly, therefore, occupies a position comparable to that of the Representatives in the Congress of the United States and in other state legislatures, and when Father first went to Albany, members of the Legislature—Senators and Assemblymen alike—were paid $1,500 a year and ten cents a mile for traveling expenses.

In New York State the Legislature is usually controlled by the Republicans, and in the Assembly of 1904 they were very heavily in the majority. The Democratic members were so few, in fact, that they were relegated to the very last row over on the left—on the Speaker's right, that is—where, Father told me many years later, it was sometimes hard to differentiate them from visitors to the chamber.

The rules of almost any legislative body are apt to be involved, but that seems to have been especially true of the New York Assembly at this time. S. Frederick Nixon, the Speaker, was a Republican from Chautauqua County, and a member of the old school of politics. He was little interested in simplifying the rules or clarifying the procedure, and new members often found it difficult or even impossible to understand just what was going on. In later years Father actually said, in referring to his first term in the Assembly, that he had no real idea of what was happening. Even new Republican members were given little opportunity to be heard, and it is interesting to note that Father did not meet Speaker Nixon personally until the Assembly, which convened early in January, was about to adjourn four months later.

Despite Father's failure to grasp much of what was transpiring he never gave up trying. He faithfully carried copies of all pending bills back to the room he and Tom Caughlan shared and studied them at every opportunity. Having no legal training, he found the going hard, and from time to time he wondered if the whole complicated business might not be too much for him. Once the Assembly had adjourned in April, however, he found his duties in the Second Assembly District much to his liking. He was renominated and re-elected in 1904, though during his second term he again found himself a part of the far outnumbered Democratic minority and still felt lost in that last row far over on the left of the chamber.

Though the Legislature of 1905 created the Armstrong Insurance Commission and empowered it to investigate the affairs of the life insurance companies, little else of consequence was accomplished. Public interest was aroused when the commission began its work, with Charles Evans Hughes as its counsel, but Father still had little understanding of the legislative complexities that surrounded him, and was more than ever conscious of what he thought was his own inadequacy. He was appointed to two committees—the Committee on Banks and the Committee on Public Lands and Forests—but he knew very little of the problems with which they dealt.

"I had never been in a bank except to serve a jury notice," he remarked years later, "and I had never seen a forest."

During his first two terms in the Legislature, Father was anything but confident that he would ever be able to play an effective part there. His lack of confidence was so great that during the summer of 1905 he thought seriously of giving up the Assembly. Tom Foley, who knew how discouraged the young Assemblyman was, let it be known that a position of Superintendent of Buildings in New York City might be obtained for him if he thought his job in the Assembly was too much for him to handle. Foley urged him not to decide at once, however, apparently quite aware that Father's determination to succeed would be aroused by the very suggestion that the job of Assemblyman was more than he could handle. And it may have been that suggestion which kept Father from leaving the Legislature. At any rate, having thought it over, he resolved not to admit even to himself that the work in Albany was beyond him, so he accepted the nomination for a third time, and threw himself energetically into his election campaign. Furthermore, when he reached Albany again in January 1906, he realized that conditions had changed. Opportunities that had been utterly lacking before now began to develop.

James W. Wadsworth, Jr., a Republican from Mount Morris, New York, and a man who was later to become a United States Senator, had first been elected to the Assembly the year before, and now, though he was serving only his second term, was elected Speaker. The Assembly was still dominated by the Republicans, but with Wadsworth as Speaker both the procedure and the rules underwent constructive revision.

Father still felt that he did not have sufficient understanding of the Legislature's more important problems, but his determination to learn had begun to bear fruit. More, perhaps, than he realized, he was coming to be at home amid the procedural complexities that had formerly troubled him so greatly. And his committee assignments that year were very helpful in further broadening his grasp of Assembly affairs. He was even given a place on the Committee on Insurance—an especially important assignment in view of the fact that Charles Evans Hughes, after one of the most widely publicized investigations New York State had known up to that time, was soon to report the insurance commission's findings.

Speaker Wadsworth and Father were good friends. Wadsworth was a Republican and Father a Democrat, so they often found themselves on opposite sides of the fence. Nevertheless, each held the other in high regard, and later in that session, when the Assembly and the Senate disagreed sharply over apportionment and John Raines, the leader of the Senate, tried to force the Senate's view on the Assembly, Father was one of the Democrats who came to Wadsworth's support, thus helping to force the Senate to adjust the matter to Speaker Wadsworth's satisfaction.

From the time of his first arrival in Albany, Father had studiously devoted himself to the work of the Assembly. During the session of 1906, however, he worked harder than ever, attending every session and spending evening after evening at the Capitol while he delved into all sorts of legislative matters. By the time that session adjourned, he had definitely gained in understanding, and when he entered his campaign for re-election that fall he was confident and really eager to continue as an Assemblyman.

At the very beginning of Father's career in the Legislature, Tom Foley had given him a bit of excellent political advice, which he had consistently followed.

"Don't speak," Foley had told him, "until you have something to say. Men who talk just for the pleasure they get out of it aren't likely to get very far."

Father had also been impressed by Foley's advice never to make a promise unless he was confident he would be able to carry it out. Furthermore, Foley strongly believed that it was always best to tell the truth. He has often been quoted as saying that most people who approach men in public life are not really looking for the truth.

" 'They like to be jollied,' " I have heard Father quote him as saying, " 'but the safest thing to do is to tell them the truth. Then, if they go about asking other people, they will find out sometime that you were right from the first.' "

As a result of this advice—which I have always felt was merely Foley's statement of a philosophy that was natural to Father, too—Father's voice was almost never heard during his first three terms in the Assembly. When he went back for his fourth term, he had gained not only in self-confidence but also in his understanding of legislative matters. He was better known and more widely accepted, and consequently was made a member of the Committee on Affairs of Cities and of the Special Committee on Revision of the Charter of Greater New York. He now began to take an active part in some of the debates, and because the amendments to the New York City Charter interested him especially, he worked hard to master the whole of that complicated subject.

Up to this time, I suspect, there may have been at least a little doubt when convention time rolled around each year that Father would be renominated. But by the fall of 1907 he had so thoroughly demonstrated his ability as a vote getter and a useful member of the Assembly that his renomination and re-election were assured far in advance. It was during the years that began about now that we children came to be so utterly sure of his invariable success at the polls. And why shouldn't we have been? From our earliest recollections his victories had always been won by very wide margins.

Children exist amid half-imaginary surroundings of their own, and the world they know is usually very different from that of the grown-ups about them. Certainly that was true of me, and therefore I have very few clear recollections of Father's activities during these years. I was only six when he began his fourth term in the Assembly, and I had no interest in political affairs, all of which were meaningless to me. In fact, I was a little unclear as to just what the Assembly was, and somewhat vaguely conceived it to be—when I thought of it at all—a large room of indeterminate dimensions in which many men were divided into two opposing groups that were forever at cross purposes.

It must be remembered, too, that Father spent only three months or a little more in Albany each year, and even while the Legislature was in session he was home each weekend. In my mind, consequently, the Assembly and Father's activities there were far less significant than they came to be as I grew older. Insofar as his experiences in the Legislature were concerned I have no recollections of any significance until I was ten or eleven, and what I recall even of that period is largely hearsay.

From what he said in later years, I know that Father's confidence in himself began to develop during his fourth term, and about this time, too, his fellow members began to recognize the fact that this big-city member—this Tammany Democrat—had his full share of ability. But other developments were under way that also had their effect on his career.

Charles Evans Hughes, besides serving as counsel for the Armstrong Insurance Commission in 1905 and 1906, had also served as counsel for an earlier commission that had been created by the Legislature to study the cost of production and distribution of gas in the city of New York. He had conducted himself with great ability on both of these assignments, and in doing so had added to his already high reputation. The idea behind both these commissions was that the Legislature would use their recommendations as a basis for legislation, but a bill which would have fixed the price of gas at eighty cents per thousand cubic feet—a figure set by the investigating commission—failed to pass. Not long thereafter the report of the insurance commission revealed so much official corruption that public feeling turned strongly against the Republicans, who had been in power in New York State without interruption since 1893.

Under the circumstances the Republicans wisely nominated Hughes as their candidate for Governor, and because of the important part he had played in bringing to light the widespread corruption in the state, he was elected. His popularity undoubtedly offset much anti-Republican feeling throughout the state, with the result that the Republicans succeeded in retaining control of both houses of the Legislature. The newly elected Lieutenant Governor, however, and all the other newly elected state officials, were Democrats.

It was on January 1, 1907, that Governor Hughes was inaugurated, but despite his widespread popularity the Republican leaders in the state were unsympathetic with his point of view. They opposed many —perhaps most—of the reforms the Governor proposed, though some of these, it is interesting to note, were later passed by a Republican Legislature when Father was Governor.

The Governor's term, in those days, was only two years, and Hughes was renominated in 1908. He was re-elected, but the leaders of his party still continued to oppose him. And when John Raines, the long-time Republican leader of the Senate, died in 1909 and Senator Jotham P. Allds was chosen to succeed him, several members of that Senator's own party charged him with accepting a bribe to influence legislation. Allds did his best to defend himself, but after a prolonged hearing before the Republican-dominated Senate he was found guilty.

It was Father's belief that the opposition of the Republican leaders to Governor Hughes was in itself enough to weaken the party. But when this was combined with the revelation of Allds' dishonesty—dishonesty which also involved many Republican county supervisors—the people of the state turned against the Republicans in the election of 1910.

John A. Dix of Thomson, New York, was the Democratic nominee for Governor, and the voters were so determined to bring about a change that not only he but also all the other Democratic candidates on the state ticket were chosen, and both the Senate and the Assembly, for the first time in nearly twenty years, went Democratic as well. In the midst of so widespread a Democratic landslide Father was naturally re-elected, and when the Legislature convened in January 1911, he began his eighth consecutive term.

A great political change had taken place, but this had to do with more than the defeat of the Republicans, for the Democratic leadership in the Assembly now changed also. For many years a kind of unwritten rule among the Democratic members of the Assembly had caused them to choose their leader from those among them who came from the "upstate" counties—that is, those counties not closely connected with the city of New York. Because of this George M. Palmer, of Schoharie County, had been the Democratic leader for years, and in 1910, when it had been necessary to choose his successor, this "upstate" idea was still so strong that Assemblyman Daniel D. Frisbie, also from Schoharie County, was elected.

When the Assembly met in 1911, the Democrats were no longer in the minority. For the first time in eighteen years they were in a position to elect a Democratic Speaker, and of course they chose their leader of the year before for that important post. But with their former leader installed as the presiding officer of the Assembly a new leader had to be chosen, and despite the long-accepted "rule" that only an upstate Assemblyman should be considered for the post, it was Father, the Tammany Democrat from the Second Assembly District in lower Manhattan, who was chosen to fill it.

Obviously he had made progress. Where, in 1904, he had been little more than a half-bewildered observer in the Assembly, now he was one of the two outstanding leaders of his party there. Nor was this all. Even after two terms as an Assemblyman he had seriously considered giving the Legislature up, but now, in addition to having been elected leader, he was also appointed chairman of the Assembly's most important committee—the Committee on Ways and Means—of which, heretofore, he had not even been a member. As he himself said later, this was "something unheard of before."

It was now sixteen years since Henry Campbell had succeeded in getting Father his first political job. He had been growing in political stature ever since his first arrival in Albany, though for a discouragingly long time he had not been conscious of it. It is unlikely, I suspect, that even up to the day he was chosen leader many of his friends would have admitted that this thirty-seven-year-old Assemblyman from the Lower East Side was a political figure of more than local significance.

Tom Foley, it is true, had long trusted Father's political ability. There is no doubt that this canny leader had had considerable confidence in Father's political future even from the first. And there were others who believed in him. Still, no really objective opinion of him prior to his re-election in 1910 would have credited him with being a political figure of much importance outside the Lower East Side and the Democratic minority in the Assembly. Now, however, in his first really great political stride, he had come to be a figure of some state-wide significance, and the tempo of his development had definitely quickened. If any specific date were to be selected as marking the greatest single change that took place in his career, it seems to me that it might justifiably be January 4, 1911, when, for the eighth time, he took the oath of office in the Assembly Chamber and turned his attention to his new duties as Democratic leader and as chairman of the Assembly's most important committee.

Father's weekly trips to and from the capital when the Legislature was in session soon acquainted him with every inch of the way, and I remember his saying that he had gone back and forth so often he always knew, from any single glance out of the train window, just where he was. Other members of the family visited Albany much less often, but nevertheless came to be almost as familiar with the way. Even yet, when I take the train up or down the Hudson, there is hardly a curve, and certainly not a tunnel or a vista, that is not familiar to me.

As I try to reconstruct Father's political activities during the 1911 session of the Assembly, I find myself in very deep water. So far as this session is concerned—yes, and the next four sessions, too—most of what I know is hearsay. But I have heard so much recounted by Father himself, and by others who took part in what went on, that I sometimes have the feeling that I was actually present and saw what, in reality, I never saw at all, and only heard about.

The 1911 session placed the heaviest kind of burden on Father's shoulders. The task of majority leader could alone have occupied him fully. For eighteen years the Democrats had been in the minority—often a small minority—and in that time they had more or less accustomed themselves to being the opposition. Now, however, they were in a position to carry out a program of their own, and as majority leader Father had a very important part to play. The Republicans naturally were always willing to take advantage of any opportunity that arose, and more than one of them was eager to match verbal swords with the new Democratic leader.

I have no doubt that Father was always conscious of the fact that many of those with whom he was associated in the Legislature had been given advantages that had not come his way. Some were college graduates, while he had been forced to leave school before completing his studies in the eighth grade. Some were widely traveled while he had seen very little outside the crowded city of New York. Some were successful business- or professional men while Father's experience in business had been only that of a minor employee. And opportunities of other kinds had come to many of them and not to him. Furthermore, he was too wise not to realize what such advantages could mean.

During these years, actually, I knew little or nothing of my father as a public figure, for I was still short of my teens. Some time was to pass before I began to see how very much out of the ordinary my father was. His manner was so simple and sincere, his purposes were so forthright, his character was so lacking in ego or artificiality that I still think of him first merely as my father, and only with an effort as the outstanding public character he is now known to have been. But even then, I am sure, I knew how incapable he was of pretense. Never, either at home, in the Assembly, or elsewhere, was he given to pretending to be anything but what he was.

This characteristic of his is accepted now, but one story in particular illustrates it better than any other. It has been widely told, I know. In fact, it has been told and retold so often that it has taken on qualities it did not possess. But I know that I know it as it happened, for it was he who told it to me.

In the course of a debate that took place during the 1911 session, partisanship was more than usually evident. A bill having to do with the removal of the Commission of Jurors in Niagara County was under discussion, and Father, who was presenting the Democratic point of view, was being opposed by three Republicans—Ed Merritt, Frederick Hammond, and Jesse S. Phillips.

Ed Merritt, it is interesting to point out, was a very good friend of Father's, though the two were often political opponents, and in this case, because the feeling in the chamber was running high, the debate was a hot one.

Unknown to Father, and probably unknown to many others who were present, Cornell University's crew was in a race that day, and at the very height of the debate Assemblyman Wade of Buffalo asked for the privilege of interrupting—a request that was promptly granted.

"Mr. Speaker," the member from Buffalo began, "I have just heard that Cornell won the boat race."

It may be that Mr. Wade was a Cornell alumnus and that the

Cornell victory was of special import to him. But to most of the others it was not exactly world-shaking, and to those who had been interrupted in the midst of so heated a debate the announcement fell flat.

"That doesn't mean anything to me," Ed Merritt remarked. And then—perhaps to soften the sharpness he had given his remark—he added, "I'm a Yale man."

It was Frederick Hammond who made the next remark.

"It doesn't mean anything to me," he put in. "I'm a Harvard man."

Jesse Phillips spoke up next.

"It doesn't mean anything to me," he said. "I'm a U. of M. man."

Father was the last of the four whose debate had been interrupted and the only one still on his feet. Because of that he may have felt called upon to make some remark in order to bring the interruption to an end.

"It doesn't mean anything to me," he remarked without a moment's delay, "because I'm an F.F.M. man."

"What is that, Al?" asked Assemblyman James J. Hoey.

"Fulton Fish Market," Father replied with a perfectly straight face. "Let's proceed with the debate."

It must have been about this time that I first met Jimmy Walker. I do not remember the incident, but he was serving his second term in the Assembly and, like Father, went to Albany every Monday morning, returning to New York each Friday afternoon. Because it was at this period that Mother, Alfred, Jr., and I often met Father at the Knickerbocker Hotel for dinner, it may be that we children first met the future Mayor of New York on one of these occasions, though Father had known him for years.

During the Legislative session in Albany they roomed together at the Ten Eyck Hotel, where Father, having seen his very slender roommate in a suit of red-and-white-striped pajamas, once described him as looking "exactly like a peppermint stick." Perhaps because Father had been forced to make his own way when he first arrived in Albany he seemed eager to help this attractive and unquestionably able young man. He introduced his youthful friend to those who might be helpful and warned him against those who might not. And instead of holding Jimmy Walker back as he had held himself he quickly recognized the younger man's ability as a speaker. Even during his first term the new Assemblyman was often effective in debate, and by the time the 1911 session began, he was of much help to the heavily burdened majority leader.

It is likely that Father was more widely known throughout the state as the majority leader in the Assembly than as chairman of the Committee on Ways and Means, but in all probability his work on the committee was more important in acquainting him with state problems and in preparing him for the greater post he was ultimately to hold. The Ways and Means Committee is of pre-eminent importance because it is responsible for all bills having to do with appropriations. Normally, in New York State, members who come from the larger cities prefer not to serve on this committee, for it deals, for the most part, with appropriations that have to do with rural districts. Father came from the very heart of the state's greatest city, and the committee of which he was now chairman was called upon to deal with very few items—possibly with none—that were of specific interest to the people of the Second Assembly District.

This mattered not at all to the committee's new chairman, however. From the first the work of the committee captured his interest, and because he seems to have been incapable of accepting any statement until it was really clear to him, he studied in great detail each item that was brought to the committee's attention. This necessitated an immense amount of work, of course, for in a state as large and populous as New York appropriations of endless different kinds are essential, and the sums involved even in 1911 were large.

Everyone who knew Father will agree, I believe, that his memory was remarkable. It was as if he were in some strange way equipped with an almost faultless method of filing away for ready reference every valuable fact that came to his attention. Time after time, even in the midst of hotly contested political campaigns, I have heard him reply to unexpected questions with facts, figures, and quotations that were astonishing because of their pointed detail and accuracy. And in his work on the Committee on Ways and Means he was never content until every detail necessary to a full understanding of any appropriation under consideration was before him. It was not enough to tell him, for example, that so many "staff members" or "clerks" or "engineers" were required by this department or that. He was certain to insist on knowing just what work these new "staff members" were to do—just where and why these hoped for "clerks" were needed—just what kind of "engineers" these were to be and why their services were essential.

Nor was he willing to permit any vagueness where appropriations for bridges, highways, or structures of any kind were concerned. He insisted on knowing where and why they were needed, what their details were, and very accurately how much they were to cost. Nor did it matter to him that the bridge, for example, might be one of small dimensions and in a remote corner of the state, or that some structure that was proposed might be of even smaller consequence. He still insisted on having every detail, which, in that almost unique way of his, he would file carefully away in his phenomenal memory. And long thereafter, when some specific fact was desired, he was almost always able to draw it forth in all its detail to the embarrassment, perhaps, of some opponent in the Assembly or some critic on the stump.

No one could guess, in 1911, that the new Democratic leader in the Assembly was about to burst his political chrysalis, and it was far too early, as yet, to see that within a few years he would step forth as the leader of his party in the nation. But as we look back now and recall the work he did in that Legislative session, it is easy to see that the future Governor of New York was in the making.

CHAPTER FOUR

From the Legislature to the New York Board of Aldermen

THE 1911 SESSION of the New York Legislature was an unusually busy one, and Father was almost overwhelmed with work. In fact, the session so clearly demonstrated that no one man could adequately perform the duties of both majority leader and chairman of the Committee on Ways and Means that two different members were assigned to these tasks in the following session, and since that time, I believe, no one has been permitted to hold both posts at once.

With so much to do Father soon learned that he would be unable to introduce and follow the progress of more than a limited number of bills. As a result most of this work was left to the chairmen of the various committees, though Father was present at every session and often lent a hand when difficulties arose. Some bills, however, he kept in his own hands—notably those which carried out promises that had been made in the Democratic platform and finance bills that were necessary to the operation of the state government. There were a few others, too, some of which had to do with the inferior criminal courts of the state—bills Father had studied and in the progress of which he was especially interested.

Though the Democrats were heavily in the majority in both houses of the Legislature, their affairs ran less smoothly than might have been expected. The reason for this, Father later explained to me, was that those Democrats who represented city districts—especially many districts in the city of New York—and those who came from upstate districts, most of which were normally Republican, had little in common. Their points of view were often sharply different, though all of them were strong in the belief that they were guided by the very soundest of Democratic principles.

This difference in outlook was especially troublesome when the new charter for the city of Greater New York came up for adoption. It was finally adopted, it is true, but party lines were shattered in the process, and Father told me long afterward that in his belief this difference of opinion among the Democrats played an important part in defeating many of the so-called "insurgents," who were mostly from upstate districts, and in returning the Assembly to Republican control the following year.

Even without any additional problems the Legislature had its hands full, but on March 25, when everyone was hard at work and the members were beginning to look forward to the time for adjournment, a tragic fire swept through several floors of a tall Manhattan loft building that were occupied by a clothing factory, and 148 women employees lost their lives. The disaster was appalling in its consequences, but it appeared doubly shocking when it became evident that it had been the result of inexcusable negligence. The city, and even the state and the nation, reacted instantly, and a widespread demand arose for effective legislation that would adequately protect the lives of working people.

My knowledge of what followed is necessarily hearsay, though I still recall the glaring headlines and the vivid newspaper accounts that told how scores of women employees of the Triangle Waist Company were trapped by a locked door in the narrow, littered aisles of the factory high above the city street. The building itself was fireproof, and the fire was soon brought under control, but the flames had spread so quickly that the trapped women, unable to reach fire escapes or other exits, were overwhelmed by flames and smoke, or were compelled to leap from windows to their deaths on the pavement below.

A determined Committee on Safety was promptly organized in New York City, and a great mass meeting was held in the Metropolitan Opera House. Here a resolution demanding Legislative action was adopted, and Henry Moskowitz, who was then connected with an East Side social settlement, and John Kingsbury, of the Association for Improvement of the Condition of the Poor, were authorized to carry it to Albany.

These two determined men promptly called on Father and on Senator Wagner, the majority leaders in the Assembly and the Senate, and in the talks which followed, a state commission for the study of factory safety was suggested, the commission's report to form the basis for the enactment of legislation aimed at protecting the lives and health of working people. The idea was promptly accepted, a bill for the creation of such a commission was written and, having been introduced in the Senate by Senator Wagner and in the Assembly by Father, was passed with practically no opposition.

The commission, when it was formed, was made up of two members of the Senate, three members of the Assembly, and four citizens chosen by the Governor from the state at large. Senator Wagner was made chairman, Father was made vice-chairman, and Abram I. Elkus, later a judge of the New York State Court of Appeals, was appointed chief counsel.

This commission had come into existence as a direct result of the tragic New York fire. The bill that authorized the commission, however, was purposely written so as to make possible a really broad inquiry into all conditions that might affect the lives or health of working people throughout the state. Protection against fire was only one of many subjects to be considered, and before the investigation was completed, business and industrial conditions of almost every kind had been examined. Industrial sanitation, industrial accidents, hours of labor, the employment of women and children, and many other subjects were studied with great care and thoroughness, and the whole system of factory licensing and inspection was examined.

It was not until the Legislature had adjourned in April that the work of the commission really got under way. Then its members visited almost every part of the state, acquainting themselves with working conditions, talking with employers and employees, discussing the problems that confronted them with state, county, and local officials, as well as with newspaper editors and others who might be helpful.

Father had never before been given any real opportunity to familiarize himself at first hand with much of his native state. He knew the city of New York as only a born New Yorker can, but he had seen very little beyond the city. Now he found it possible to acquaint himself with almost every corner of the state. As chairman of the Assembly's Committee on Ways and Means he had so carefully studied every appropriation bill that had come up for consideration during the preceding session of the Legislature that his knowledge of the state was far from narrow, but now for the first time he was to have the opportunity of actually seeing and studying the entire region from New York Harbor to Niagara Falls, and from the Pennsylvania line to the Canadian border.

Viewed at this distance, it is easy to see how important this was in Father's career. It was impossible for anyone to realize it at the time, but the detailed knowledge of New York State he gained as vice-chairman of the Factory Investigating Commission was of inestimable value to him later.

Much of what he saw delighted him, for many portions of the Empire State are very beautiful. To a person acquainted at first hand—as Father was at this time—with little except the crowded and unbeautiful surroundings of the Lower East Side, the state's great rural areas, its spreading lakes and forest-covered mountains, its broad, rich river valleys, its many busy cities and peaceful villages must have seemed to be almost a fairyland. Sometimes, of course—in cities, towns, and even in rural areas—he found conditions less to his liking. Beautiful though most of the state is, it soon became apparent that it was not only in the great manufacturing cities that working conditions needed correction. Hours of labor could be as long and as deadening amid the beauties of upstate New York as among the loft buildings of Manhattan.

It was not until the Legislature convened in 1912 that bills based on the commission's studies came up for consideration, and by then the Republicans had regained control of the Assembly, though in the Senate the Democrats were still in the majority. Despite this change Father retained his position as vice-chairman of the Factory Investigating Commission, and in that capacity it was up to him to urge the adoption of the bills that were based upon the commission's report.

There was considerable opposition to this legislation, unfortunately, for several misunderstandings had arisen and many businessmen were fearful that drastic and unjustifiable laws were being proposed. Still, the commission's report was a carefully prepared document, and many forward-looking businessmen were convinced that reasonable laws governing working conditions and hours of labor would prove to be an asset to everyone concerned.

To any person accustomed, as most of us now are, to working conditions as they exist today, it may appear surprising that only a little more than forty years ago the Factory Investigating Commission was able so widely to find in the state of New York working hours so excessive and working conditions so bad. There were many considerate employers, of course, and in numerous factories and other places of business working conditions were good and hours of employment reasonable. Much too often, however, such conditions did not prevail.

Not only in city factories, but also in small-town plants and even in rural canneries, women and children had to work as many as sixteen hours a day and seven days a week. And, strangely enough, the cannery owners of the state of New York had in some way come to be so influential politically that no state regulations existed to control conditions in their highly seasonal businesses.

These facts and others like them were readily brought to light by the commission, and ultimately a number of bills were taken up for consideration by the Legislature. One of these was based upon the need for limiting hours of labor, and in the form in which it was brought before the Legislature, it called for all business and manufacturing establishments in the state to grant their employees at least one day of rest in seven. The opposition that had been aroused by the commission's activities had considerably weakened by the time this bill was introduced, but when it came up for debate, the cannery owners succeeded in having an amendment offered that specifically would have exempted the canneries from its terms.

Father was not the only proponent of this particular piece of legislation, and there were others as opposed as he to the proposal advanced at the instigation of the cannery owners. It was Father, however, who took the floor in an effort to defend the bill as it had been originally written.

I was not among the visitors to the chamber on this occasion and, because I was only ten at the time, would have missed the real significance of what occurred even if I had been there. I often heard the matter discussed in later years and heard from others besides Father of the surprisingly short but utterly unanswerable speech he made.

"Mr. Speaker," he began when he had been given the floor, "I have carefully read the commandment 'Remember the Sabbath Day, to keep it holy,' but I am unable to find any language in it that says 'except in the canneries.'"

He made no further argument. He stopped at that point and sat down. And the members of the Assembly, surprised that anyone should speak for so short a time, remained silent for a long moment. Even Speaker Merritt was apparently caught by surprise, and for as long a moment he made no move on the rostrum. Then others had their say and it was some time before the vote was taken. In effect, however, Father had spoken the final word, and when the bill was passed, the canneries were not exempted.

The factory legislation that was enacted during the 1912 session was of unusual importance, but the session was short and, in Father's opinion at least, otherwise uninteresting. The national political picture, on the other hand, was of the utmost interest and was to have a profound effect not only on the Federal government, but also on the political situation in the state of New York.

Theodore Roosevelt had been succeeded as President in 1908 by his long-time friend and supporter, William Howard Taft. By 1910 the two had clearly drifted apart, and in 1912 Roosevelt made a determined effort to defeat Taft for the Presidential nomination of the Republican party. Failing in this, he initiated the organization of the Progressive party, became its candidate for President, and brought about the three-cornered contest which resulted in the election of Woodrow Wilson and the first Democratic Presidential victory in twenty years.

Because of this dramatic national contest political occurrences in New York were largely lost to sight. Despite this a series of interesting developments took place in Empire State politics. Governor Dix, who had been elected in 1910, naturally hoped to be renominated by the Democrats in 1912. Many Democratic leaders felt, however, that he could not be re-elected, and William Sulzer, a member of Congress from New York City, was consequently nominated. Father, I think I should say at this point, was not one of Sulzer's supporters—a fact that came to have more significance in 1913 than it had in 1912—and the Progressive party, which had been organized because of national political developments, immediately began to have an important effect on the political situation in New York State.

Taking the nation as a whole, the Republicans were clearly the majority party. But the Taft-Roosevelt fight and Roosevelt's nomination as the Progressive party's Presidential candidate effectively split the Republican strength. As a result Wilson was elected President, though with fewer votes than were cast for his two opponents. And in New York State, where Sulzer was victorious, he polled only 649, 559 out of a total of a million and a half, the others being more or less evenly divided between Job E. Hedges, the Republican candidate, and Oscar Straus, who ran on the Progressive ticket.

I still remember the excitement of that election. Our whole family was delighted by the extent of the Democratic victory, both nationally and in New York State. In the State Assembly, for example, out of a total membership of 150, 105 were Democrats. Because of the split in the Republican ranks many districts that had always been inclined to send Republicans to Albany now found themselves represented by Democrats, and when the Assembly convened on Tuesday, January 7, 1913, it was Father who mounted the rostrum as Speaker.

Grandmother and Mother, as well as my sister, my three brothers, and I, were all present in the Assembly Chamber when the 1913 Legislature convened. Many years have passed since then and I am quite unable to remember just how I felt. I was eleven years old—no longer a little child—and when I saw Father take his place on the rostrum and, with the gavel in his hand, bring the Assembly to order, I began to realize that this very human and very simple, unaffected man was more than just my father.

I do not recall in detail what took place. Even had I been asked to describe my surroundings at the time, I could hardly have done so. But I still remember the crowded Assembly Chamber. Scores of Assemblymen were everywhere—some in their seats, some gathered in groups of twos and threes and fours about the floor, some half lost among the visitors while they chatted with friends and relatives and political supporters. Greetings were being endlessly exchanged. Men I had never seen before, as well as some I vaguely recognized and a few I actually knew, came up to speak to Father before he went to the rostrum, and to speak to Mother and Grandmother. Now and then some of them even spoke to my brothers, my sister, and me.

Newspapermen, some with pencils and folded paper in their hands, seemed to be asking questions of everyone—of Father and other Assemblymen, of visitors I could not identify, even of Mother and Grandmother. And yet, despite the bewilderment I felt, it began to dawn on me that, among all the hundreds of people who were present, it was Father who was at the center of what was going on. Men continually congratulated him and shook his hand. They asked him questions and seemed intent on his replies. And presently he left us. For a time he disappeared from sight, lost, so far as I was concerned, among those who crowded around him. And then I saw him again as he made his way to the rostrum.

As I look back now, it seems to me that this may have been the moment I first began to recognize in Father at least a little of his true dimensions. And how clearly I remember the loudness and the sharpness of the sound when he raised the gavel and quickly brought it down, calling the Assembly to order for the first time in his new capacity as Speaker.

In later years I often heard him say that when he mounted the Assembly rostrum that day he imagined that he had reached the very apex of his political career. He often said, as well, that his year as Speaker was a period of almost constant turmoil, and I know that the session of 1913 was the longest and one of the stormiest on record. Before that year was out, the Legislature brought a State Supreme Court judge to trial (though he was exonerated), impeached the Governor, and sent a newspaperman to jail for contempt of the Assembly. And yet, despite the bitterness and heat that grew out of these activities, that very Legislature is to be credited with enacting an astonishing amount of much needed reform legislation.

Father had worked under very heavy pressure when he was majority leader and chairman of the Committee on Ways and Means, but now, as Speaker, he was fully as busy as he had been then, and the session, instead of lasting a little more than three months, continued, with occasional recesses, until Christmas.

Though Father served in the Assembly from 1904 to 1915—twelve terms—the Republicans were in the majority during all that time except in 1911 and 1913. It was not until 1911 that Father came to be accepted as a powerful political figure. From that time on, he was recognized as one of the Legislature's most effective members, though undoubtedly his period of greatest influence was the year he served as Speaker. It was then that the last of the legislation proposed by the Factory Investigating Commission was passed, thus completing what Henry Moskowitz once called "the most enlightened labor code ever placed on the statute books of any state." But though this and other useful legislation must be credited to the Legislature of which Father was the leader, that fact is often overlooked because of the furor that was aroused by the impeachment of Governor Sulzer.

Two years earlier the Legislature had passed a bill that proved, in its final form, to be an unsatisfactory compromise. Originally suggested as a direct primary law, this act actually provided for the nomination of many candidates by direct vote in party primaries. For the nomination of those who were to run on the state tickets, however, the party convention system was retained. The law also contained many other provisions, but any objective examination of it suggests that at least one result of it had been to create difficulties for fusion tickets and independent voters.

As is sometimes the case when comprises go too far, this law was not accepted very enthusiastically by anyone. The "liberals" still favored the direct primary for all nominations, while members of Tammany and many others much preferred the party convention system. However, Governor Sulzer, early in April 1913, sent a message to the Legislature urging the passage of a law abolishing the party convention system, but he failed to get the support for which he obviously hoped.

I cannot speak of Governor Sulzer with much firsthand knowledge. I have heard him described, by men who knew him, as an overly self-confident and egotistic person. Apparently with some justification, he has been called a bit of an actor—even a poseur—and though I saw him on only two or three occasions, and certainly cannot claim to have known him, I have not forgotten his great and somewhat unruly shock of red hair.

For years—first as a member of the Assembly and then as a member of Congress—he had had Tammany support, but in sending his message to the Legislature he was clearly presenting a point of view that belonged less to the recently victorious Democrats than to their liberal and Progressive opponents. Because of this both the Senate and the Assembly, by large majorities, refused to pass the bill for which he asked. Furthermore, they then passed a substitute measure which the Governor, in his veto message, referred to as an insult to the electorate.

It is not surprising, with such differences of opinion coming into the open, that the Governor and the Legislature began to find themselves even more widely in conflict. Early in the session some opposition had manifested itself in relation to several of the Governor's appointments, but now, with the fight over the primary law so clearly met, the Senate refused to confirm a long list of Sulzer's appointments, and on May 3 the Legislature adjourned.

Checked though he appeared to be, the Governor refused to concede defeat. Instead he endeavored to arouse the public in support of his defeated primary bill and called the Legislature back into special session in an effort to force the bill's enactment. Under the circumstances it hardly appears remarkable that the proposal he favored was soundly defeated again, but there can be little doubt that the developments which followed surprised the Governor as well as the public.

Under the Constitution of the state of New York no measures may be considered by a Legislature called in special session except those proposed by the Governor in his message. Now, however, the Governor sent a message that had to do with the Corrupt Practices Act. To his astonishment, I suppose, this opened a door that led the Legislature into an entirely new field, for a resolution was promptly offered and adopted authorizing an investigation of the campaign fund that had been raised in the Governor's behalf the year before. Moreover, witnesses testified that Sulzer had made false reports on the contributions he had received, and evidence was presented to show that some of the money had been used for speculative purposes.

With all this spread upon the record the Legisalture recessed on July 23, whereupon the Governor declared the special session adjourned. The Legislature reassembled, however, and the Assembly, on August 13, took up the matter of impeachment.

Father, as I have already said, had not supported Sulzer for nomination as Governor, and had found little in the man's program to support. Father was not alone in his lack of enthusiasm for the Governor, but now he was frank to admit that he was almost equally lacking in enthusiasm for the proposed impeachment proceedings. Father's idea of "regularity," I am confident, had some bearing on his point of view. He understood how greatly the impeachment of a Democratic Governor by a Legislature dominated by the same party would benefit the Republicans. But he found it impossible to argue with the facts that had already been disclosed and therefore reluctantly supported the resolution by which the Assembly voted, seventy-nine to forty-five, to impeach the Governor on eight counts.

Under the law the Assembly's part in the affair ended there, for the Court of Impeachment consisted of the judges of the State Court of Appeals and the members of the State Senate. Before this body a very strong case was presented. The Governor made no defense—failed even to take the stand. Found guilty on three counts, he was automatically removed from office, and was succeeded by the Lieutenant Governor, Martin H. Glynn.

Though he had offered no defense, Sulzer now made an effort to regain at least some portion of his lost public support. Running for the Assembly that very autumn, he was successful in being elected in the Sixth Assembly District, where, as a candidate of the Progressive party, he soundly defeated both his Republican and Democratic opponents. Furthermore, the Republicans gained control of the 1914

Assembly, defeating in the process many Democrats who had voted for Sulzer's impeachment. Perhaps this was at least partly due to the fact that, at the time, many people believed that the impeachment was more the result of Tammany's displeasure than of Sulzer's dishonesty. The time has now long passed, however, since I have heard anyone question the essential justice of the Court of Impeachment verdict.

The November elections of 1913, which gave the Republicans control of the 1914 Assembly, left the Senate still under the control of the Democrats. As a result the 1914 Legislature accomplished comparatively little. The 1913 Legislature, which had recessed after the Sulzer trial, reassembled in December and, following the recommendations of Governor Glynn, enacted several highly constructive measures.

The first of these was a direct primary law that abolished the old state convention system. A second bill simplified the ballot. A third had to do with the direct election of United States Senators. A fourth provided for a workmen's compensation law. And the fifth, which was to play an important part in Father's further progress, provided for submission to the people of a measure calling for a state constitutional convention.

Few legislative milestones were set up by the Legislature in either 1914 or 1915. In 1915, however, an event of real importance took place. Having been authorized by the vote of the people in the elections of 1914, the Constitutional Convention met in Albany, and on April 6 it began a serious and thoughtful attempt to rewrite the basic law of the Empire State.

I have already referred to the fact that in the state of New York such conventions, if approved in advance by the vote of the people, are called every twenty years. And in this case 116 Republican and 52 Democratic delegates were elected when the convention received the necessary popular support. Though overwhelmingly Republican those who were chosen nevertheless included many of the state's leading figures in both political parties, and Father was among them, representing the Senatorial district that included our Oliver Street neighborhood.

Senator Elihu Root, a national as well as a state figure of great prominence, became chairman. George W. Wickersham, who had been an Attorney General in the Cabinet of President Taft, served as leader of the Republican delegation, and Judge Morgan J. O'Brien, who had served as a judge of the Supreme Court of New York for thirty years, was chosen to lead the Democrats.

The task of the convention, as outlined by Senator Root in his opening speech, was to revise the state constitution, eliminating its obsolete portions, reducing the document to more compact form and incorporating amendments and improvements agreed upon by the delegates. Almost from the first the task proved difficult and when, at last, the work of the convention came to an end, the constitution, which, among other things was to have been condensed, had, in Father's words, "assumed the proportions of the New York telephone directory."

Great ability was demonstrated by many of the delegates—a fact which, in the years since then, has often been forgotten, for when the revised constitution was finally voted on by the people it was rejected— and for five months they labored arduously at their difficult task. Reactionary influences were constantly exerting pressure, and there was an almost uninterrupted struggle between the convention's liberal and conservative groups.

Among the delegates were men of wide legal experience. A large number, in fact—Elihu Root, George W. Wickersham, Henry L. Stimson, Morgan J. O'Brien, and more besides—would have been included in any fair-minded list of the nation's leading lawyers. Father had had no legal experience whatever. But in his years in the Assembly he had studied the government of the state so thoroughly and had come to understand it so well that, despite his lack of formal legal training, he played an active and consistently constructive role in opposing reactionary changes and in aiding in the preparation and adoption of liberal reforms.

When the convention met, he was unacquainted with many of its leading figures. Before it adjourned, however, he had come to know most of them intimately, and to count as friends not only leading Democratic delegates he had not known before, but also many Republicans—Root, for example, as well as Wickersham, Stimson, and others, many of whom came gladly to his assistance when, as Governor, he had occasion to ask their help. Most of these men were later willing to acknowledge Father's ability and usefulness in the convention.

"Of all the men in the convention," Elihu Root said when its work had been completed, "Alfred E. Smith was the best informed on the business of New York State."

"Root planted the crop," said Charles Evans Hughes, who was an

associate justice of the Supreme Court of the United States at the
time, "and Smith watered it."

And George W. Wickersham said even more when he referred to
Father as "the most useful man in the convention."

While the Constitutional Convention was in session, Mother and all
five of us children spent a good deal of time in Albany, and my brother
Alfred actually played a part in the convention itself as a volunteer
page boy. We children were occasionally permitted to visit the Assembly Chamber, where the convention met, but I must admit that,
so far as I was concerned, the debates I heard were more or less meaningless. I know, too, that though in our rooms at the Ten Eyck and
over our meals we must have heard Father explain what the convention's problems were, his remarks were either too complicated for me to
grasp or my mind was elsewhere. It seems to me that the outstanding
event of that summer was not the convention itself, but the news we received as the convention was reaching its conclusion—news that told
us that Tammany Hall's executive committee had chosen Father to
enter the approaching 1915 primary as a candidate for the office of
Sheriff of New York County.

Here was something that struck all of us children as being really
dramatic, though we didn't know what a sheriff's duties would be in a
city like New York. Arthur and Walter—my two younger brothers—
were not conscious of the fact that they did not know. They had seen
too many movies not to sense what a "Western" sheriff was, and they
imagined that Father was about to begin wearing chaps and a som-
brero, with a kerchief about his neck and with large six-shooters in
holsters hanging from his cartridge-laden belt. "When you are Sheriff,"
they asked, "can we be cowboys?" They learned the answer to that
question later, and also found out that Father's costume was to be the
same as it had always been, though I remember that some of Father's
friends humorously presented him with a revolver which he actually
had occasion to use, though only once. That was when he was called
upon to start a race by firing a blank cartridge from it in Madison
Square Garden.

When the Legislature had adjourned the preceding spring, Father
had had no idea that he was about to end his career in the Assembly.
By the time the Constitutional Convention adjourned on September
10, however, he knew that he was about to enter a political contest

such as he had never before had to face. Heretofore his campaigns had always been conducted within the somewhat narrow limits of the Second Assembly District. Now he was running for a county office and had to look for support throughout the whole of Manhattan.

He said later that he probably made more speeches in that campaign than any previous candidate for the office had ever made, but my own memories have less to do with the campaign than with the "old Home Night" that was celebrated on election evening on Oliver Street.

The Citizens Union, a nonpartisan and strongly anti-Tammany organization, supported Father in that campaign, and the New York *Tribune,* the city's leading Republican paper, published an editorial commending Father and expressing regret that he was leaving the Assembly.

When the returns began coming in on election evening, it was soon evident that Father had won. In fact, an overwhelming victory was indicated very early, and the celebration on Oliver Street promptly turned into a very enthusiastic occasion. The street was crowded for hours that evening, and Father spent a great deal of time shaking hands with the men and women—and even the children—of the district. People filled the street from curb to curb. Delegations representing numbers of different nationalities appeared to offer their congratulations. Even nearby Chinatown, though the Chinese were not voters, took part in the celebration, bringing many of their colorful lanterns and bright hangings over to Oliver Street.

I remember the eager scamperings of scores of children and listening to solemn speeches by heads of delegations. And I especially recall the endless handshaking friends and acquaintances who made their way up and down the six stone steps that led to our front door. Nor have I forgotten that when the returns had proved beyond any shadow of doubt that Father had been elected we had our picture taken in the parlor—Father, Mother, and the five children. And that picture brings back the details of the occasion vividly. It even suggests a little of the carnival atmosphere of Oliver Street that evening, for in it a few twisted bits of colorful serpentine paper are shown beneath our feet in the corner of the parlor.

In the picture Father is shown wearing a wing collar, a bow tie, and a derby—a black one, incidentally, and not the brown one that later became so famous. The rest of us appear to have been much less individualistic. Everything we wore now appears quite hopelessly out of date, and one wonders why anyone should have chosen such things. All our shoes, for instance—except Mother's—were high, and mine were very high indeed, and buttoned as well. And the hat I wore convinces me, I am glad to say, that my taste in such matters has changed as much as have the times.

The office of Sheriff was not one Father really enjoyed. During the preceding twelve years he had come to be an influential and constructive legislator whose political understanding and experience had elevated him to a position of importance in Albany, but as Sheriff he had duties that were much less stimulating than his work in Albany had been. The new office provided no real challenge, and yet the position had its advantages.

As an Assemblyman, Father had received a salary of fifteen hundred dollars a year, though members of the Legislature were also given ten cents a mile for necessary travel. Now his salary was twelve thousand dollars a year—as much in twelve months as he had been paid during eight years in the Assembly. And that was the smallest part of his new income, for in addition to this salary the Sheriff of New York County was then given half of all the fees collected by his office throughout his term.

Naturally, we children were not told what Father's income was. But we began to enjoy many conveniences and even luxuries we had never been able to afford before—our first automobile, for instance. Father also enlarged and improved the Oliver Street house. Still, I had no real idea how much our economic situation had improved. It was not until Father's autobiography was published in 1929 that I learned that during his two years as Sheriff his income from fees alone amounted to about $105,000. I think I should point out, however, that his term as Sheriff gave him the only opportunity he ever had during his political career to accumulate any substantial savings. He was the last holder of the office to whom any portion of the fees was paid, for during his term the Legislature did away with that long-established but finally outmoded system.

Having reached my fourteenth birthday just before Father's induction as Sheriff, I was beginning to have a little better understanding of politics. Its intricacies were still beyond me, but the fascination politics had always had for Father began to be apparent to me. Only a few months after he entered his new office, I graduated from St. James' School, and soon thereafter the family went to Patchogue, Long Island, for the summer. Then, not long after we returned to Oliver Street, I was sent to the Ursiline Convent School in Bedford Park.

For the most part the girls in the school were day pupils who went home when classes were over at three o'clock. But there were two dormitories for boarding students, and I was assigned to one of these, along with some twenty other girls, a few of whom came from places as distant as South America. Pupils whose homes were no farther away than mine were permitted to leave school on Friday afternoon provided we returned on Sunday evening, and we were also at home for Christmas and Easter, as well as during the summer.

Taught by Ursiline nuns in black costumes, with big white bibs and with white bands across their foreheads, we studied Latin, history, English, algebra, and Christian doctrine, and living, as we did, in dormitories where we had only as much privacy as was made possible by curtains that could be drawn about each girl's bed and washstand, we found ourselves much less active as individuals than as parts of a carefully directed group.

This new life was very different from the one I had known at home, and under the circumstances I learned comparatively little about Father's new activities. If my school life in itself was not enough to explain my outlook, I need only add that during Father's second year as Sheriff the United States entered World War I, and the world we children had assumed to be fully formed and more or less immutable began to undergo such changes as history had seldom recorded before. At the time, I gave Father's new position little thought and was much more interested in the many speeches he made in behalf of government loans than in his work as Sheriff.

When Father was elected to his new post, John Purroy Mitchel was Mayor of New York, and in 1917 he made a bid for re-election on an Independent ticket. He was a man of real ability and, in addition to having many Republican followers, he was being supported by many independent Democrats. Because of this it was obvious to every politician in New York that he would be hard to defeat, and when John F. Hylan, a county judge of Kings County (Brooklyn), was nominated on the Democratic ticket, every effort was made to strengthen the ticket he headed.

Two years earlier Father had been elected by a large majority, and with his great political popularity in mind the Democratic leaders, who knew very well that the city ticket needed all the help it could get, urged him to run for the office of President of the Board of Aldermen, and Father agreed. He readily obtained the nomination, and I believe it fair to say that it was he, more than any other, who was most effective in the campaign that followed.

His opponent was Robert Adamson, a well-known newspaperman with whom Father had long been friendly. As a political writer for the New York *World* for ten years Mr. Adamson had come to have a wide political acquaintance, and he had later been secretary to Mayor Gaynor and to Gaynor's successor, Mayor Kline. He had also managed Mayor Mitchel's previous campaign and had been appointed Fire Commissioner as a result. But he had never run for political office before, and in view of Father's reputation as an effective opponent in debate—a reputation that had been thoroughly established in the Assembly—it is remarkable that Adamson challenged Father to a joint debate.

When the challenge came, Father accepted, for that kind of thing was to his liking, and the debate was held in a Brooklyn club. Adamson spoke first. "What," he concluded, turning to Father, "are your qualifications for the office of President of the Board of Aldermen?"

In later years I was often with Father when he addressed political gatherings, and I am convinced that he was never more effective than when he was replying directly to some questioner. He had what sometimes seemed to be a kind of intuitive ability to read the collective minds of his audiences, and the simple and often forceful directness of his replies always seemed to make a favorable impression.

"My qualifications," he began when he rose to reply to Adamson's question, "are twelve years as a member of the New York Legislature and four years as Democratic floor leader there. I was for one year Speaker of the Assembly. I was six years on its Cities Committee, which revised the New York City Charter. As chairman of the Committee on Ways and Means I personally prepared the state budget. It cut down expenses by fifteen million dollars as compared with the last of Governor Hughes's administrations.

"I was vice-chairman of the committee which obtained our existing excellent factory protection laws. I was a member of all the important committees of the last Constitutional Convention. If there is any man in the city with the same Legislative experience, let him speak. I will be glad to surrender my nomination to him and go back to Fulton Market."

When Father completed his reply, the applause of the audience made it plain to Mr. Adamson that his question had been less than wise.

It may not have been very widely known at the time—may, perhaps, not have been known at all except to a few intimates—but Father was not impressed by the ability of Judge Hylan, the Democratic candidate for Mayor. Nevertheless, he energetically campaigned in behalf of the whole Democratic ticket, and because his own success was reasonably assured far in advance, he spent more time in campaigning for others than for himself.

Many influences were at work. For one thing, the campaign took place during the war, and the Socialist vote—perhaps in protest—was very large. Wartime shortages, too, no doubt had caused much dissatisfaction with the Mitchel administration, and Tammany, of course, had had many long years of experience in city elections. Thus the Democratic ticket was successful. Mayor Hylan was elected, and so was Father, along with a majority of the members of the Board of Aldermen.

It was on January 1, 1918, that Father was inaugurated as President of the Board of Aldermen, and our Oliver Street neighborhood made the most of the occasion, for City Hall lies no more than three or four minutes' walk from where we lived. The celebration that drew so many people to the street before our house surpassed even the "Old Home" celebration that had marked Father's election as Sheriff, but as I think of those days now I am much more impressed by Father's remarks at the first meeting of the newly elected Board of Aldermen than I was by the neighborhood gaiety that filled Oliver Street with so many of Father's friends and supporters.

As I have said, the Democratic Aldermen formed a majority of the Board. Among the others were not only the usual Republicans, but also—and for the first time—a number of Socialists. Father was conscious of these members, of course, and was acutely aware of the significance of their presence. He made no attempt to belittle either their influence or their number. Instead, when he brought the first meeting to order, he clearly had the Socialists in mind.

"To the majority party," he said, "I desire to say that the people of the city in no uncertain terms placed upon us a grave responsibility. The glory that comes from what we do of benefit can be claimed by everybody. Those things which are neglected constitute our sins of omission.

"I have a keen understanding of the relationship to the body of the minority and the minor minority—meaning the Socialist members. The people rule negatively as well as affirmatively, and a good, healthy, vigorous minority is the necessary check on great power.

"The rules of the board are intended for the protection of the rights of minorities as well as to expedite the business of the majority. In that spirit, I will interpret them with a desire to do equal and evenhanded justice to all."

That point of view, I fear, has not invariably been apparent in American politics, and it would be interesting if we could know what might have been the result if Father had completed his four-year term in his new position. But that was not to be. Before eight months had passed it became clear that he would be a candidate for the Democratic nomination as Governor, and exactly one year from the day on which he assumed the position of President of the Board of Aldermen of the city of New York, he took the oath of office as Governor of the Empire State.

CHAPTER FIVE

Tammany Hall and Election
as Governor

WORLD WAR I was approaching its final phases when Father began his four-year term as President of the Board of Aldermen, and wartime activities and demands were pressing New York City to the limits of its capacity and energy. Because of this the problems that arose in connection with the city's administration far exceeded those of normal times, though the war dominated the news of the day and these local difficulties were given less than normal attention by the press. Not long after the new administration had taken office, however, a cold spell blocked the Hudson River with heavy concentrations of drifting ice, and thousands of tons of badly needed coal that had reached the freight yards on the New Jersey side could not be brought across to Manhattan. The situation quickly threatened to grow serious, and news of it appeared prominently in the papers.

Mayor Hylan was away at the time and because the President of the Board of Aldermen becomes Acting Mayor in the absence of the Mayor, Father was faced by the problem which milder weather was slow to solve. This experience ultimately served him in good stead, for it provided him with much pointed information, on which, as Governor, he later based his approval of the plan for a vehicular tunnel under the Hudson that would make possible a route into the city that would be less subject to interruption. This introduction to one of the city's problems also later played a part in the evolution of the Port of New York Authority's wonderfully comprehensive plans for developing and improving the vast community that occupies portions of two states at the mouth of the Hudson. Father was able to make little more than a good beginning in his new position, however, before it became evident that he was being considered as a potential Democratic candidate for Governor in the election that was to take place in the autumn of 1918.

As every New Yorker knows, the voting strength of the Democrats in the Empire State is most heavily concentrated in New York City while that of the Republicans is mostly to be found elsewhere in the state. Because of this it is not hard to see why Democratic candidates on state tickets always hope to make a strong appeal "upstate" and why Republican candidates hope to do the same in the city. It is not that either side expects to win outright in "the enemy's" territory. That is rarely done. If the opposition vote is reduced where it is largest, however, a candidate who is strongly supported elsewhere is closer, by that much, to victory. With this in mind it is understandable that Tammany leaders are often willing to go out of their way to keep from giving the impression that they wish to force candidates they prefer on upstate Democrats. Knowing that Tammany support may actually prove to be a handicap outside the city, they are often hopeful that the candidates they favor will first be proposed upstate.

Tammany Hall is a most misunderstood organization. It takes its name, though only indirectly, from an Indian known as Tamanend—or Tammany—who was a former "sachem" or chief of the Delawares. I know nothing about him except that his name is said to have been a Delaware term meaning "the affable," or "the friendly one." In fact, there may never actually have been any such chief. I must say, however, that "the friendly one" would serve very well to describe several of the Tammany leaders I have known, and whether or not this Delaware chief ever actually existed, we know that even before the American Revolution there were Whig societies that were known as "Sons of St. Tammany" and "Sons of Liberty." With strong revolutionary leanings these societies commonly used Indian words in their rituals with the idea, apparently, of suggesting that the organizations were purely American in character.

The successful outcome of the Revolution brought about the decline of these patriotic societies, but on May 12, 1789, just twelve days after New York City had seen George Washington inaugurated as our first President, a certain William Mooney founded the "Secret Society of St. Tammany or Columbian Order." It may be that Mooney had been a member of some earlier Tammany society with revolutionary interests, but the new organization he founded was nonpolitical in purpose. It was successful, and in 1805 it was incorporated as a benevolent society. In 1811 it built a meeting place—which it called the Wigwam—near City Hall, and the society continued to occupy it until 1867, when it moved to new quarters on Fourteenth Street, where it was still to be found when Father was President of the Board of Aldermen. This Society of St. Tammany, however, is not the political organization that has played so great a part in New York City. For more than a century and a half it has existed, as it still exists today, only as a benevolent and nonpolitical society, but it rents its hall to the Democratic County Committee of the county of New York, and this committee, many of whose leading members are also members of the Society of St. Tammany, is the political organization that is almost universally referred to as Tammany Hall.

It may be that these facts are not well known, but even fewer people realize that though Tammany Hall has been deep in politics since the days of Aaron Burr the organization was controlled by committees and not by individual "bosses" until the emergence of Boss Tweed—William M. Tweed—in the decade following the Civil War. And this first real boss of Tammany, along with a group of obviously willing lieutenants, succeeded in plundering the city so extensively that even yet Tammany's reputation has not entirely recovered.

Tweed was ultimately sent to jail, where he died, but the committee system he had overthrown did not return. First John Kelly and then Richard Croker became bosses in their turn, and in 1902, after a series of political reverses, Croker gave up his leadership and returned to his native Ireland. His successor was Charles F. Murphy, a man whose character differed sharply from that of his predecessor.

The earlier leaders of Tammany—Tweed, Kelly, and Croker—have never been much more than names to me, but our family knew Mr. Murphy well. Father's first meeting with him took place on a sand bar at Quogue, Long Island, during the summer of 1908. This meeting appeared at the time to be nothing more than a casual contact, and Father never felt it had been anything but that, though accounts were later written suggesting—and even saying—that it was very much more. We had taken a cottage that summer at a place now known as Hampton Bays, but then called Good Ground, not far from Mr. Murphy's summer home, and Father was swimming when the two were introduced. I have since read that because of what Tom Foley had said about Father, Mr. Murphy was interested in him even as early as that. That is possible, but Father, I know, had no knowledge of it, and I know, too, that he and Mr. Murphy did not come to know each other well until 1911, when Father was majority leader in the Assembly. It may have been about then that I first came to know this unusually silent leader of Tammany Hall.

As those who are acquainted with the eastern end of Long Island are aware, a short canal has been cut through a narrow portion of the island, connecting Shinnecock Bay with Peconic Bay, and close beside the highway bridge that spans the canal there has been for many years a hostelry known as Canoe Place Inn. The inn that stands there now bears no resemblance to the much smaller one I knew as a child. Whatever the older place lacked in size it made up in more intimate qualities. Every room in the old inn was very small, and there were not many of them, either. Even the dining room was small, and I remember that there were no menus. But then no menus were needed for no choices were possible. One merely took what was provided, though no one ever complained for the food was always excellent. And at the time I am trying to recall, this little inn, whose location was then much more remote than it is now, had come to be a favorite meeting place for an important group of politicians from New York. This no doubt was due to the fact that Mr. Murphy's summer home was only a few minutes' drive from the inn, but even when the Murphy home was closed—on Thanksgiving or Decoration Day, for example, or on off-season weekends—politicians and their families sometimes gathered at Canoe Place Inn, and then Mr. Murphy himself was often present.

Political problems always took precedence when these meetings occurred, but having had no part in such discussions, I remember much more clearly that we children learned to play hearts in the little parlor of the inn. Nor were we sent off merely to play alone. Father and Mother often played with us, and so did Mr. Murphy. Sometimes there were others, too—Senator Wagner, for example.

It was not only there that we saw Mr. Murphy. During several summers when we had our own cottage at Good Ground, he often took us children about his extensive farm, letting us pet the animals or look in the hens' nests for eggs. He was taller than Father, and heavier, though he was anything but portly. And he was meticulous in his appearance. There was nothing of the shirt-sleeved politician about him, and nothing that was casual. Even when he went with us to the stable, the hen house, or the pasture he was certain to be dressed as neatly and conservatively as he would have been in the city.

He was smooth-shaven, and his glasses were rimless pince-nez of a kind now almost never seen. His hair was thin and gray by the time I knew him, and though his natural dignity made it easy for him to keep people at a distance, he was always friendly with children. His voice was the lowest and gentlest I have ever known a man to have.

Father always called him "Commissioner." To most people, however, he was "Mr. Murphy," and though he remained leader of Tammany Hall for a longer period than any of his predecessors he bore no resemblance to the popular idea of a political boss.

Born in New York City in 1858, he became a streetcar driver as a young man. The salary he received was small, but somehow he managed to save a little money, and with it opened a saloon. He ran it carefully, maintained good order there, and ultimately became the proprietor of several places, which he is said to have defended as "poor men's clubs." In 1892 he succeeded a certain Edward Hagan as Tammany leader of the Eighteenth Assembly District, and in 1897 he was appointed a member of the board of Commissioners of Docks and Ferries. He served in that capacity for five years, and when Richard Croker retired as leader of Tammany Hall, Mr. Murphy succeeded him.

Father, who came to know him intimately, often said that Mr. Murphy was not the boss at all in the commonly accepted meaning of that term. He surrounded himself with men of ability—leading lawyers, well-trained men of business, and others—and he was inclined to accept their conclusions. In fact, he often expressed his belief in them by asking, "If these men do not understand this thing, who does?"

"He was a good adviser," Father once wrote, "and if he placed his confidence in a man he allowed that man to make decisions."

This did not mean, of course, that Mr. Murphy had no ideas of his own. He was keenly interested in constructive social legislation and unhesitatingly gave his full support to the bills that were based, for example, on the conclusions of the Factory Investigation Commission. He also favored the widows' pension bill and other legislation of that nature. Far from attempting to dictate he often succeeded in advancing ideas that he favored by quietly and diplomatically encouraging others to propose them. And that, I suspect, was the method he chose in preparing for the gubernatorial election of 1918.

Throughout the spring of 1918 the progress of World War I dominated developments of every other kind, and with Father so recently installed in his new position in the city administration, I gave little heed to any other possible political office for him. School occupied my time for five days a week, and on the remaining two days I worked in a canteen that Mrs. Hylan, the wife of the Mayor, and Mrs. William Randolph Hearst were operating at the corner of Fortieth Street and Fifth Avenue. It was run for men in uniform, and because of its location was almost always a busy place. I have no idea how much food we dispensed—sandwiches and coffee, doughnuts, pie, ice cream, and other things—but the total wasn't small, and those who prepared the portions we handed out across our service counter were busy every moment of the time. I remember that the portions Mrs. Hearst always heaped upon those plates were quite the most generous we served. In no time at all I learned to tell, merely by the sizes of the pieces of pie she cut and by her more than ample servings of ice cream, when she had donned her apron and gone to work.

Father took a summer cottage at Good Ground again that year—a cottage that was close to the houses that stood beside it. However, it was convenient to the water and was only a short drive from Mr. Murphy's big, rambling house, which explains why it was chosen. Two other political leaders also had cottages nearby—Nicholas J. Hays, the Tammany leader of the Harlem district, and Judge Morgan J. O'Brien—and I learned to play bridge that summer with their daughters, Nora, Catherine, and Helen Hays, and Estelle and Maud O'Brien. And Mr. Murphy's daughter Mabel, though she was older, played with us as well.

I do not remember just how soon after we reached Good Ground that my brothers, my sister, and I first began to realize that Father might become a candidate for Governor. He had been President of the Board of Aldermen for only about six months when we left for the Good Ground cottage, and because we knew he had been elected for a four-year term we probably did not stop to think of the possibility of any other office. Our elders, however, were surely looking further ahead, and Mr. Murphy, I later learned, was hopeful that the upstate Democratic leaders would select some potential candidate for Governor who would be especially strong in the Republican-dominated areas outside New York City.

Because of the primary law that had been passed just after the impeachment of Governor Sulzer, candidates on state tickets were no longer chosen at party conventions, though that did not mean that political gatherings of that nature had been utterly eliminated. Officially recognized party conventions were no longer permitted. Someone, however, had to choose those who would contend for the nominations in the primaries, and this task was naturally assumed by the leaders of the two great political parties, who met in "unofficial conventions" for that purpose. In 1918 a group of Democratic leaders, one of whom was Mr. Murphy, held a preliminary meeting at the Syracuse home of William F. Kelly, the leader of Onondaga County, even before the unofficial convention was held. They hoped to be able to agree on an upstate candidate, but it soon became obvious that no agreement could be reached, and after another meeting that was held in New York City, they decided that though a Tammany Hall candidate would be acceptable this would be the case only if enough upstate leaders first expressed their willingness to support him.

In the course of these discussions fifteen or twenty individuals had been considered, most of whom were none too strongly supported, and no one of whom could be agreed upon. No publicity attended these discussions, but word of what had taken place was given to the leaders who made up the unofficial convention when it met in Saratoga early in August.

Father was one of the leaders who attended the Saratoga meeting, though everyone soon saw that he was also an important contender for the gubernatorial nomination. This placed him in a very awkward position, for under the circumstances he did not feel free to further his own candidacy and he felt even less free to oppose any of the others whose names were being considered. He therefore confined himself largely to his room at the Grand Union Hotel. Meanwhile the potential candidates were being considered and one by one were being eliminated.

The meeting lasted for three days—an exciting three days for Father, as he later admitted. But it was not only he who was excited. We at Good Ground were excited too.

I doubt if we had realized, prior to the Saratoga meeting, that Father was a really serious contender for the nomination. Once we became aware of it, however, we thought of little else, and when Tom Campbell, our Oliver Street friend and neighbor, told Mother that he was so interested in the outcome that he was about to leave for Saratoga, my brother Arthur, who was eleven at the time, begged her to let him go along, assuring her with all his youthful enthusiasm and conviction that if only he could be there he would be sure "to bring home the bacon." And not only did Mother let him go, but also, shortly after he got there, Father's candidacy was agreed upon and it was Arthur who called Mother on the phone and gave her the exciting news.

The Saratoga decision, important though it was, did not make Father's nomination certain. But as a result of it he was entered in the primary by the regular Democratic organization, and therefore his prospects for success were excellent. He was opposed by William Church Osborn, a prominent New York lawyer, whose name appeared on the primary ballot as a result of a petition filed by a group of independent Democrats. Despite the strength of Father's position Mr. Osborn's opposition was not to be taken lightly. Eminent both as a lawyer and a businessman, he was widely known in the field of politics. He had been a member of the New York State Constitutional Convention of 1894, had been legal adviser to Governor Dix in 1911, and had been chairman of the Democratic State Committee from 1914 to 1916. A man of widely recognized ability, he was certain of much support. Early in the evening of the day the primary vote was cast, however, it began to be clear that Father had won. His lead was so promptly seen to be overwhelming that he left New York City at midnight—well before the final results were tabulated—for Binghamton, where, at the Broome County Fair on the following day, he began his campaign against the Republican incumbent, Governor Whitman.

Except for weekends, I was back in school throughout the whole campaign. I must admit, however, that the newspaper accounts of Father's speeches and the reports of his other activities interested me more than my schoolbooks did. And when I went home for the weekend before Election Day, it was with the understanding that I would not return to school until the election was over and the returns were in.

Unexpected difficulties had arisen in the campaign. It is true that Governor Whitman, the Republican candidate, was felt by some observers to have weakened his position in the state by aiming too obviously at the somewhat remote 1920 Republican nomination for the Presidency. Still, he was running for a third term as Governor and he was not alone in being conscious of the fact that if he were victorious he would surely be a strong contender for the Presidential nomination.

This possibility was not directly a part of the campaign. In the immediate situation, it was more to the point that Whitman had done very well in his two earlier Gubernatorial campaigns. He had defeated Governor Glynn in 1914 by 145,000 votes, and in 1916 he had defeated Judge Samuel Seabury by 149,000. In view of these successes few observers expected him to make a poor showing. And Republican prospects were certainly not dimmed by the fact that the widespread influenza epidemic of 1918 greatly reduced the number of people at many public gatherings before which Father spoke while campaigning in upstate New York. Some meetings were called off entirely, and sometimes Father found that the "great crowds" he was supposed to be addressing consisted, for the most part—and once or twice entirely— merely of a few political leaders and the newspapermen who had been assigned to cover his campaign.

He spent three weeks upstate, but in that time he was able to speak to large gatherings in public auditoriums only in Buffalo, Albany, and Ithaca. Elsewhere he often spoke in the open, it is true, but throughout the campaign the epidemic greatly reduced the number of those who heard him. It even cut down the vote when Election Day finally arrived, though that, as it turned out, worked to Father's advantage, for the New York City vote was not correspondingly reduced.

In later years Father came to be much better known to the voters of the state than he was during the 1918 campaign. He had had a wide acquaintance among upstate political leaders, newspapermen, and businessmen, and many of these people, having known him in the Assembly or having met him when he was going about the state as vice-chairman of the Factory Investigation Committee, recognized his ability. He was less well known, however, among the people at large, and many of them were strongly opposed to him because of his Tammany connections. He understood all this and recognized the fact that the support he might gain in areas remote from the city of New York would be the result of the voters' ideas of his record and his personality.

Even in New York there has always been more or less opposition to Tammany, and that has been doubly true upstate. It was only to be expected, therefore, that the Republicans would make the most of Father's long-time Tammany connections. The chairman of his personal campaign organization, however, was Abram I. Elkus, a non-Tammany Democrat who had not only served as counsel for the Factory Investigation Committee, but also had later been appointed Ambassador to Turkey by President Wilson. Furthermore, Father was aided by the fact that many non-Tammany specialists in social welfare and progressive citizenship were members of the committee that Mr. Elkus headed, while Father's "board of strategy" included many names to which no one could object.

Tammany Hall was very strong in New York City, and regular Democratic organizations throughout the state were also helpful. John F. Gilchrist, an old Oliver Street friend and member of Tammany Hall, was chosen to act as the connecting link between all these interested groups, and both Tammany and non-Tammany organizations worked to further Father's campaign.

Father had had years of experience as a campaigner and had always been an effective speaker. Unlike many public figures he never spoke from prepared manuscripts. He always knew just what he intended to say, and sometimes was willing to give newspaper reporters detailed advance information about some coming speech. Invariably he spoke merely from penciled headings he had jotted down in longhand on envelopes. He preferred envelopes for this purpose because he found it convenient both to pencil his notes on them and to enclose special and related information inside—clippings, for example, or direct quotations that he might care to read. His speeches were never outlined in any other way, and the penciled headings on the envelopes were often hardly understandable to anyone but himself.

From the time he first entered politics he had always found it easy to make himself heard without the aid of microphones. He explained this by saying that he had "a good loud voice," but there was more to it than that. His voice was naturally loud and there was a roughness about it, but it was resonant and understandable as well.

His manner of speech was highly individual and utterly unlike that of the polished orators of his youth. Poetical passages and flowing perorations were not for him. He was always clearly conscious of the points he wished to make, and he was always well prepared, but he was quite naturally informal. He was fluent and, in his own way, often eloquent. Neither his fluency nor his eloquence, however, were the result of form or polish. They were the result, instead, of his sincerity and deep conviction. The informality of his approach always left him free to take advantage of unexpected developments—even of interruptions—and I never saw him leave any platform without having made the points he had had in mind when he began to speak.

He had his share of bitter opponents in the 1918 campaign. The Anti-

Saloon League, for example, attacked him heavily, insisting that in some unexplained way he was tied up with the liquor interests. He was even attacked because of his religion, though not on the scale that he later experienced. In some rural areas this worked in his disfavor, though elsewhere these attacks were resented and proved helpful to him.

Having completed his campaign upstate, he returned to New York City a week before Election Day. It is interesting to recall that no exceptional issues played any decisive part in the campaign. The war dominated everything, and everyone was solidly back of the immense military effort the country was making. On that account nothing connected with the struggle affected the campaign. New York State policies were discussed, of course, and Father criticized Governor Whitman's administration for extravagance. When Whitman attempted to belittle Father's years of public service, saying that he had "never earned a dollar with his hands," the Governor drew only a single sentence in reply.

"When my opponent was a student at Amherst," Father pointed out in his very next speech, "I was working from dawn to dark in the Fulton Fish Market."

Far more impressive was a statement he made in concluding a speech at the Women's University Club of New York. His audience consisted entirely of women, and in addressing them he first outlined the whole story of the suffrage movement in New York State and then outlined his ideas of the basis of representative government. He was speaking as a candidate for office, and he concluded what he had to say with that in mind. His audience, he knew, was not a typical one. The women who composed it were college graduates, and though they had had little experience in politics they were cultured, well educated, and well informed. On that account he knew that they would be impressed not only by his experience and ability, but also by his sincerity and honesty. As I have already remarked, Father seems to have had a kind of instinctive understanding of the collective minds of his audiences, and it was that understanding, I believe, that now dictated the conclusion of his speech.

"I have spent twelve years in the Assembly in the state of New York," he told them, "and I know the state government. I want to say to you here and now that if I am elected I will do what my conscience tells me is best for the state of New York. If I do wrong, you may be sure that it will not be from ignorance, and you can hold me responsible."

His two final speeches of the campaign were in the main auditorium of the Brooklyn Academy of Music and in the larger auditorium of Carnegie Hall. He was a born New Yorker, and both the Brooklyn audience and the greater Manhattan one were made up very largely of his enthusiastic adherents. I attended these two meetings but all that I remember about them is that both auditoriums were crowded almost to suffocation with so many of Father's cheering supporters that, in my inexperience, I felt certain his overwhelming victory was assured.

Any election has its elements of suspense, and though from my earliest recollections our family had always eagerly awaited every election outcome, we all were doubly eager this time. We knew that Father had never before been confronted with so great a contest or one in which so many factors new to us might influence the outcome. As I have already said, Father's re-election to the Assembly each year had always been practically assured. We had never feared the results. Our greatest interest had usually been in the extent of his majority. When he had run for Sheriff he had been forced to look for support throughout the whole of Manhattan, and when he had run for President of the Board of Aldermen he had had to campaign throughout all five of the city's counties. Accustomed to the narrow limits of the Second Assembly District, our whole family had been much impressed by the greatly extended territory covered in these two campaigns. Now, however, with the entire state of New York to be considered, Election Day took on proportions so huge and complicated in our minds—or at least in mine—as to be difficult to grasp. Later, as Father ran again and again for Governor, I came to be familiar with every part of the state. I came to know the political potentialities of every county from the so-called "southern tier" to the St. Lawrence River, and from Montauk Point and the state's eastern border to the Great Lakes. I even came to have a considerable understanding of what might be expected in every city, every county seat, and practically every other community of consequence in the state. Yet on the evening of Election Day in 1918 I had little knowledge of what most of the state might actually do. I knew that the upstate counties were certain to be strongly Republican while New York City was sure to be the opposite, but I had never before followed the tabulation that told the whole complicated story of returns throughout the state, and I was soon overwhelmed by the intricate and apparently conflicting nature of the returns.

Throughout the city the regular Democratic political organization had been hard at work for Father, and in addition the Citizens' Committee had been organized to support him. Made up largely of independent voters and former members of the Progressive party, it included many Democrats who were not affiliated with the regular organization, and even some Republicans who hoped for a change in Albany. This was the committee of which Abram I. Elkus was chairman, and not only its headquarters but the headquarters of the state Democratic organization were in the Biltmore Hotel, where our whole family went on the evening of Election Day to get the election returns.

We arrived at the Biltmore when only the earliest returns had begun to come in—Mother, Grandmother, Aunt Mamie, and all of us children—and had dinner there in a private dining room. Father was busy and did not join us, but I remember that Mrs. Jimmy Walker and Mrs. Gilchrist did. Dinner, however, meant little to any of us. The election returns were what we had come to hear, and by the time dinner was over and we were back in the crowded headquarters rooms again, figures were coming in rapidly.

The first returns were from the state's larger communities, and for a time the figures were almost entirely from New York City itself. These were greatly in Father's favor, and as the reports continued to come in, his lead increased until it assumed immense proportions.

It is important to remember, in considering any state-wide vote in New York, that New York City, in addition to being the stronghold of the Democrats, contains more than half of the entire population of the state. The population is greater now than it was in 1918, but even then the proportions were more or less what they are now, the population of the city then totaling about five and one-half million while that of the entire state was only about ten million. And because the city returns were among the earliest to come in, for an hour or two after the polls had closed, Father's lead grew until it assumed overwhelming proportions.

There at Democratic headquarters everyone, naturally, was a Democratic partisan, and our delight and enthusiasm grew by leaps and bounds. It was still early in the evening when people started to crowd around Father, shaking his hand, congratulating him, and calling him

"Governor." And it seems to me now that he was the least excited of us all.

I realize that I could hardly have been called a cool and objective observer. My seventeenth birthday still lay a little way ahead, and though I had begun to consider myself quite grown-up, I was still a good deal short of that. Therefore Father's attempts to restrain our enthusiasm seemed to me more an expression of his modesty than of his political understanding.

"Wait now," he said again and again when overenthusiastic friends came up to congratulate him on his victory. "Most of the returns so far have been from places that are on our side. But the returns will soon be coming in from the small cities and towns upstate. Give the other fellow his day in court before you decide just what the result will be."

And, sure enough, as the hours passed and the returns continued to come in, Father's immense lead began to be reduced. I attempted to be philosophical about it at first, recalling what I had been told about the strength of the Republicans upstate. By now practically all the returns were in from the Democratic strongholds, and though now and again some previously unreported election districts gave Father a big majority, most of the returns that were arriving did exactly the opposite. By midnight, in fact, his lead had been so greatly reduced as to frighten me, and many who were far more experienced than I began to grow concerned as well. Throughout all the crowded rooms the gay enthusiasm of early evening had noticeably lessened.

Headquarters remained crowded all night long, and it was not until eight o'clock in the morning that Mother and I left. Grandmother, however, was unable to stay that long. By three o'clock she was almost exhausted and Father asked Aunt Mamie to take her home, and Arthur, Walter, and Catherine must have been sent home about then too, though I did not think of leaving, and neither did my brother Alfred.

Because we had been accustomed to Father's uninterrupted victories for so many years, some of those upstate returns were almost too much for us to grasp. When precinct after precinct in Manhattan had given Father immense majorities, we had accepted the figures as a matter of course. We merely laughed, for instance, when the returns from the Oliver Street district came in and we learned that Father had carried it by a vote of 387 to 2. It is true that Father had never done quite that well before even there in our own home district, but the figures did not appear at all astonishing to us. However, when upstate returns began to show figures that were very nearly as extreme the other way, it was not only I who found them hard to believe. About two o'clock in the morning, for instance, when one of Father's friends who was getting the returns in Park Row far downtown heard that the city of J᎑᎑᎑᎑estown had given Governor Whitman an overwhelming majority, he got in his car and hurried up to the Biltmore. Just why he had been so affected by the Jamestown returns I do not know. Other upstate reports had been somewhat similar. The Jamestown figures, however, had especially bothered him, and he seemed intent on driving there at once. It is true that he did not know just where Jamestown was, and he may not have known exactly what he hoped to do there, either. When Father told him that the place was four hundred miles away and could not be reached by auto in much less than two days, he reconsidered and drove back downtown to Park Row.

Our optimism declined as Father's early lead began to melt away. At first I could hardly believe that the trend against him would continue, but it did, and I became increasingly concerned. There was nothing I could do, but in my youthful desperation I made a solemn promise that if Father were elected I would not eat a piece of candy for five years!

I was just about seventeen and I was fond of candy. Furthermore, five years is a long time when one is young. But I was utterly sincere when I made that promise, and I am glad to be able to say that I kept it, though now and again, I must admit, I was sorely tempted.

The crowd at headquarters shifted and changed somewhat as the night wore on, though it did not seem to grow much smaller. The returns were coming in by telegraph and telephone, for radio had not yet begun to play a part in such affairs. Nowadays anyone can remain comfortably at home, tuning in the returns with no trouble whatever. But then those who wished to keep in touch with developments could do so only at the comparatively few places where the telegraphic reports were being received and compiled. Otherwise it was necessary to wait until the early editions of the papers came out. Therefore, interested people kept coming in throughout the night and were able, under various pretexts, to crowd even into the "private" rooms in which those who were closest to Father gathered together over the growing figures. Now and again, these "private" rooms became so crowded that we would slip out one by one to some new room that had been cleared, and there reassemble in more comfort. I remember that

r. and Mrs. Alfred E. Smith
the time of their marriage,
May 6, 1900.

Alfred E. Smith when he was
Speaker of the New York
State Assembly in 1913.

Mrs. Alfred E. Smith, Sr.
(Catherine Mulvehill Smith,
the Governor's mother),
about 1918.

after one move Mrs. Jimmy Walker, who was with us all night long, assumed the post of doorkeeper. Father was with his campaign manager elsewhere, and Mrs. Walker was being reasonably successful in keeping people out of the room to which we had just moved. Presently, however, an insistent knock came on our door, though Mrs. Walker made no move to open it. But the summons came again—even more insistent this time.

"Who is it?" Mrs. Walker demanded, though still with the door tightly closed.

"Jimmy Walker," came the reply.

"Ah," she said as she turned the lock and opened the door a little way to let him in, "her master's voice!"

By six o'clock in the morning Father's lead had been cut alarmingly. The figures which had earlier seemed almost overwhelming had actually been cut to hardly more than three thousand. Furthermore, the New York City vote had all been tabulated, and no single community that could be expected to favor Father very heavily remained unreported. There were important upstate areas from which no returns had yet been received, and several counties in central New York State as well as those in the so-called "southern tier" were unaccountably slow in sending in their figures. No one could guess just what was going on. Messages from upstate Democratic leaders began to suggest the possibility of fraud. Father's lead had been cut so greatly that even a small change might give the lead to Governor Whitman. It is hardly surprising, therefore, that after considering the situation carefully Father and some of his closest advisers—Alfred J. Johnson, who was then City Chamberlain, Senator Robert Wagner, Judge George Van Namee, and Jimmy Walker, who was then a state Senator—decided to leave at once for Syracuse, where the Democratic upstate headquarters had been established.

None of us had had a wink of sleep but we did not think about that now. Father went off to take a shower and to change his clothes, and at eight-thirty we saw him and his party off on the Empire State Express, after which, tired and silent, we drove downtown to Oliver Street. We were almost exhausted, but rest did not come easily, for though the reports that still came in from time to time continued to show that Father was maintaining a narrow lead, his margin of advantage remained so small that almost until the very last a reversal was quite possible.

Having arrived in Syracuse, Father and the others talked by telephone with Democratic headquarters in many of the upstate counties, checking the returns and making certain that the ballot boxes were being protected everywhere. We learned later that one county leader with whom Father talked admitted that he was at home getting a bite to eat. He insisted, however, that the ballot boxes were perfectly safe. He was certain of it, for he had left his wife in the office of the county clerk and she was sitting on them.

By Thursday the returns were practically complete, and Father still retained a lead. It had even grown a little, and now amounted to about seventy-five hundred, so he returned to New York. The "soldier vote" —the absentee votes, that is, of New Yorkers who were in uniform— had yet to come in, and there was still a great deal of excitement at the Biltmore Hotel. Ultimately the Secretary of State in Albany reported that the soldier vote had arrived and had been tabulated. And, to our immense relief, these final ballots increased Father's lead to about fifteen thousand.

It was entirely clear by now that Father had won, but Governor Whitman was unwilling to concede the election. Instead he obtained a court order for a review of the returns in several election districts in New York City. The returns in our Oliver Street district, for example, seemed especially doubtful to the Governor, and for a very simple reason. Three hundred and eighty-seven ballots had been counted there for Father, and only two for Governor Whitman, but under the law, eight Republicans had to be present to man the polls.

The Republican leader of the district quickly explained the matter when he was summoned to headquarters. Having been unable to find eight Republicans in that district who were willing to work at the polls in opposition to Father, it had been necessary, as is possible under the law, to import them from other districts, where, naturally, their votes had been cast.

When Father asked the Democratic district captain about the vote, that loyal person was more concerned about the two votes that had been cast against Father than about anything else.

"That result is strictly on the level," he insisted. "I am not concerned about the ballot boxes. They can open them up and do what they like with them. But I would like to know who the two people were who voted against you, and I'll find out, too."

One of those votes, it later turned out, had been marked by a woman who lived in Cherry Street and who had gone to school with Father. This being her first vote, she had made a mistake which she herself later explained to the captain of the district. And the other vote, Father was later told, had been cast by a man who believed that his son could have had a position in the Police Department except for what he thought was Father's refusal to help.

As a result of the court order Governor Whitman had obtained, a number of ballot boxes were taken to court so that the records might be reviewed. No irregularities appeared, and the only real result of the court proceedings was to delay the arrival of Father's certificate of election until late in December.

I did not go back to school until the Monday following Election Day, and even then, with Thanksgiving, Christmas, and Father's inauguration on New Year's Day in Albany all crowding in upon us, I doubt if I made much progress with my studies. Then, too, one Saturday when I was home from school, Father took my sister Catherine and me uptown in order to buy each of us a fur coat!

We went directly to B. Altman & Company, at Thirty-Fourth Street and Fifth Avenue, but there, to our surprise, we did not go to the fur department, as we had naturally expected we would. We went, instead, to the office of Michael Friedsam, the president of the firm, who was a friend of Father.

"It's cold in Albany," Father explained, "and we have to have a couple of fur coats."

And Mr. Friedsam helped us pick them out—a brown muskrat coat for Catherine and a three quarter-length gray squirrel coat for me. And to my great delight Father also let me get a matching gray squirrel hat—a kind of tam o'shanter, which may or may not have been as becoming as I thought.

I recall no other period into which, in so short a time, so many different events were crowded. That very tense election was followed within less than a week by the Armistice, which ended World War I. Then came Thanksgiving, and a little later, within two days of each other, my seventeenth birthday and Christmas.

Throughout all this I had to attend school and accompany Mother on shopping trips, for we were to leave for Albany between Christmas and New Year's. And it was not merely that we were to go there for the inauguration. We were to go there to live, at least for the next two years—to live in the Executive Mansion that is provided by the state of New York for its Governors. I need hardly point out how many preparations had to be made before we could consider ourselves ready for so great a change.

During those crowded weeks I was in a flurry of anticipation. Our coming move from Oliver Street to the Executive Mansion alone took on a kind of fairylike aura. Then, too, the Inaugural Ball, the inauguration itself, and endless other coming events seemed infinitely exciting to me.

But just after Christmas, Father came down with a bad cold. For weeks there had been reports of the widespread epidemic, and with Father's inauguration less than a week away it was influenza that we feared. Luckily his illness proved to be only a cold. Within a few days it was noticeably better, and late in the morning of December 30, which was Father's forty-fifth birthday, we took the train for Albany —Father, Mother, Grandmother, and the five children. There was also another member of the family on the train—Caesar, our great Dane, a huge and vigorous animal, but very friendly and harmless despite his size and energy.

It had long been the custom in Albany for the outgoing Governor, as the end of his term approached, to invite the new Governor and his wife to the Executive Mansion so that they might learn, at first hand, what plans to make prior to the actual time of their arrival at the official home they were to occupy. Governor Whitman, however, had extended no invitation, and even now that we were about to arrive in Albany for the inauguration, Father could not be positive that we were to go directly to the Executive Mansion. It was not until we actually alighted at the Albany station that we learned that we were expected there, and still there was no word from Governor Whitman. But Mrs. Martin H. Glynn, the wife of former Governor Glynn, and a welcoming committee met us at the station and escorted us to the mansion.

The station was crowded, for our arrival time had been published in the papers, but when we entered the cars that were to take us to the Executive Mansion, Caesar created a problem, so Alfred, Jr., announced that he would walk to the mansion with Caesar on a leash, and off he started, getting away from the station even before we did. Presently we were on our way, and because it is not far from the station to the mansion, we shortly arrived under the escort of the welcoming committee, and having said good-by to them, we found ourselves in the large hall of the official residence we were to occupy.

I think it is fair to say that in those days there was little that was especially attractive about the Executive Mansion in Albany, and I am glad that so many improvements have been made since then. It was large, and while many of its features were impressive when we lived there and many of its furnishings were handsome, others were not. Some, in fact, missed dowdiness—if they missed it at all—by very narrow margins though no such appraisal of the place would ever have occurred to me on that late December afternoon when, as a family, we first entered the front door of the Executive Mansion and found ourselves in the spacious hall.

Later I learned to know the mansion intimately, but now I was merely conscious of the various rooms that opened from the hall. Off to the left were the library, the dining room, and the breakfast room. And to the right lay the morning room, the music room, and the drawing room. A broad staircase led upward from the hall to unseen portions of the mansion, and directly before us as we entered was a fireplace—a most impressive fireplace, it seemed to me, for it far surpassed in size the one we had had in Oliver Street. And it was real, as ours at home was not, and a wonderful fire was blazing there.

I had no opportunity to take in more than a few of our surroundings at the moment, for a gentleman who was standing before the fireplace as we entered came forward at once to greet us. I recognized him as Governor Whitman and realized that the uniformed officer who stood with him was his military aide.

The Governor greeted Father first, shaking hands with him, and then, one by one, we others were introduced. The military aide was introduced as well, and as we stood there talking—or remaining silent as my sister, my brothers, and I did—Alfred, Jr., with Caesar still on the leash, arrived from the station.

Knowing how powerful Caesar was, and how energetic he must have been after several hours of being cooped up on the train, I can imagine that my brother had found it difficult to hold that leash, and I am sure that the walk from the station was a very rapid one. I suspect that Alfred was a bit out of breath and can understand why, the moment he and Caesar entered the door, he was impelled to unsnap the leash and let the dog go free.

Neither Governor Whitman nor his aide was expecting the arrival of such a visitor, and they were facing the other way when my brother arrived. When Caesar was released, however, he made an almost elephantine bound for Father.

Governor Whitman and his aide were naturally startled.

"What——" began the Governor, throwing up one hand.

Father took a firm hold on Caesar's collar.

"Don't be frightened, Governor," he laughed. "It's only the Tammany tiger come to take possession of the Executive Mansion."

To our surprise Mrs. Whitman had left the Executive Mansion before we arrived—because of a previous engagement, Governor Whitman said. And now, having welcomed us, he, too, left the Mansion while we began to settle into place.

Though the Governor's official mansion in Albany was not a beautiful residence in 1918, I was not aware of it when we first arrived. I did not notice that much of the furniture and many of the rugs were badly worn, and that the excessive use of red and green on furniture, curtains, rugs, and walls made the place look as if it were decorated for a kind of perpetual Christmas. The walls were of rough plaster painted red, though there seemed to be a kind of metallic finish to the paint, and we children soon learned that by sliding our feet across the deep pile of the rugs we could generate a surprising amount of static electricity and create quite a spark by approaching the wall with one finger—or, better still, by similarly approaching someone else's unsuspecting ear.

The entrance hall had two big chandeliers, from each of which hung electric lights with frosted-glass coverings that were globular in shape but open at the bottom. Elsewhere, too, were other fixtures and furnishings whose design left much to be desired, and some of the atmosphere of the mansion may be suggested by the fact that a great deal of the china and glassware, together with at least one clock and I do not know what else, had originally been purchased for the New York State Building at the San Francisco Exposition of 1915.

Let no one imagine that I detected any shortcomings in the mansion when we first arrived. To me it was a palace. How could I have felt otherwise? What but a palace—though possibly a modest one—could have a reception room, a drawing room, a morning room, and a music room? Then, too, there was a dining room capable of seating thirty-two, a library, a breakfast room, and there were nine bedrooms, each with its own bath.

We had always thought—and we were right—that our house in Oliver Street was a really comfortable place, with quite enough room for the family. It is true that we got along with only one bathroom until Father became Sheriff, when, in addition to the two floors we had always occupied, we took over the third floor and Father also built on two additional rooms and a second bath. But here in the Executive Mansion each bedroom had a bath! And there were fifteen servants, with Harry Whitehead, a most thoughtful and efficient person, acting as major-domo.

On the second floor there was a very pleasant sitting room, or a library and sitting room combined. And there was also a huge bedroom that could only have been intended for Father and Mother. The rest of us searched about a bit before we made our selections, fascinated but a little muddled by our new surroundings, and quite unaccustomed to the idea of so many servants.

And bells. There were buttons to press in every room, but I had never rung bells before to get anything done for me. It took some time to grow accustomed to the idea, and then a little more time to learn not to overdo it.

We had dinner in the big dining room that evening—just the family, though later a few friends and state officials dropped in.

The inauguration was set for New Year's Day, when, at noon, the formalities would be carried out in the Assembly Chamber in the state capitol, but the term of an outgoing Governor in New York State comes to an end at midnight December 31, and in order that the new Governor's authority may go into effect the moment that of his predecessor ends, it has long been customary for the oath to be taken privately before the public ceremony is held. And because it was Father's birthday, Judge John W. Hogan, of the New York State Court of Appeals, was asked to administer the oath of office that evening before the fireplace in the reception hall of the Executive Mansion.

The ceremony was not a formal one, and only the family and a few friends and officials were present. But I especially remember the words as I first heard Father repeat them with the Bible in his hand there before the fireplace in the reception hall.

"I do solemnly swear, that I will support the Constitution of the State of New York, and that I will faithfully discharge the duties of the office of Governor according to the best of my ability."

His voice went on through the second portion of the oath, but to me that first sentence was more important than the rest.

I knew that in taking that oath Father was making a promise before God—a promise no one ever meant more deeply or more solemnly than he.

CHAPTER SIX

In the Executive Mansion — The Fight with Hearst

FATHER'S FIRST INAUGURATION as Governor took place in the Assembly Chamber of the state capitol just after noon on January 1, 1919. The ceremony was both dignified and official, but it was nevertheless merely a matter of form. Governor Whitman's term had expired at midnight the night before, and because Father had taken the oath of office semi-privately in advance he had actually been Governor of the state of New York for over twelve hours before the oath of office was publicly administered. Oddly enough, his first public appearance as Governor, as if to offset this delay, had taken place at the so-called Inaugural Ball on New Year's Eve two or three hours before Governor Whitman's term had actually expired.

The Inaugural Ball was not just what its name implied. Actually it was a charity ball given annually in Albany. Each time a Governor is inaugurated, however, this annual affair becomes the Inaugural Ball, and because of the attendant publicity it attracts a large number of guests.

Father and Mother were the guests of honor, but Alfred, Catherine, and I were with them. I still remember that evening as gay and colorful, but I see it in perspective now and realize it was only a prelude to the events of the following day.

It was sometime after noon on New Year's Day that Mother, Grandmother, and we five children were taken to the platform that had been erected in the Assembly Chamber. Every corridor in the Capitol was crowded, and the chamber itself appeared filled to capacity as we entered, though the doorkeepers were still permitting additional guests to enter. It was reported that thousands who hoped to be there were unable to get in, and even that former Governor Dix was barred by one of the doorkeepers as "unknown." Brother Baldwin, however, who had been one of Father's teachers at St. James' School thirty-five years before, had come to Albany for the occasion and he succeeded in entering though Governor Dix failed. And Father, I know, was immensely pleased at this evidence of friendship and this reminder of his Lower East Side boyhood.

The Assembly Chamber was elaborately decorated for the inauguration with evergreens and with the national colors. A gaily uniformed band was playing patriotic music in the gallery, and when we took our places on the platform we found ourselves surrounded by state officials, by the commanding officers of both the military and naval forces of the state, and by leading members of both the Senate and the Assembly. But the most exciting of all to me were the officers who had been sent to represent the Old Guard of New York City. They stood out vividly as they entered the Assembly Chamber in their white and heavily gold-braided tunics, their blue trousers, and—most spectacular of all— their immensely tall fur shakos.

The ceremony began at twelve-thirty, but there were many formal preliminaries. Just before the actual appearance of the Old Guard, for example, the following formalities—as nearly as I remember them— took place:

"Mr. Secretary of State," intoned the Sergeant at Arms.

"Sergeant at Arms," replied the Secretary.

"The Honorary Escort of the Governor," the Sergeant at Arms announced, "the Old Guard of the city of New York."

"Sergeant at Arms," ordered the Secretary of State, "will escort the Honorary Escort of the Governor, the Old Guard of the city of New York, to their official positions."

Then, following the entrance of these unique officers, other official individuals and groups were seated in their turn. And finally the Sergeant at Arms announced the retiring Governor and the new Governor.

I shall never forget the thrill I felt as Father and Governor Whitman entered the Assembly Chamber and walked together down the wide aisle to the platform. Until the moment of their entry the chamber had been filled with the kind of subdued roar that always seems to issue from such a gathering. As the two Governors made their way down the aisle, however, the roar grew less and less and throughout the crowded chamber there was an almost universal shifting of position and an obvious craning of necks. Then, as Father and Governor Whitman reached the platform, a few ragged cheers broke out in the chamber, followed by a spontaneous shout of greeting.

My eyes were on Father and I can see him yet as he smiled and waved his hand. Presently the chamber fell silent as Monsignor Joseph A. Delaney pronounced the invocation.

The Secretary of State and master of ceremonies was Francis M. Hugo, of Watertown, and following the invocation he introduced Governor Whitman, who, in a short and well-phrased speech, dwelt for a moment on the responsibilities of office, and then welcomed the incoming Governor.

It was now that Secretary of State Hugo administered the oath of office—the same oath that Father had taken in the reception hall of the Executive Mansion on the evening of our arrival, though the simplicity of that earlier occasion was lacking. Every person in the Assembly Chamber was standing silently, and our family—Mother, Grandmother, and the five children—stood at Father's left, more than a little awed and somewhat overwhelmed. My heart was in my throat, and my mind was filled far less with thoughts than feelings—feelings that left me conscious of nothing but Father's familiar voice. I heard the words he spoke as if they were a prayer that I myself was silently repeating.

A pause followed, and the chamber was filled with a rustle of sound as everyone sat down. Then came the voice of the Secretary of State once more—"I have the honor of introducing His Excellency, the Governor of the state of New York."

Father's inaugural speech was very short. In five minutes, or even less, it was over. He thanked Governor Whitman for his courtesy "and for making pleasant the change from his administration to mine." He thanked other officials and members of the Legislature, and referred to his long acquaintance with Albany, which had made his most recent arrival there "somewhat like a home-coming." He referred to the recently concluded war and to the fact that, though the fighting had ended, many internal problems remained to be solved. "I am mindful," he continued, "of the burden of responsibilities which this office places on my shoulders." And presently he reached his conclusion:

"With a firm resolve to make myself worthy of the great honor bestowed on me by the people of this state, I ask that Divine Providence grant me the health, the strength, and the will to do the right as I am able to see it."

It was over, and we were surrounded by a veritable crush of well-wishers. Father's hand was shaken by scores of friends and acquaintances, and then we were outside, somehow, and in the cars that were to take us back to the Executive Mansion, while the air shook to the detonations of cannon as they fired the first salute that was ever given in Father's honor.

No one knows better than I that Father approached his new responsibilities sincerely determined to promote to the best of his ability the interests of the people and the state of New York. He was competent in the playing of the game of politics, but over and over again I have seen him gain even political ends by refusing to think of any personal political advantage. In discussing the point of view he held during his first term as Governor he once made the statement that his actions were never influenced by thought of a second term. And that was true—true, that is, in the sense in which he meant it, that no action of his as Governor was ever dictated by selfish political reasoning. For Father deeply believed that the greatest political advantage lay, in the last analysis, in wholehearted, unselfish service to the people and the state.

Though he was new to the office he now held he was very familiar with New York State problems, and from the first he surrounded himself with men of real ability, choosing them often without regard to their political affiliations.

"The greatest contribution a man can make to his own success in high office," he once told me, "is to gather about him intelligent men who thoroughly understand their business and are deeply but impersonally interested in it."

Guided by this philosophy, he brought many capable men into the service of the state, though his appointees sometimes surprised those who had to deal with them, as one illustration demonstrates.

Father had not been Governor very long when the Rome Brass and Copper Company, of the city of Rome, in Oneida County, found itself confronted with a long-drawn-out, ill-tempered strike. Conditions became so threatening that a representative of the company, whom Father had known in the Legislature, asked him to send state police to Rome to intervene. Father replied that he would not hesitate to send the police if law and order could be preserved in no other way, but he also said that, in his opinion, the company's officials should first discuss ways of settling the strike with some representative of the state Department of Labor. The officials of the firm agreed, and Father, who had recently appointed Miss Frances Perkins a member of the state Industrial Commission, announced that he had selected her to act for him.

Miss Perkins was less well known in those days than she later came to be, though Father had known her ever since 1912, when she served as an investigator under Abram Elkus on the New York State Factory Investigating Committee. The company officials with whom she was now called upon to deal, however, were shocked at the very thought of discussing their labor problems with a woman. However, there was nothing else they could do, and after Miss Perkins had presided at a meeting to which she had called representatives of both the company and the union, one of the company's officers was so impressed by her ability that he asked the company's attorney to learn from Father "where he found that woman."

Labor problems were numerous throughout 1919, and Father succeeded in resolving several. He didn't follow any particular formula, and was inclined to suit the actions he took to specific problems as they arose, but even before he was inaugurated he realized that many problems demanded prompt attention.

The war had interfered with many normal activities. Public construction had been brought to a halt. Labor costs had risen enormously. Hundreds of thousands of men were being discharged from the military service and had to find work. The cost of living had skyrocketed, and a number of lesser problems had to be solved. Wherever the thoughtful person looked, in fact, there were difficulties, and Father, realizing how complicated and difficult the situation was, and realizing, too, that the regular departments of the state government were confronted with problems of their own, seized upon a suggestion made by Mrs. Belle Moskowitz, who had been chairman of the women's division of the Citizens' Committee at the time of his election, and decided to create a special Reconstruction Commission to study and to make recommendations for needed legislation.

Here, obviously, was a task to be approached without thought of politics, and the thirty-four names Father selected represented every important field of endeavor. Ability was the primary criterion in these appointments. Bernard Baruch, Charles H. Sabin, Felix Adler, and Charles P. Steinmetz were among those chosen. Abram Elkus was elected chairman, Mrs. Belle Moskowitz was secretary, and Robert Moses, who was later to be not only of inestimable help to Father but was also to develop into an invaluable servant of the state, was the committee's very effective "chief of staff." And among the committee members were men and women who stood high in the professions, in social service, in banking, business, and education.

It would be hard to imagine where any opposition to such a group would originate, but opposition nevertheless promptly materialized. Father, wondering how the cost of the commission could be financed, learned that seventy-five thousand dollars that had been appropriated for special war activities still remained unexpended, and he asked the Legislature to transfer this to the commission. Unfortunately both houses of the Legislature were controlled by Republicans who were unwilling to be of help, and his request was denied. The work of the commission was so important, however, that the members of the commission themselves unhesitatingly financed the work.

Father always felt that the Republican members of the Legislature thought of him in his first term as nothing more than a "political accident" and, in addition, that they did not take the work of this Reconstruction Commission seriously. The commission's task was enormously important, however, and was so prolonged that its final recommendations, along with its complete report, were not ready for presentation to the Legislature until 1920.

Among many lesser matters its proposals included a permanent policy for dealing with unemployment in the state and a program for public improvements. In view of what occurred more than ten years later, it is interesting to note that the suggestion was also made that these public works should be planned so as to be undertaken or broadened in the event of business depression and unemployment. Americanization, public health, housing, and food production were studied, and proposals affecting all these and many more state problems were advanced. An executive budget, a longer term for the Governor, and a short ballot were all proposed. And, finally, a program for the reorganization of the state government itself was suggested, thus launching a prolonged battle that did not end in victory for Father until 1928, just before he went out of office for the last time.

It seemed odd to me even then that though Father was intimately acquainted with many members of both the Assembly and the Senate, and was personally on the very best terms with scores of Republicans and Democrats alike, he still was confronted with such stubborn opposition. Men who frequently came to see him at his office in the Capitol or even at the Executive Mansion, and who, I know, held him personally in high regard, nevertheless opposed him obstinately on the floor of both houses of the Legislature. Recommendations made by the Reconstruction Commission seemed especially unpopular with them, and that was true despite the fact that Charles E. Hughes, who had formerly not only been Governor of New York State but also, in 1916, had narrowly missed defeating Woodrow Wilson for the Presidency, appeared with Father at the City Club of New York, where both of them spoke in support of the commission's proposals.

Though living in the Executive Mansion was very different from life as we had known it in Oliver Street, my brothers, my sister, and I soon began to feel entirely at home there. Walter and Arthur, the youngest of the family, became acquainted with a score of other children in the neighborhood, who soon were running in and out of the Executive Mansion as freely as others had in Oliver Street.

All of us were now going to school in Albany, and as young people usually do, we made new friends and promptly found new interests. Each one of us occasionally felt a touch of homesickness. That would have been true, I suppose, even had the Executive Mansion been one of the fairy castles of our more youthful dreams. But under the circumstances we soon felt happy and at home in our new surroundings.

Father was far more familiar with Albany than we were, though, as Governor, he had less freedom than he had enjoyed as a member of the Assembly. And, too, unpleasant developments that were to grow to serious proportions were apparent to him before six months had passed.

William Randolph Hearst, who was an enthusiastic supporter of Mayor Hylan, had supported Father, too, though less enthusiastically, not only in his campaign for President of the Board of Aldermen, but also in his race for the governorship. By early summer in 1919, however, and as Father often said, "for no reason I was ever able to understand," the Hearst papers in New York began to attack Father in most violent terms, contending, among other things, that he was personally responsible for a sharp increase that had taken place in the price of milk.

I still don't know the reasons behind this attack, though Norman
Hapgood and Henry Moskowitz in *Up from the City Streets,* a book
they wrote about Father, explained it by saying that Hearst was angered
by Father's failure to make him a member of the state committee to
receive the returning soldiers. What they said appeared both in the
World's Work Magazine and in book form before Father completed his
final term in Albany, but I never heard him refer to it.

Whatever the reason for the Hearst attack—and I am not so naïve
as to assume that no reason existed—it was both prolonged and
violent. These charges insisted New York City was being supplied
with milk exorbitantly priced so as to enrich the "milk barons" by
wringing pennies from the thin pocketbooks of the poor. Father, these
attacks insisted, was furthering the interests of the "milk barons," who
were repeatedly pictured in vicious cartoons as fat, dishonestly pros-
perous, and utterly callous in their dealings with their half-starved and
downtrodden customers. Over and over again these cartoons portrayed
gaunt and hollow-eyed women and children as they paid their last
pennies for the "bad" milk for which Father, in some way or another,
was supposed to be responsible. He was even cartooned amid the tomb-
stones of imaginary children for whose deaths he was held to blame.

Anyone in public life is quite properly fair game for cartoonists, and
Father's sense of humor enabled him to enjoy cartoons of himself that
antagonized me. In the Hearst attacks, however, cartoons that were
downright vicious were published, while distorted editorials and
"slanted" news accounts repeatedly returned to the attack. At first
Father paid little attention. The attacks were so exaggerated as to be
senseless. But they did not stop. They kept on and on, and merely as the
result of endless reiteration they began to have serious effects even on
some whom Father had regarded as supporters. Still, he might have
continued to say nothing had it not been that his mother was taken
very ill.

Father frequently had occasion to go to New York City, and he never
went without finding time to go to Middagh Street in Brooklyn. And
now, during Grandmother's illness, he began to realize how troubled
she was by the Hearst attacks. She said little about them, but her concern began to be apparent.

At least one published story pretends to report in much detail many
troubled comments she is supposed to have made while she was deliri-
ous, but nothing of that kind occurred. Every member of the family

was irritated by the attacks, and we no doubt expressed our annoyance in various individual ways, but Grandmother said comparatively little. She was seriously ill, however, and Father may have felt that the accounts she had already seen were still troubling her.

If so, that may have played a part in his decision to answer the attacks. I never heard him object to honest criticism of anything he had done or failed to do. In fact, even on lesser matters than this I sometimes felt that he should reply when he refused to do so. Many of his political friends, however, strongly urged him not to get into a fight with Hearst. "He's too powerful," they said in effect. "Nobody has ever dared challenge him and you had better not."

"But what he is saying about me isn't so," Father argued, "and I'm not going to let him get away with it."

It was with this in mind that he began to discuss the matter with some of his more combative friends and it was not long before a Citizens' Committee, headed by Colonel Jefferson de Mont Thompson, was formed in Father's behalf. With that step taken Father challenged Mr. Hearst to meet him on the platform of Carnegie Hall, there to substantiate, if that was possible, the statements his papers had been making.

The meeting was called for the evening of October 29, 1919, and Father well knew what he might expect. Despite the publicity that had attended the challenge, he was sure Mr. Hearst would not appear. In a book entitled *Progressive Democracy,* by Henry Moskowitz, a reference is made to the "scurrilous communication"—which I do not recall ever having seen—in which Hearst refused the challenge.

"Of course," Father said almost as soon as the chairman had presented him and he had begun to speak, "I am alone. I don't know whether the chairman of the committee expected that I would be alone, but I knew that I would . . . because I know the man to whom I issued the challenge . . ."

And then, for the better part of an hour, he went over the various points that had been made in the Hearst attacks—the milk strike of the previous January—the published statement in which a Hearst paper had said that Father "was responsible for the starvation of the children in New York, because he refused to reduce the price of milk"—another statement in which Father was untruthfully said to have appointed a representative of the "Milk Trust" to office—and more and more and more until he pointed out in his conclusion what "makes me come down here, into the city of New York, before this audience, and urge them to organize in this city to stay the danger that comes from these [Hearst] papers, to the end that the health, the welfare, and the comfort of this people, of the people of this state, may be promoted, and we may get rid of this pestilence that walks in the darkness."

It seems strange, at this distance, that bitterness so deep should have played any part in Father's political career. He was not a bitter man, and were it not for the printed record, I would find it difficult to recall these unpleasant details. Over and over again I have heard Father say "I do not oppose individuals. I merely oppose ideas when I believe them to be wrong." In this instance, however, the man and the ideas could not be separated, and even ten years later, when he wrote his autobiography, Father's point of view appeared very little changed.

"On that memorable night," he wrote in 1929, "I cleared up in the minds of the people of New York City and the rest of the country any misgivings they might have that these attacks might be true, and I taught Mr. Hearst and his cohorts a lesson. It was the first chime in the death knell of Hearst's political power in the eastern part of this country."

That is true, I am sure, but some time was still to pass before the final chime was rung.

CHAPTER SEVEN

Renominated but Defeated

FROM THE TIME of our arrival in Albany I had been given a special task which made it possible for me to participate, in a minor way, in many events from which Alfred, Catherine, Walter, and Arthur were usually willing, or even glad, to be excused.

The "social calendar" at the Executive Mansion was not crowded during Father's first term as Governor. Still, there were social events that required both thought and attention, and almost at the moment of our arrival in Albany, Father suggested that it might be good for me to act as Mother's social secretary. A well-trained social secretary, I have no doubt, could have been very helpful, but our plans called for no elaborate entertainment, and the dinners and teas and other affairs that were given went off smoothly enough. Now and again I naturally had to check up at the Capitol on matters of precedence so as to know how to seat official guests at dinner, but aside from such small problems things usually went along with little effort, for Harry Whitehead had been at the mansion for years and took everything in stride.

It had long been customary for the wife of the Governor to be "at home" one day a week from about the middle of January to the end of March—a period which usually coincided with the Legislative session —and one of the tasks I assumed in connection with these functions was to make certain that one lady from some political family and another from some family that had no connection with politics were present to pour. These affairs soon came to take on a regular pattern and so they created no problems, but the more formal dinners—though they were never numerous—could be quite another matter.

Early in February the Legislative Reception was held—the largest affair of the year. Large as this was, Father never permitted it to be held on as large a scale as had formerly been common.

A story that has often been told about Father has to do with the very first Legislative Reception he ever attended. It was during his first term in the Assembly, and being new to such entertainments, he naturally assumed that because it was the Legislative Reception few people except members of the Legislature and their wives would be present. To his surprise he found when he arrived at the Executive Mansion that thousands of guests were entering and departing. He and the friends with whom he had come were ushered in, presented to Governor Odell, to Mrs. Odell, to the members of the Governor's staff, and then were ushered out again with remarkable celerity.

"Well," Father is said to have remarked as he and his friends went back to their hotel, "if I ever get to be Governor and give a Legislative Reception, it will be for the members and their families only."

That had been merely a remark. The thought of ever actually being Governor could hardly have occurred to him at the time. But now, fifteen years later, he remembered what he had said, and the Legislative Receptions that were held throughout all his terms as Governor were just what he had said they would be.

I especially recall the first one he gave. Limited though it was to the members of the Legislature and their families, it was still a very large affair. The Executive Mansion was crowded with guests, most of whom I did not know at all, and standing beside Father, I finally found an opportunity to comment on that fact.

"It seems so strange," I said, "to have a party for so many people and really to know so few of them."

It may be that Father had a twinkle in his eye when he replied, but I did not see it.

"The only advice I can give you," he said quite solemnly but under his breath, "is not to let anyone take your plate just because he looks like a waiter. If you do, you may find that he's really an Assembly-man."

That first year Father also gave an official dinner for the chief judge and the six associate judges of the New York State Court of Appeals. Neither Mother nor I were present, for no ladies were invited, but I arranged the seating. And as a result of that little effort I learned, to my surprise, that in the Empire State, the Supreme Court is not supreme. It is the Court of Appeals which stands at the apex of the state's judicial system, and the Supreme Court is one of lesser jurisdiction.

The 1919 campaign in New York State gave political observers an inkling of what might be expected in the coming national elections of 1920. Political prejudices and partisan appeals that everyone had known were out of place during the war expanded immensely with the sudden release of wartime pressures. Throughout the war Americans had been wonderfully unified, but the moment the fighting ended, conflicting interests of different kinds began to shatter the nation's one-time unity. It was not merely that Republicans and Democrats began to draw apart once more. Under our system that is normal and constructive, provided there is reason and honesty in the expression of their opposing points of view. In 1919, however, it was evident that partisanship was rapidly getting out of hand and, in addition, various groups began to grow vociferous and troublesome as they furthered their special aims.

Whenever such conditions arise, the "ins" are apt to be the major target of attack, as the national elections of 1920 were later to demonstrate. Even in 1919, and in elections that should have been directed only toward the solution of local or state-wide problems, national and even foreign interests influenced the outcome. And so widespread was the desire for a change that the regular Democratic organization was soundly defeated even in New York County—the island of Manhattan —where it has always been very strong.

When the Legislature met early in January 1920, Father's first term was half over. Even the 1919 Legislature had opposed most of his proposals, but with the Assembly now much more heavily Republican than it had been the year before, it was plain that this opposition, if it were to change at all, would merely be intensified. The Republican leaders in the Legislature had begun to look upon "the political accident" who occupied the Executive Mansion in a new light. They had become convinced that Father was intent on furthering a really constructive program, one that would be greatly to his credit and to that of the Democratic party. They knew, too, that his administration of the state's affairs in the previous twelve months had made a most favorable impression on the voters. Therefore, with the important elections of 1920 not very far ahead, they determined to increase their opposition.

The events I have in mind took place in 1920, but I am recounting them after the passage of thirty-six years. It seems to me that in the light—or perhaps I should say the shadow—of the "anti-Red" developments of the early 1950s they may prove that Mademoiselle Bertin, Marie Antoinette's milliner, was not far wrong when she said, "There is nothing new except what is forgotten."

In the New York State election of 1919 voters turned in large numbers from the Democrats to the Republicans, and many went a long step further. They voted the Socialist ticket, and actually elected five Socialists to the Assembly.

Socialists have at no time been numerous in New York State affairs, but this was not the first time any of them had succeeded in being elected to office. I have already told, for example, how Father recognized the existence of the Socialist "minor minority" in the New York City Board of Aldermen when he first presided as President of that body. Now, however, a great cry went up warning all and sundry that the safety of the state, and perhaps the nation—my memory is hazy on that point—was endangered by these enemies of society, these Socialists, these Reds.

The Socialist party had long since made a place for itself in the state —a small place and one lacking influence, but one that was quite within the law. And there was no doubt about the accuracy and legality of the vote that had elected five Socialists to the Assembly. But under the influence of the alarm that was now sounded, the Assembly, when it convened, refused to permit the Socialists to be seated, arguing that the Legislature was within its rights in excluding them because, under the state constitution, that body was admittedly the judge of its own membership.

Technically this claim was true. Still, the constitutional provision under which the Legislature decided to act had been intended for use merely to combat fraud or other wrongdoing on the part of any member of the Legislature. Certainly it had not been written in order to authorize the exclusion of any properly elected member no matter how unique, or even offensive, his political ideas were, provided they were within the law.

The opposition to Socialist members had begun the year before when a joint Legislative committee—the so-called Lusk Committee—had been created to investigate the activities of certain unnamed and vaguely described "enemies of the government"—an expression that was interpreted by some to mean anyone whose governmental ideas were "radical." Father had no doubt that the decision to expel the

Socialist members was, as he said, "preconceived," and he also said that he "regarded the trial during which the Republican leaders sought to establish the unfitness of these members as a mere formality intended to lend color and give virtue to the undemocratic and un-American performance of their expulsion from the body."

Father's effectiveness, I am sure, was often traceable to the promptness with which he went into action. And his promptness played a part in this affair, though, as Governor, he had no actual authority in the matter.

The Socialists were expelled from the Assembly on a Friday, and that evening Father decided to issue a statement in reference to the matter. The next morning he called a meeting of the Democratic leaders of the Senate and the Assembly, who, at first, were doubtful of the advisability of opposing the action the Republicans had taken. Father soon convinced them that it should be done, and they stood with him in the matter. With this backing he prepared a statement which he handed to newspapermen that evening.

"Although I am unalterably opposed," the statement read, "to the fundamental principles of the Socialist party, it is inconceivable that a minority party, duly constituted and legally organized, should be deprived of its right to expression so long as it has honestly, by lawful methods of education and propaganda, succeeded in securing representation, unless the chosen representatives are unfit as individuals.

"It is true that the Assembly has arbitrary power to determine the qualifications of its members, but where arbitrary power exists it should be exercised with care and discretion, because from it there is no appeal.

"If the majority party at present in control of the Assembly possesses information that leads them to believe that these men are hostile to our form of government and would overthrow it by processes subversive of law and order, these charges in due form should have been presented to the Legislature and these men tried by orderly processes. Meanwhile, presumably innocent until proved guilty, they should have been allowed to retain their seats.

"Our faith in American democracy is confirmed not only by its results but by its methods and organs of free expression. They are the safeguards against revolution. To discard the method of representative government leads to misdeeds of the very extremists we denounce and serves to increase the number of enemies of orderly, free government."

Father's statement, while it made his own position clear, did not succeed in returning the Socialists to their seats in the Assembly. They were subjected by the Legislature to a trial that went on for months, and though the Bar Association of New York appointed Charles Evans Hughes, Morgan J. O'Brien, Louis Marshall, Joseph M. Proskauer, and Ogden L. Mills to defend them, the Socialists finally lost. The decision was not reached until September, and by then other events of importance had taken place. At that time, however, Father issued a proclamation calling for special elections in each of the affected districts so that new Assemblymen might be chosen to serve at least for the remainder of the term, throughout all of which, up to then, five Assembly districts had been deprived of representation.

The Legislature—and especially the Lusk Committee—had had other ideas in mind than merely those that were connected with the five Socialists. The committee, having "investigated" what the members called "revolutionary radicalism," published a list which undoubtedly included the names of a few extreme and possibly dangerous radicals, but which also included the names of others—Jane Addams, for example—whose liberalism, under any reasonable definition, could not possibly be classed as dangerous. And early in the Legislative term the committee recommended legislation that would have interfered with freedom of speech, that would have necessitated special loyalty tests for teachers, that would have regulated school courses in the interest of what the committee mistakenly imagined good Americanism to be, and that otherwise would have limited basic American rights. Three such bills were actually passed, though Father vetoed them all.

"The bill unjustly discriminates against teachers as a class," he wrote in one of these veto messages. "It deprives teachers of their right to freedom of thought, it limits the teaching staff of the public schools to those only who lack the courage or the mind to exercise their legal right to just criticism of existing institutions. The bill confers upon the Commissioner of Education a power of interference with freedom of opinion which strikes at the foundation of democratic education."

"The safety of this government and its institutions," he wrote in another of these veto messages, "rests upon the reasoned and devoted loyalty of its people. It does not need for its defense a system of intellectual tyranny which, in the endeavor to choke error by force, must of necessity crush truth as well."

From the time the Legislature convened, Mother and I attended every Monday-evening session of the Senate. Sometimes these sessions were slow and colorless, but now and again they were full of interest, and by following them regularly we found ourselves increasingly absorbed in the give-and-take of politics. Interesting though the sessions were, I was glad when they came to an end, for Father had promised to take Alfred and me to San Francisco for the Democratic National Convention. The thought of such a journey was exciting. After all, except for a few trips to Atlantic City and elsewhere in New Jersey and into nearby Connecticut, I had never been outside New York State.

A week before Mother and I left Albany for San Francisco, Father, who took Alfred with him, left for French Lick, Indiana, to attend a preconvention meeting of Democratic leaders. Later our party assembled in Chicago, where we went aboard a special car that was attached to the Overland Limited.

In addition to Father, Mother, Alfred, and me there were Mr. and Mrs. Murphy; Judge and Mrs. James A. Foley, who were Mr. and Mrs. Murphy's son-in-law and daughter; Charles W. Berry, the adjutant general of the New York State National Guard; and William Humphreys of Albany, a close personal friend of Father who was not in politics at all, and may appear to have been even more out of place on that private car when I add that he was a Republican.

This was my first extensive journey away from New York, and it was my first experience at a national convention. Father and Mr. Murphy were old hands at such affairs. Just how many conventions Mr. Murphy had attended I do not know, but Father had been at the Democratic National Conventions in St. Louis in 1904, in Denver in 1908, in Baltimore in 1912, and in St. Louis in 1916.

Traveling for the very first time across the United States, I was awed by its immensity. Illinois and Iowa, so far as I was able to see, were not so very different from portions of New York State I knew. But I was not really prepared for such vast and treeless expanses as we crossed in western Nebraska and Wyoming, and the mountains, when we reached them, were utterly unlike the only mountains I had ever seen before.

Finally the prairies and mountains were behind us, along with Great Salt Lake and the arid uplands of Nevada. California may not have been exactly as I had imagined it, but the ferry from Oakland to San Francisco struck a familiar note, and once we had reached the St. Francis Hotel I almost felt at home. Delegates from New York were all about, and we found as many friends in the lobby, the corridors, and the elevators as we might have encountered at the Ten Eyck in Albany or the Biltmore in New York.

It was Father's contention—and in my inexperience I certainly could not take issue with him—that the convention held a minimum of interest. Since I knew little about conventions, the sessions I attended were often more or less meaningless, though I saw a good deal that caught my interest. I knew Father did not hold William Jennings Bryan in very high regard. Still, Bryan was a figure of importance in the Democratic party, and I was very attentive when he rose to speak. Bryan's debate with W. Bourke Cockran of New York was one of the high points of the convention. Bryan, of course, was a "dry," which Bourke Cockran was not, and their debate concerned the stand the party should take on that troublesome issue. It was generally conceded by those whose opinions I heard that Cockran not only had the better of the argument, but also that this fluent member of Congress from New York proved himself superior as an orator to the three-times Democratic Presidential candidate, though the party platform, when it came to be written, reflected neither fact.

It may be well, at this point, to interrupt my fragmentary account of events that occurred at the Democratic Convention at San Francisco to refer to a minor happening that took on added meaning in the light of later events.

The delegates had hardly more than arrived in San Francisco when those who were connected with the New York delegation were invited to attend a reception aboard a battleship that was in port. A large group went, for this was an unusual social event, and we were received not only by the ship's officers, but also by Assistant Secretary of the Navy Franklin D. Roosevelt, a handsome young man—he was only thirty-eight at the time—who had served from 1910 to 1913 as a Senator in the New York State Legislature.

Father and the young Assistant Secretary chatted briefly about acquaintances and experiences they had had in common in Albany eight or ten years before, and on the quarterdeck of the battleship that day I was one of many who met Franklin Roosevelt for the first time. Had I been able to look even a little way into the future I surely would have been more alert in my observations. As it was, I was impressed only as any other young girl would have been at meeting an Assistant Secretary of the Navy, and one so handsome, so debonair, and with a family name so universally known. It was impossible to know, of course, that before the convention adjourned this very person would be named as the Democratic candidate for the Vice-Presidency, and the more remote future was utterly inconceivable.

It is interesting, sometimes, to look back at the beginnings of events that have attained significance in our times. As they originate and gradually unfold, even great developments may sometimes seem to be of little consequence, and may appear to evolve so slowly as to be almost motionless. In retrospect it is often possible to see that they actually moved with the swiftness of the wind.

Only two years before the convention met in San Francisco, my sister, my brothers, and I had been very excited to learn for the first time that Father might *possibly* become the Democratic candidate for Governor of New York. Much had happened in those two years, and though I did not realize it then, I am able now to see how little time had passed. Then, one evening there in San Francisco, I was told something so thrilling—so overwhelming in my eyes—that when I went to bed that night I lay wide awake but nevertheless in a dream.

The very next day, W. Bourke Cockran was to nominate Father as New York's choice for the Presidency of the United States!

I had been told that this was just a gesture—that any number of states were to offer "favorite sons"—that there was no chance that Father would actually be selected as the Democratic candidate. I knew these statements were true, I suppose, though I had no idea whatever that this was Mr. Murphy's method of trying out the wind. So when I went to bed and lay there wide awake I dreamed such dreams as sleep had never brought me and imagined a future the like of which had never occurred to me before.

I slept at last, but awoke early, and could hardly control my impatience until Mother, Mrs. Murphy, Mrs. Foley, and I were in one of the temporary flag-draped boxes that had been built all about the convention auditorium.

Conventions are often notoriously slow in getting under way, which was certainly the case that morning. I was utterly convinced that *this* time all records for slowness had been broken. The chairman seemed intent on everything but what interested me, and his voice droned on and on until it seemed to me that the delegates should rebel.

Mr. Cockran had come to Father the evening before and explained what he had in mind.

"I am about to achieve the joy of my life," Father later quoted him as saying. "For as long back as I can remember I have been fanning the wind at national conventions, either against somebody or against something. At last I have an opportunity to be *for* somebody."

And then he had taken Judge Morgan J. O'Brien off into another room and had kept him there until three o'clock in the morning while he rehearsed the speech he intended to make.

With such a speech in prospect is it any wonder that I was impatient with the chairman? And even when the nominations began, my patience continued to be taxed though the New York delegation was finally recognized and the Honorable Bourke Cockran appeared upon the rostrum.

Some men are naturally distinguished, and W. Bourke Cockran was one of these. He was in his sixties at the time, I believe, and his hair was white, but his appearance gave no suggestion of age. Meticulously dressed, a little portly, perhaps, but with a glow of eagerness and health about him, he stood for a moment looking out upon the crowded convention hall. Confident and utterly at ease, he seemed to me, even before he spoke, to be the very beau ideal of oratory.

When he began to speak, the flavor that marked his diction was not immediately apparent. Every sentence was perfectly formed, every reference was flawless. Little by little, however, it began to be obvious that though what he said was being presented in cultivated English it was cultivated English as only a cultivated Irishman could speak it.

I cannot repeat more than a portion of the speech he gave, though I—and not I alone—hung on his every word. I suspect that in the succeeding years there was not a single member of our family who could not repeat at least the conclusion of the speech word for word. And many a time I have heard Father gleefully repeat it with a most successful imitation of Mr. Cockran's accent. It was not an event that I could easily forget, but I especially remember Mr. Cockran's ringing voice when, having named Father and recounted his accomplishments, he came to his conclusion.

"We offer him to you as President of the United States," he cried. "We will accept no compromise in the convention. If you take him we will give you the state of New York, and if you reject him we will take him back and run him again for Governor."

That last word had hardly rebounded from the rafters when the waiting band burst forth with

East Side, West Side,
All around the town,

and for the very first time "The Sidewalks of New York," which later came to be almost universally recognized as Father's personal "theme song," was played in a political convention. And to my unbounded delight the New York delegation, along with many others, made their shouting, singing way up and down the convention aisles with the New York banner and Father's picture on a pole to lead the way.

Despite the wakeful dreams I had had the night before, Father's nomination proved to be no more than I had been told it would be. I still recall Mr. Cockran's speech with deep appreciation, but the various favorite sons all gave way in the crowded hours that followed and James M. Cox and Franklin D. Roosevelt (whose nomination Father had seconded) emerged from the convention as the Democratic candidates for President and Vice-President.

Father, Mother, Alfred, and I returned to Albany by way of Los Angeles, the Grand Canyon, and Denver, and I, for one, brought home with me a much more adequate understanding of the varied immensity of this land of ours. I returned, too, with a better understanding of Father's place in its affairs and of the greatness of the task that confronted him in Albany.

His renomination as Governor was assured, though his campaign, when it began late in September, was largely overwhelmed, so far as the news accounts were concerned, by the Presidential campaign in which Cox and Roosevelt, on the Democratic ticket, were opposed by Harding and Coolidge on the Republican.

No one in our family lacked confidence in Father's re-election. We knew that his victory two years before had been won by a very narrow margin. On the other hand, there was considerable evidence that Father had gained some strength upstate. He was now running for office for the seventeenth time, and never yet had he been defeated, so it is no wonder that we who were closest to him were confident.

I was back in school throughout all but the last week of the campaign. When Father completed his upstate tour and, during the final week, turned his attention to New York City, we all went with him. There, once more, I heard his Friday-night speech at the Academy of Music in Brooklyn, and his Saturday-night speech in Manhattan. And once again, when the polls had closed and dinner was over on the evening of Election Day, we hurried to Democratic headquarters at the Biltmore.

Two years before, the election had dealt only with state and local affairs. Now, however, the Presidential election dominated everything, and lesser offices were given little attention in the first great rush of returns. From the first, Harding and Coolidge seemed to be carrying everything. To our astonishment report after report told of election districts even in the Democratic stronghold of Manhattan Island going Republican, and when the returns showed beyond any shadow of a doubt that Harding had actually won in Mr. Murphy's own home district, even the most hopeful of us began to see the handwriting on the wall.

We knew that Harding had been elected before we learned how Father had come out. Ultimately we learned that Harding and Coolidge had been given a total national vote of sixteen million to only nine million for their Democratic opponents—that the Republicans had even carried sixty-one out of the sixty-two Assembly districts in New York City, while only one had gone for Cox and Roosevelt. That single district, which had remained so staunchly in the Democratic column, succeeded in giving us at least a little gloomy pleasure, for it was the district Father had represented for so long in Albany—the Second Assembly District, in which Oliver Street lay.

Unlike two years before, we knew the outcome reasonably early. The returns on the vote for Governor were slow in coming in, and even there in the Democratic headquarters signs of pleasure were now and then evident as the figures began to mount in Father's race against Nathan L. Miller, but the outcome soon became apparent. For the first time in seventeen campaigns Father was defeated though where Harding and Coolidge had won by a gigantic national landslide and had rolled up a lead even in New York State of 1,088,000, Father lost to Nathan Miller by only 74,000.

In 1918 William Church Osborn had unsuccessfully opposed Father in the primaries. Now he sent a friendly telegram.

"Even in defeat," it read, "you came closer to swimming up Niagara Falls than any man I have ever seen."

After thirty-six years I know how great an accomplishment that was. I did not understand that to be true in November 1920, however. I had learned that the Executive Mansion was very far from being a fairy castle, but it began to take on added charms when I realized that we would have to leave it. Father was remarkably philosophical as he accepted the outcome of the election. I now know that he must have felt some personal satisfaction in the support he had received, but my brothers, my sister, and I were young, and defeat was hard to accept. We could not know, of course, how very great Father's career in politics was still to be.

CHAPTER EIGHT

Out of Politics and Back Again

THE FACT of Father's defeat on the evening of Election Day in 1920 did not burst upon us suddenly. The returns quickly made it clear that Harding and Coolidge had won. In fact, it was not long before the landslide proportions of their victory began to be obvious, but the early reports were so exclusively concerned with the vote for President and Vice-President that only fragmentary figures on other contests were available. Experienced observers were able to guess with some accuracy how the Presidential landslide would affect many state and local elections, and Father's defeat was no doubt evident to him and to a great many others before it was to Mother, Alfred, Catherine, or me.

Brought up on uninterrupted Election Day victories as all of us had been, defeat was hard to accept, and so far as I was concerned, it was as if I had unexpectedly run into a stone wall. I was so severely jolted that, for the time being, I had no clear sense of direction, and the defeat was a heavy blow to Father too.

"It was definitely fixed in my mind," he wrote later in reference to this defeat, "that my political career, so far as public office holding was concerned, had come to an end."

Nevertheless, he was quick to send a telegram of congratulations to Judge Miller. And he promptly invited the Governor-elect to come to Albany sometime before the inauguration so that they might go over in detail whatever seemed likely to be most useful to the new state administration.

Though Alfred, Catherine, and I had come to New York with Father and Mother, Walter and Arthur had been left behind in Albany. They were as deeply interested in the outcome of the election as the rest of us, but it fell to me to call them on the phone and give them the bad news. It was Arthur who dejectedly answered when the call went through, but the conversation that followed was not at all what I expected it to be. The boys had already been given the news, and their minds were on a personal problem that was obviously troubling them a great deal.

"Do we have to go to school tomorrow?" Arthur asked plaintively.

"Why, I suppose so," I replied. "Don't you want to?"

"No," he replied. "They'll all kid us about Pop getting licked."

Somehow an account of this conversation got out, and when it appeared in print, I was credited with wisely replying that they might as well go—that their prospective tormentors would still be waiting for them the next day. But that was not what occurred. When Arthur told me to ask Mother if they could stay at home, I understood just how they felt and took it on myself to say they could.

It would be difficult, I think, to find two men more different than Father and Governor Miller, but each held the other in really high personal regard. Political opponents though they were, their personal relations were always cordial, and when Mother invited Mrs. Miller to come to the Executive Mansion so that she might be better able to make her plans, Father called Judge Miller on the phone.

"I'd like to know," he explained, "what kind of a party you'd like to have. Are there any particular guests you'd like to have us invite, or should we make it just a family affair?"

"Oh, just the family," Judge Miller replied. "We would much prefer it that way."

They came early in December, and as they had suggested, it was a family affair—just Governor-elect Miller, Mrs. Miller, and ourselves. When they came the next time, it was on the day before Governor Miller's inauguration, and though we received them in the big hall of the Executive Mansion, we had already moved to the Ten Eyck Hotel, where we remained until after the inauguration ceremonies were over.

Governor and Mrs. Miller, I should add, had a delightful family of seven daughters, one of whom—she was about ten—was keeping a diary. And Father was later told by Governor Miller himself what was set down in that diary the day he was inaugurated.

"January 1, 1921," the entry read. "Saw Al Smith today."

The rest of the page was blank.

We returned to 25 Oliver Street when the inauguration was over, and after two years in the Executive Mansion all of us felt the limitations of the old house. While we had been in Albany, each of us had had a big bedroom and a bathroom. Now space was more restricted. Catherine and I shared a room at the rear of the house on the third floor, and we had no private bath. The house had been thoroughly done over, however, and was bright with new furnishings.

Not long after the election Father had been offered the position of chairman of the board of directors of the United States Trucking Corporation at fifty thousand dollars a year, and on January 2, 1921, two days after his term as Governor had ended, he assumed his new responsibilities in the company's office on Canal Street. Convinced, as he was, that his political career was over, he threw himself wholeheartedly into his new work—a task that was especially challenging because the company was losing money as a result of the postwar slump in business. He made a careful study of the company's operations, and before the year was out its methods had been reorganized, its department heads had been given wider responsibilities and more authority, and the company was rapidly being brought back to a paying basis.

Meantime my brothers, my sister, and I all returned to school in New York City—Alfred at Fordham University in the Bronx, Catherine and I at Mount St. Vincent in Riverdale, Arthur and Walter at a boarding school on Fifty-Seventh Street. Shortly after we had moved back to New York, when Father came home one evening from his Canal Street office he found something definitely lacking in the house at 25 Oliver Street. There was nothing wrong with the new furnishings. The new cook and the new maid had done all that anyone could ask. At dinner, however, Father shook his head.

"Well, Katie," he said, "we're right back where we started—just the two of us sitting down to dinner."

I do not find it hard to guess how lonely the meal was for both of them. And though Mother said nothing of what she planned to do, both Walter and Arthur were home for dinner the following evening, for she had promptly taken them out of boarding school, entering them in day school, instead, so that Father would not find the house in Oliver Street so empty and quiet when he reached it from the office.

Though Father felt definitely that his political career was over, it was not an idea that was very widely accepted. He had no sooner left Albany than President Wilson appointed him a member of the National Board of Indian Commissioners, and a few months later Governor Miller telephoned from Albany to ask him to accept an appointment as a member of the Port of New York Authority, which the states of New York and New Jersey had established under the terms of a treaty between them. The New York State Association—a nonpolitical body—asked him to lend his influence to that of the association to further the reorganization of the state government along the lines originally prepared by the Reconstruction Commission he had appointed in 1919.

I was never able fully to understand where Father found the time for these public duties, but he always managed to do so and succeeded in fulfilling other commitments as well. In addition to these public duties and to those he had assumed as chairman of the board of the United States Trucking Corporation, he somehow also found the time to serve as a director of the Morris Plan Corporation, of the wholesale coal firm of Pattison & Bowns, and of the National Surety Company.

He later admitted that these new activities took all his time, but, in a way, politics had demanded more. Now, at least, he was free to spend Sundays and most of his evenings at home, and he thoroughly enjoyed the summers of 1921 and 1922, which we spent at Sea Gate, Coney Island.

Though he imagined himself to be through with politics, many of the Democratic leaders in the state continued to keep in touch with Father. By the spring of 1922 they were coming to see him in ever increasing numbers. The problem confronting them concerned an organized and generously financed movement for the nomination of William Randolph Hearst for Governor of New York State on the Democratic ticket. It is true that Hearst had few friends upstate, but Mayor Hylan, who had been re-elected to a second term in New York City, was enthusiastic in his support of the publisher, and the upstate leaders realized that, by way of the patronage Hylan controlled in Greater New York, he might succeed in obtaining the nomination for Hearst. This was a possibility many Democratic leaders plainly feared, and on that account they began beating a path to Father's office, hoping to convince him that he should lead the forces that were opposed to Hearst.

Over and over again Father was told that the fight against Hearst could not succeed without his help. In fact, he was told that unless he himself actually became a candidate Hearst could not be stopped. He shook his head at that, however. His political career, he felt, had been long enough. Furthermore, he had come to realize not only that business was enjoyable, but also that his new activities were making it possible for him to provide adequately for the future—something politics had given him little opportunity to do. Finally Norman E. Mack of Buffalo bluntly explained that unless Father was willing to co-operate with the upstate leaders, Erie County, in which the city of Buffalo lies— and undoubtedly not that county alone—would surely select a delegation pledged to Hearst.

Confronted with this situation, and with the frequently repeated argument that his refusal to enter the contest was nothing less than an avoidance of his duty, Father's determination to stay out of politics was very greatly weakened. And at this stage of events Franklin D. Roosevelt, who had been the Democratic Vice-Presidential candidate two years before but who was now a private citizen, added his arguments in the following open letter to Father:

> *Hyde Park, Dutchess County*
> *New York*
> *August 13, 1922.*

Hon. Alfred E. Smith
25 Oliver Street
New York City.

Dear Al: Over a month ago I wrote to the conference of Democrats in Syracuse, urging that the Democratic party of this state must put its best foot foremost in the selection of candidates this year. It appeared to me then that the sentiment of the overwhelming majority of Democrats was for your nomination again for the office of governor.

Today, a week before the filing of designating petitions for delegates to the state convention, I am of the same opinion. I have been in touch with men and women voters from almost every upstate county and there is no question that the rank and file of Democrats want you to run.

Many candidates for office are strong by virtue of promises of what they will some day do. You are strong by virtue of promises of what you have done. People everywhere know that in 1920, while you lost by a narrow margin in the landslide, you received a million more votes in this state than the presidential ticket.

More than that, your support came not only from Democrats but literally hundreds of thousands of Republicans and independent men and women who knew that you had given to this State an honest, clean and economical government, and had consistently opposed the privilege seekers and the reactionaries.

These voters are not satisfied with the present conduct of affairs by Republican leaders in Washington and Albany. To them will be added many more who are now sorry that they voted the Republican ticket in 1920. You represent the hope of what may be called "the average citizen."

Something must be done, and done now. In every county the chief topic of political conversation is: "Will Al Smith accept if he is nominated?" Already unauthorized agents are saying that you will not accept, and many are being deceived and beginning to lose interest as a result. It would surprise you to know what enthusiasm would spring up overnight if we knew you would accept the nomination.

Frankly, I don't want to see things go by default in this most hopeful year, and that is why I am writing you before the primary petitions are filed. I am taking it upon myself to appeal to you in the name of countless citizens of upstate New York, Democrats, Republicans, Independents, men and women, to ask you to say now, not later, that if nominated for governor, you will accept.

We realize that years of public service make it most desirable that you think now for a while of your family's needs. I am in the same boat myself —yet this call for further service must come first. Some day your children will be even prouder of you for making this sacrifice than they are now.

You represent the type of citizen the voters of this state want to vote for for governor, and you can be elected. The decision must be made now, as I have tried to point out. That is why—reluctantly to be sure, for I know what unselfishness it will call for on your part—I am asking you personally and publicly to accede to the wishes of so many of your fellow citizens.

Very truly yours,

FRANKLIN D. ROOSEVELT.

Father's determination to remain on the sidelines had been greatly weakened even before he received this letter, but it was in the reply he now made that he first announced his willingness to accept the nomination if it was offered him.

Dear Frank: I have your letter of August 13th and I have carefully read it. I appreciate your kindly sentiments, and they compel me to talk to you from my heart. I would not be entirely frank with you if I did not admit that evidence has been presented to me which would indicate a desire on the part of the Democratic rank and file that I again take the post of leadership. It has been and still is my desire to remain in business life for the reason you state in your letter—for my family's sake—but during the past twenty years I have been so honored by my party that even the members of my family would be dissatisfied if I did not answer the call.

Therefore, considering the facts as I know them, and answering your letter, I feel myself that I would be ungrateful if I were to say that I would be unwilling to assume the leadership. The state convention will be composed of elected representatives of the rank and file of the Democratic party throughout the state. They will undoubtedly come to the convention alive to the sentiment in their respective districts. If a majority of them desire me to accept the nomination for governor and lead the party in this state to what seems to me to be a certain victory, I am entirely willing to accept this honor from their hands and to battle for them with all the energy and vigor that I possess.

With kind regards to your mother and Mrs. Roosevelt and all the children, I am

Sincerely yours,

Al.

Up to the time this reply was published, Hearst's nomination as the Democratic candidate for Governor seemed almost certain. Once Father's willingness to run became known, the picture changed. Where, until that moment, Hearst's supporters had hoped to see the publisher nominated for Governor, they were quick to see that that was now impossible. They did not withdraw his name, however. They merely changed their plan and began to present him as the logical Democratic candidate for the United States Senate.

The state convention was held in Syracuse that year, and because of a bad attack of neuritis Father found it hard to get there. For several weeks it was very difficult and painful for him to walk, and though Mother and I did everything we could to ease the way for him, it was quite an effort for him to get to Syracuse and to the eighth floor of the Onondaga Hotel, where he had reserved a suite. Once there, however, though he was quite unable to move about and did not leave the suite during the whole period of the convention, he was able to keep in touch with all the more important developments.

Even before we reached Syracuse, Father's nomination for Governor was assured. Nowhere was there any important opposition to him. But though that was certain, much pressure was brought to bear to get him to accept Hearst as the party's nominee for the United States Senate. The major portion of Hearst's strength was clearly traceable to the influence of Mayor Hylan. Elsewhere, however, there were party leaders who, though they cared little for Hearst, were convinced that a Democratic victory could hardly be achieved without the support of the Hearst papers. And this, they contended, would be too much to expect unless Hearst was flattered and conciliated by being given the Senatorial nomination. As practically everyone understood, there was little likelihood that could be done unless Father was willing to withdraw his opposition.

Father, however, refused. Though leader after leader came to see him there in the hotel and urged every kind of practical argument upon him, he would not change his stand. Even Mr. Murphy, the powerful leader of Tammany Hall, was in favor of permitting Hearst to have the Senatorial nomination, though he made no direct attempt to influence Father in the matter. In fact, he stayed away, apparently because other leaders had told him how firm, and even angry, Father's opposition was. Tom Foley saw Father regularly and brought report after report about developments as they occurred.

Years later Father himself clearly explained his attitude at Syracuse. "I frankly served notice on the leaders," he wrote in 1929, "that if his [Hearst's] nomination was brought about I would have to decline the nomination for Governor. In view of our past relations, in view of his bitter attacks upon me as well as upon the Democratic party for so many years, I was unable to reconcile myself to both of us being put on the same ticket."

The position in which Father found himself was a very strong one. He had made no bid for the nomination. He had made it clear from the first that while he was willing to accept it he would do so only as a matter of duty and on his own terms. Otherwise he was determined not to reduce his income by 80 per cent or more and cut himself away from the opportunity his business connections had given him to accumulate a competence for himself and for his family.

From morning to night since the time of our arrival he found it necessary to state and restate his position. It was not easy to oppose so many friendly political leaders, but he kept at it, and he seldom seemed to lose his sense of humor. There was little that Mother and I could do to help. Most of those who came wished to speak to Father alone, but sometimes there were groups and delegations that asked to see Mother or Mother and me, and I particularly remember one such call. I was in my room with Mother and two women visitors when the telephone rang. I answered it and an unfamiliar voice explained that a delegation in the lobby would greatly appreciate it if Mother and I would join them.

I had no idea who they were or what the call was all about, but naturally I was unwilling to antagonize anyone, so I replied that we would be down presently.

Mother and the ladies who were with us understood politics well enough to accept the situation when I explained it, and having powdered our noses and carefully adjusted our hats, we left and made our way to the elevator. But just before we reached it, the door of Father's sitting room opened and he poked his head out.

"Where are you going?" he asked.

I told him about the delegation that was waiting.

"Well," he replied, "they aren't there any longer, so don't go down."

"What do you mean?" I asked.

"I mean they never were there," he chuckled. "I'm the one who called you." He laughed with almost boyish pleasure at the joke he had played. "You didn't recognize my voice, did you?"

It may have been on that day, too, that Tom Foley, who had never for a moment failed to keep himself abreast of developments, gave Father his final bit of carefully considered advice. No one knew better than Mr. Foley how much pressure had been brought to bear on Father, and no one, I am sure, understood better the comparative strengths of the contending forces. Now, having considered the situation carefully, he put his head in at Father's door. Father was momentarily alone, fortunately, and he beckoned his visitor in, but Mr. Foley did not enter. He merely poked his head inside, and the message he had come to bring consisted of a single word.

"Stick!" he remarked, whereupon he withdrew his head and closed the door.

"That meant," Father told me later, "that he knew I was right and that I'd win."

The Hearst supporters were still busy testing their strength, but already they were beginning to learn that the nomination could not be had. Later a well-authenticated rumor ran through the lobby and the corridors of the Onondaga Hotel. A telegram, we heard, had come from Mr. Hearst withdrawing his name. I never heard what the message contained. But obviously it was a full concession of defeat—a defeat that became very definite when we learned that shortly after the arrival of the telegram Mayor Hylan and his most intimate supporters caught a train for New York City.

Thus Father not only became a candidate for office again, but he also dealt a hard blow to William Randolph Hearst's political influence in the Empire State. These were the really important accomplishments of that convention. As a kind of afterthought the delegates chose Dr. Royal S. Copeland, Health Commissioner of New York City, to run in the primary for nomination as the Democratic candidate for the United States Senate. In the absence of Mr. Hearst's chief supporters this move was accepted without opposition.

Our whole family had accepted Father's retirement from politics as an actuality, and we had succeeded in adjusting ourselves to the changes this entailed. But Father had no sooner replied to Franklin Roosevelt's letter than we once more found ourselves surrounded by the old, familiar atmosphere, and when the campaign of 1922 actually began, it almost seemed as if there had been no break in Father's political activities.

It was clear as soon as the campaign got under way that it would be entirely different from the one two years before. Then the national election had so dominated everything that state and local problems were largely lost to sight. Now Father and Governor Miller were able to explain and to defend their points of view on the more important problems that confronted the state without having their statements buried in the back pages of the papers or obscured by the presence of more highly publicized accounts of other matters.

Father had long been in favor of reorganizing the state government, and felt that a constitutional amendment was necessary for that purpose. Governor Miller, though he agreed that a governmental reorganization was highly desirable, contended that the necessary changes could be made without modifying the constitution. Father also advocated a constitutional change that would permanently establish an executive budget—an idea Governor Miller opposed. Then, too, there were clear-cut differences between them on the control of public utilities, with Governor Miller favoring centralized state control while Father contended that local problems in this field were best left to the localities affected.

I have already referred to the fact that when Father was Governor he had vetoed several bills which, in his belief, would have interfered with freedom of thought and freedom of speech, and that would have compelled teachers to submit to a loyalty test. Governor Miller, however, had accepted and signed these bills when the Legislature had passed them again, though he was now clearly unwilling to answer Father's criticisms of these laws. Instead he based his campaign very largely on the economies his administration had put into effect.

Father spent four weeks on his campaign, as he had done two years before, devoting the first three weeks to the upstate areas and the final week to New York City, and it was obvious from the first that he had lost none of his political appeal. It is true that the great metropolitan dailies, with the exception of the New York *World* and, interestingly enough, the Hearst papers, supported Governor Miller, but when the polls closed early on the evening of Election Day and the returns began to come in, it soon began to be apparent that Father had won. As a matter of fact, the final figures showed that he had received a plurality of 387,000—the largest any Governor had ever been given in the entire history of New York State. Furthermore, every other Democratic nominee on the state ticket was also elected though, due to what Father always felt was the state's unfair system of apportionment, the Republicans retained control of the Assembly, and the Senate went Democratic by only a single vote.

It was on Father's forty-ninth birthday—December 30, 1922—that we returned to Albany and to the Executive Mansion. We had spent Christmas at the Biltmore Hotel in New York—a very happy Christmas, in view of what awaited us—and had arrived in Albany in the midst of a snowstorm which had already covered the streets with slush.

The weather was most unpleasant, though none of us felt that the day was, for despite the snowstorm a great crowd had assembled at the station and Father, the chief actor in this "home-coming," marched on foot with a great parade of welcomers all the way to the Executive Mansion.

We were cordially received in the big hall of the mansion by Governor Miller and the other outgoing Republican state officials, and once this reception was over, each of us almost automatically settled into place—each of us, that is, except a pet monkey Father had received as a Christmas present and brought along. The inquisitive little creature had no sooner been released than he began a thorough exploration of the mansion, and was lured back to his cage only with the greatest difficulty. That monkey, incidentally, may have played some part in encouraging Father to establish the menagerie that ultimately came into existence behind the mansion—a menagerie that later grew to somewhat surprising proportions. Even during Father's first term he had gathered together a number of ponies, dogs, and birds. Now with his pet monkey and our usual assortment of dogs he made a beginning on what came to be called the "Executive Mansion Zoo." Always interested in animals, he was willing to accept young racoons, deer, elk, bears, rabbits, foxes and other animals and birds that were occasionally found and sent to him by employees in the state's Department of Parks and by friends, and in this way his private zoo grew until it contained an estimable exhibit of animals that were native to New York as well as some others that came from more distant places. As these creatures grew in size and strength—and that was something the bears and elk very rapidly did—many of them, outgrowing the limited facilities Father was able to create, were given to various zoos in the state where they could be more adequately cared for.

Any really objective examination of Father's career as Governor of New York will show that he is to be credited with many constructive accomplishments, but no one knew better than he that his unusual success was due, in very large part, to the length of time he remained in office.

Early in the history of New York several Governors served for equal or greater lengths of time—George Clinton, the first Governor, for instance, as well as John Jay, Daniel D. Tompkins, and DeWitt Clinton, that very well-known nephew of the state's first governor. For more than a century before Father was returned to Albany for his second term, no Governor except David Hill had served for any really extended period of time, and a kind of custom had been established whereby Governors appeared to be limited to a maximum of two terms. Father, however, had not only served one term before his re-election in 1922, but also was now well started on another, which, though no one could have guessed it at the time, was to be followed by a third and even a fourth.

Years later, in looking back over his career, he himself divided his accomplishments as Governor into three major parts: first, the reorganization of the state government; second, the preservation of individual, political, state, and legal rights; and third, welfare legislation.

In the many years that have passed since Father was laboring to reorganize the government of the state of New York, it has been easy to forget how greatly that reorganization was needed. In almost a century and a half of existence the state had permitted the establishment of 187 governmental agencies, many of them improperly and inefficiently organized, and several whose functions overlapped in haphazard ways. It was almost impossible under such a scheme of things to administer the state government with real efficiency or with much economy, and Father favored a plan which, though it necessitated an amendment to the state constitution, would require these various agencies to give way to nineteen distinct departments. Furthermore, these departments were to be established by name in the proposed amendment, and the Legislature was thereafter to be prohibited from adding other departments to them. In addition he proposed the establishment of the executive budget, which the state had never had, and he also proposed, among other lesser changes, that the term of the Governor should be lengthened from two years to four, with elections to that office to be arranged so as not to coincide with the national elections.

As even a hurried glance will show, these were major proposals, and it is not surprising that the 1923 Legislature succeeded in accomplishing little along these lines. Then, unfortunately, the Legislature of 1924 fell wholly under the control of the Republicans. Still, the amendment to consolidate the various departments was then passed by the Senate, and was finally approved by the Assembly with only minor changes.

Under the terms of the constitution this amendment then had to be sent to the office of the Secretary of State to await repassage by the Legislature of 1925. And before that body met for the first time—before it was even elected—Father had been called upon to play a very important part in one of the most exciting political dramas that was ever staged by the Democratic party.

Though I was not conscious of it at the time, the problems that confronted Father grew much more complex after he became Governor, and especially after he returned to Albany in 1923. The events that preceded 1919, for example, are reasonably clear if they are considered merely on a day-to-day basis, and to some degree that is also true for the next four years. But from the time Father's second term as Governor began, events and developments were so numerous and complicated as to make a simple chronological account almost impossible. It is on that account, and despite the approach of more dramatic happenings, that I go back for a moment to November 1923, when Colonel George F. Chandler, the superintendent of the state police, called on Father in the Executive Office at the state capitol and announced that he had decided to resign.

Though Father had made the mistake of opposing the state police at first, he had long since changed his mind. Their record of accomplishment had been remarkable despite their limited numbers, and Father had come to admire them greatly. He knew that the efficiency of the body was very largely due to Colonel Chandler's executive ability and to his success in the selection of officers. And up to this moment he had known nothing of the colonel's wish to resign.

The conversation which followed was not a short one, for Father had no wish to see the state of New York lose so competent a servant. Learning that Colonel Chandler had definitely decided to return to the practice of medicine, which he had given up only because he had so deeply felt the importance of organizing the newly authorized state police, Father finally agreed to accept his resignation.

"But," he asked, "whom should I appoint as your successor?"

Colonel Chandler had obviously given some thought to that matter, for he answered the question without a moment's hesitation.

"Captain John A. Warner," he replied. "He's now Captain of Troop K at White Plains."

Father made a note of the name, and on Thanksgiving day a telegram was delivered to the captain:

I HAVE TODAY APPOINTED YOU SUPERINTENDENT OF STATE POLICE. KINDLY REPORT TO ME AT THE EXECUTIVE CHAMBER DECEMBER 1.

When the appointment was announced, the newspapermen naturally asked Father about the new superintendent.

"I never saw the man in my life," he replied, adding that he was confident of the new superintendent's ability because Colonel Chandler had so unhesitatingly recommended him.

But he was wrong when he said he had never seen the man he had appointed. Only a few weeks earlier Father, Mother, Catherine, and I had attended a dinner given at Briarcliff Lodge by Sophie Irene Loeb, the well-known newspaperwoman on the staff of the New York *World,* who was largely responsible for the Widows' Pension Law of New York State, and Captain Warner had been one of the guests. He had not been in uniform, however, and for reasons that will appear later, my memory of his presence there was better than Father's.

Though Father had not been one of the really serious contenders for the Democratic Presidential nomination at the San Francisco Convention of 1920, he had no sooner been re-elected Governor in 1922 than it became clear that his Presidential chances in 1924 would be far better. Mr. Murphy, who by now had been the leader of Tammany Hall for more than twenty years, had long hoped to play an important part in the selection of a Democratic Presidential candidate, and he was convinced that in the years since 1920 Father had become a national figure. Mr. Murphy was a silent man, and it may be that no one ever learned in full detail the plans he had in mind, for though he seemed in the best of health when he left Tammany Hall on April 24, he died from a heart attack at his home the following morning.

To Father, Mr. Murphy had been much more than just the leader of Tammany Hall. He had been a close friend and an always dependable adviser for whom Father had felt a very deep affection. Thus his death struck Father a severe blow, and merely as a matter of practical politics his loss created problems.

Mr. Murphy had been the unquestioned leader of Tammany Hall for many years, and no "natural" successor was available. In a way Father was the natural leader of the Democratic party in New York State.

Tammany Hall, however, was another matter, and though Father and many others hoped that Mr. Murphy's son-in-law, Surrogate James A. Foley, would accept the leadership, he refused, and the Tammany Hall executive committee finally selected Judge George W. Olvany, of the Court of General Sessions.

The death of Charles Murphy, as I have said, was a heavy blow to Father, but an even heavier one was soon to follow. Father's mother—my grandmother—had twice suffered from attacks of pneumonia, but now, early in May 1924, she fell ill with a third attack. It was serious from the first though at one time she appeared to be recovering. But on Sunday, May 18, she died.

"It was the first real sorrow," Father said later, "that I had ever suffered."

Throughout these very weeks the pressure of political developments had enormously increased. Under the circumstances Father felt impelled to take a few days' rest, but politics did not. For one thing the New York *World,* under the direction of Herbert Bayard Swope, had initiated a campaign aimed at bringing the 1924 Democratic Convention to New York City—an idea that Mr. Murphy himself had encouraged, though Father had been less enthusiastic. He understood that both Mr. Swope and Mr. Murphy felt that if the convention were to be held in New York his chances for the nomination would be enhanced, but he was not convinced they were right. He realized, of course, that he, as an interested party, might not be the best judge of the matter. Therefore he bowed to the judgment of his friends, but in the light of later events it became evident that his reaction was sounder than theirs.

Many months before New York was chosen as the convention city, it was clear that Father would not be the only prominent contender for the nomination. William Gibbs McAdoo, who had been acting chairman of the Democratic National Committee during the Presidential campaign of 1912 and had later served as Secretary of the Treasury in Woodrow Wilson's Cabinet, was fully as prominent and much more active. There were many others also. Never before, in fact, had so many contenders permitted their Presidential aspirations to appear. A couple of weeks before the convention actually met, the New York *Times* listed thirty-five names.

After the passage of more than thirty years I find it difficult—almost impossible—to describe certain conditions as they existed in 1924. For one thing the entire nation was concerned almost beyond belief with the pros and cons of prohibition, which—unwisely, as events proved—had been written into the Constitution of the United States in the well-intentioned but ill-advised Eighteenth Amendment. In effect for more than four years before the Democratic Convention met in 1924, this troublemaking law had utterly failed to settle the liquor problem—had, instead, created endless new difficulties and a constant series of ill-tempered arguments. As yet the "drys" were still in control and anyone who in any way questioned the Eighteenth Amendment, the Volstead Act, or any other related "reform" was almost certain not only to be labeled a "wet," but to be damned as one. And Father, who was as sincere a believer in temperance as anyone and who certainly did not believe in permitting the return of the saloon, was down in the black books of the Anti-Saloon League as a "wet."

This alone was an almost insurmountable barrier to his success in 1924. A few more years had to pass before the honesty of purpose and the logic of his point of view on prohibition were accepted by most of the people of the country. But, as if this were not enough, thousands of Americans all across the country, though especially in the South and West, had so far forgotten or misinterpreted the basic principles of sound Americanism as to become members of the so-called Ku Klux Klan. This was an anti-Negro, anti-Catholic, anti-Jewish, and anti-foreign-born society which had taken its name from an organization that had existed for a time in parts of the South during the harsh Reconstruction days following the Civil War.

In any free society one must expect to come across groups that express extravagant points of view. The occasional presence of such groups, in fact, may actually prove that real liberty exists. The Ku Klux Klan of the 1920s, however, was not concerned with liberty. And in the lurid light of its fiery crosses there was an idea that was the very antithesis of the beliefs on which our country had been founded. Due to a strange psychological urge I do not pretend to understand, appeals to prejudice were especially effective during the years that followed World War I, though American common sense never permitted the Ku Klux Klan to develop as far as Fascism did in Italy or Nazism in Germany. Nevertheless, it was evident many months before the Democratic Convention met that the Klan was certain to have much influence and that this would be directed against Father because he was a member of the Roman Catholic Church. It soon became perfectly clear that Father would be the Klan's most important target, though there were others who were also opposed by the organization. For example, Senator Oscar W. Underwood of Alabama, the most prominent Southern contender for the nomination, had publicly assailed the Klan months before the convention opened, and in doing so had earned the society's enmity. Furthermore, there were other potential candidates who did not meet the very narrow specifications of the Klan. Even McAdoo, according to a report that appeared in the New York *World* on March 17, 1924, was momentarily criticized in Georgia as a "straddler" by some of the Klan's more radical members. He was campaigning against Senator Underwood in the Georgia primaries at the time, and in reply to a reporter's question as to his attitude toward the Klan, which was expected to support him, he expressed himself as standing "foursquare with regard to this and every other order . . . for freedom of speech, freedom of the press, freedom of religious worship, and the right of peaceable assemblage."

It may appear surprising that so mild a statement should have aroused any criticism whatever, but it did. As the New York *World* pointed out, Senator Underwood had already made his bold attack on the Klan, so McAdoo was not hurt. There was no one else to whom the members of the Klan could turn.

The years in which our Presidential campaigns are held are always rich in interest, but that was especially true of 1924. Warren G. Harding, who had been elected by so great a landslide in 1920, had died in office on August 2, 1923, with his administration under a cloud. This had been due, in part, to the dishonesty of one member of his Cabinet and the questionable activities of another, but Vice-President Calvin Coolidge, who now succeeded to the Presidency, had in no way been connected with the scandal. It is true that he had entered the White House only a short ten months before the Republican National Convention of 1924 met in Cleveland, but no significant opposition developed, and on the first ballot cast by the delegates he was nominated to succeed himself. A Vice-Presidential candidate proved harder to find, but General Charles G. Dawes was ultimately nominated, and the Republican Convention completed its business and adjourned more than two weeks before the Democratic Convention met in New York.

The Klan, as I have said, was certain to play an important part in the convention, but so was prohibition, and in view of the strength of the nation's "drys" it is necessary for a moment to look back at an action Father had taken in 1923.

Those who have become adults since the repeal of prohibition are not likely to understand how dominant that issue was in the 1920s. Though liquor had been outlawed by the adoption of the Eighteenth Amendment, prohibition still played a very important part in American politics. The Anti-Saloon League was immensely powerful and was ever ready to oppose anyone in public life whose outlook differed from that of the league. Because of this extreme point of view problems relating to prohibition had arisen in many states, though few of these grew to such proportions as the one that troubled New York.

The Federal law under which the Federal prohibition-enforcement agencies operated, and by way of which the Eighteenth Amendment was actually enforced, was known as the Volstead Act. This applied throughout the United States, but under the powerful influence of the Anti-Saloon League most of the states had also adopted prohibition laws of their own—laws which more or less paralleled the Volstead Act. In New York State a prohibition law known as the Mullan-Gage Act had been enacted.

Father had never been a believer in prohibition. He understood and was opposed to the evils that attended the sale of liquor, but he believed these evils could most effectively be opposed by education and the adoption of carefully considered local laws.

"The radical drys look upon drink as a moral problem," he told me on one occasion, "but I look on it as an economic one. Before the Eighteenth Amendment was adopted, this whole question was growing less. In a way it was solving itself. But now that the amendment has been passed, the only practical way of improving the situation in this state would be to legalize the sale of light wine and beer. Then we would be in a much better position to destroy the demand for strong drink. In time a new generation would grow up that would be acquainted only with these lighter drinks, and we would then be better able to decide two questions: first, whether we cared to abolish the lighter drinks too; and second, whether such a step had become possible."

He always held to this belief, but in 1923 the Legislature voted to repeal the Mullan-Gage Act, and Father had to decide whether to approve or veto their action. This, as the Republican leaders thoroughly understood, confronted Father with a dilemma. Many friends and advisers urged him to veto the bill, and one, with his mind on the 1924 Democratic Convention, went so far as to suggest that a veto would help Father nationally.

"I hope," he replied with a touch of sharpness in his voice, "that as long as I live I'll never do anything because it may help me to preferment or place rather than because it is what I believe to be right."

This was the point of view that dictated his decision in the matter, and he made his attitude crystal-clear in the unusually long message he wrote when he took his final action.

"Much has been said in the public prints," he wrote as he approached the conclusion of that message, "with respect to the effect my action on this bill may have upon my own political future. I have no political future that I am willing to attain by the sacrifice of any principle, or any conviction of what in my mind is for the welfare and the benefit of this state and nation.

"Because I believe there is nothing to be gained either for the nation or for the state by the retention of this statute, [the Mullan-Gage Law] while on the other hand I believe that its repeal is of distinct benefit in the preservation of the rights of our people . . . and being mindful of the responsibility placed on me by the electorate of this state, grateful for their overwhelming vote of confidence, devoted as I am to the welfare of the country and to the happiness and prosperity of the state, I have after careful thought arrived at the conclusion that the bill before me should receive executive approval, and I therefore approve the bill."

It is probable that the signing of this bill, more than any other single thing, made Father a leader of the "wets," but he did not sign it for that reason.

George Van Namee was Father's secretary in Albany, and during the years when the two were so very close, he had a better opportunity than almost any other person to learn how Father reached his decisions.

"In all the time I spent with him," George once remarked, "I never heard him say, when a bill was placed before him for his signature, 'What will this mean for me?' The only question he ever asked was, 'Is this law good for the people of this state?'"

And George once quoted Father as having said, "'I am satisfied that as long as I do what I believe to be right I won't have to worry. I am sure that any law that is good for the people is good for me too.'"

I know Father was convinced of the truth of that, for on scores of different occasions, and in many different ways, I heard him express that same thought. In a way, I believe, it was the basis of his political philosophy.

CHAPTER NINE

The 1924 Democratic Convention—The Smith-McAdoo Fight

THOUGH IT WAS OBVIOUS to every political observer that Father would be a serious contender for the Democratic nomination when the Democratic Convention of 1924 met, he consistently refused to interrupt his work as Governor in order to further his Presidential prospects. Even up to the time the Legislature adjourned some two months before the New York convention was to meet, he still objected to the organization of any movement that would promote his Presidential chances.

The Legislature adjourned on April 10 that year and, in doing so, left hundreds of bills on Father's desk. Consequently, with these to study and to sign or veto within the period of thirty days that was set by the state constitution, he had his hands full. In addition to this really pressing task he was faced by the fact that the Democratic State Convention was scheduled to meet in Albany on April 15—only five days after the Legislature had adjourned—and that this convention was to select the delegates at large as well as their alternates, who were to attend the Democratic National Convention, which was to open in New York City in two months. They met and attended to these duties but they also adopted a resolution favoring Father for the Democratic nomination.

It was after the passage of this resolution that Father arrived to address the convention, and to the surprise of those who were present, he gave his attention primarily to state problems. But as he approached his conclusion he referred to other matters.

"I want to step out of my character as Governor," he said, "and have a personal word with you. I heard the resolution that you passed. In fact, I read it before it came up here.

"It would be a difficult task for any man to stand before an audience of this kind and be able to express adequately the appreciation he would have to feel for the great compliment, the great honor, and the great distinction that comes to him to be spoken of as the choice of his party in the greatest state in the Union for the highest office in all the world.

"If I were to tell you that I haven't heard anything on this particular subject for the last year, you wouldn't believe me because it wouldn't be true. I have heard a great deal about it, but in the frankness that ought to exist among friends and comrades together, let me say this to you: I have done absolutely nothing about it, either inside or outside of the state, and I do not intend to do anything about it. The man who would not have an ambition for that office would have a dead heart. But I stand exactly in the position that I stood in on the floor of the Constitutional Convention in 1915 when I said that the man who used one office and neglected it in order to climb to a higher one was not deserving of the one he had.

"I am going to do nothing about it, because there is nothing I can do. In the first place I haven't got the means to do it. In the second place I haven't got the time to do it. For the next thirty days I will be just as busy as any man could possibly be in the consideration of the nine hundred odd bills left for my attention by the Legislature. Then, within a reasonably short time, after five solid months without a vacation, I will have to turn my attention to the administrative details of some of the departments of government.

"This work I propose to do right up to the time the convention starts. If I fell down on this job, I would never forgive myself and I would not ask forgiveness from anyone else. If the required number of delegates in the national convention takes your view of it, I will be honored beyond the power of expression to lead the forces of my party in the next campaign.

"In conclusion I want to leave just one thought with you. If my nomination is brought about and it results in a triumph for the party, you can say to every delegate that you meet at the convention in New York City that I promised you in the capital city of this state before God Almighty Himself that neither they nor you will ever have any cause to regret any confidence they or you see fit to repose in me."

With only two months left before the Democratic Convention was to open, political activities took on added urgency. Among all the many candidates whose names were beginning to appear in the news accounts, McAdoo was quite the busiest as he went about his search for delegates. Father, on the other hand, refused to enter any of the state contests, though early in April his name had appeared in the Wisconsin primaries. This had been done without his knowledge, but he had won twenty-three of the state's twenty-six delegates and easily took the lead over McAdoo, whose name was also entered.

Even earlier than this it had become clear that Father and McAdoo would be the leading contenders when the convention opened, though no one pretended to know which of the two would win. The New York *World* for March 20 carried a story which quoted McAdoo supporters as saying that a deadlock was a possibility, and on April 5, when observers had had a little time to study the meaning of Father's unplanned primary victory in Wisconsin, the following series of headlines in the *World* gave an inkling of how this might occur:

Figuring Is Upset by Smith Victory

Spontaneous Move to Governor in Wisconsin

Forces Politicians to Reckon with Him

Underwood Camp Happy

Hope for Aid of Smith's Supporters against McAdoo

Though Father had opposed the early organization of any political committee designed to further his Presidential aspirations, such a body ultimately had to be set up. Long before this was accomplished, it was clear that Father would be an active contender in the convention, but no one knew in detail how great his strength might be until the New York State Smith Committee was organized and went to work late in May.

Father was known all across the country as a member of Tammany Hall, and much of his strength in New York politics derived from that connection. As a potential Presidential candidate, however, he would have an advantage if some nationally known New York State Democrat who had no Tammany connections were to head the committee to be formed. A difficulty immediately arose though, for in all the state of New York only one Democrat existed who was not a member of Tammany Hall and yet was nationally known. This was Franklin D. Roosevelt, who, after having served for three years in the New York

State Senate and seven years as Assistant Secretary of the Navy, had been nominated in 1920 as the Democratic Vice-Presidential candidate. He had been defeated in the Harding landslide, but the campaign and his family name had established him as a national Democratic figure. And, coming as he did from Hyde Park, he had never been a member of Tammany—had actually fought the New York organization during his service in the Senate. Unfortunately he had been the victim of an attack of infantile paralysis in 1921, and there was some doubt that he would be physically able to attend to the many duties the chairmanship of the committee would entail.

At this point Judge Joseph M. Proskauer, Robert Moses, and Mrs. Belle Moskowitz, three of Father's closest associates and advisers, made the suggestion that solved the problem. If, they said in effect, Mr. Roosevelt will permit his name to be used as chairman of the New York State Smith Committee, we'll do the work or will see that it is done by other members of the committee.

Oversimplified though this explanation may be, it was essentially in this way that the chairmanship of the committee was decided.

By the time this decision was reached, Father had succeeded in clearing his desk in Albany. He had disposed of some nine hundred bills, had attended to endless administrative duties, had accepted resignations and made appointments, and had turned his attention to scores of other diverse and complicated problems. I often sat with him in the Executive Chamber, watching as he went over the never ending list of documents and reports he was forced to study. He usually did this work silently, though sometimes he would explain or make humorous remarks about the problem before him. I especially remember one incident, and though it occurred several years later, after my marriage to Major John A. Warner, the new superintendent of the New York State Police, I may as well tell it here, for Father never changed and similar stories might be told about him at almost any stage of his career.

He was going over a list of appropriations, and I was sitting on the arm of his chair, looking over his shoulder. The paper before him had a long list of items on it, most of which were familiar to me, but as my eye ran over the list, one item caught my attention.

"New barracks for state police," it read, "seventy-five thousand dollars."

I had not been married very long, and was as eager as any other bride would be to help her new husband, so I leaned forward and put my finger on that particular item.

"Don't forget that one," I insisted.

I don't recall that he said a word, but he paused and followed the words "New barracks for state police" with his pen almost as if he were about to underline them. But then, suddenly, he drew a bold line through them, striking them out. His action jarred me for a moment, but before I found my tongue I saw that he was writing something to take the place of what he had deleted.

I leaned closer as he wrote, and presently I made it out.

"Palace," he had inserted, "for cops and horses."

Father could be sharp and even angry on occasion. More than once I have known him to take state officials to task because of something they had done badly or had not done at all. That was not typical of him, however. Sometimes he would bring an entirely serious conversation to an end with a bit of song, "Mother Machree," perhaps, or even "Yes, We Have No Bananas." And even during the busy weeks he spent at his desk in Albany before we all went to New York he retained his sense of humor. I often wondered how he did it, with endless papers before him, with callers always waiting to see him, and with George Van Namee coming in every few minutes, it seemed to me, to say that some politician or newspaperman was on the wire from New York or Chicago or almost any other place hoping for some statement that would "influence the situation" or make a headline. Ultimately he succeeded in clearing his desk and, with the whole family and George Van Namee besides to bear him company, left for New York. We went directly to the Biltmore Hotel, and throughout the following weeks we stayed there while more callers than I had ever seen before arrived and departed in what sometimes seemed to be an absolutely uninterrupted stream.

The McAdoo supporters were making great claims. For instance, a statement in the New York *Times* for June 3 read as follows: "Supporters of McAdoo will number 32 out of 52 members of the Comittee on Permanent Organization of the Democratic National Committee." The report then qualified the statement by explaining that that was what certain McAdoo supporters were saying.

Occasionally the claims were made with no qualification whatever. Certain McAdoo supporters were quoted as saying that 505 votes would be cast for McAdoo on the first ballot. It was the Smith supporters—Bob Moses, perhaps, or Judge Proskauer—who insisted that that figure was at least fifty too high.

The Ku Klux Klan was in the headlines almost every day, and so was prohibition. Even the Republicans were troubled by them, though not to the degree that the Democrats were. But the Republicans faced a problem that was exclusively their own—a problem that resulted from Senator Robert M. La Follette's determination to run for the Presidency on an Independent ticket. There was no chance that he would be elected, but he claimed he would carry several states and a great many observers thought he might.

In view of what occurred when the convention finally met, it is interesting to recall what some of the forecasts were.

"Underwood Sees Klan as Chief Issue," a headline in the New York Times read on June 8. And the very next day another Times headline read:

McAdoo Men Admit Deadlock Is Likely

The deadlock, if it were to come, would be between Father and McAdoo. That much was clear. But if it came it would be largely because of the Klan's anti-Catholic position, so all of us were immensely interested when Father was asked, as Governor, to review a Flag Day Parade of the National League of Masonic Clubs and associated bodies. He accepted, naturally, and even wore two Masonic emblems on his lapel while he was on the reviewing stand. He was cheered by many of the marchers and was even hailed as "Our Next President" by some of them.

The New York papers reported this incident in more or less detail, but the story attracted comparatively little attention because the final list of instructed delegates appeared in print at the same time—a list which the New York Times gave as follows:

WILLIAM GIBBS MCADOO	294
ALFRED E. SMITH	123
JAMES M. COX	48
SAMUEL M. RALSTON	30
WOODBRIDGE N. FERRIS	30
OSCAR W. UNDERWOOD	29

There were ten others on the list, and the number of delegates for each of them ranged down to six. John W. Davis, with sixteen instructed delegates, was among them. There were still more potential candidates—thirty-five in all, according to the New York *Times* of June 15.

With all these names now in the picture observers began to hint at the probable outcome. On the very day the long list of names appeared in the *Times,* for instance, another series of headlines in the same paper read as follows:

> Davis and Ralston Looming in Race
> as "Dark Horses"
> Becoming Formidable in the Event of
> a McAdoo-Smith Deadlock.

And on June 16 another *Times* headline read:
> Davis "Second Choice" of Many Delegates

The so-called two-thirds rule then prevailed in Democratic conventions, and a mere majority was not enough for victory. The votes in the convention would total 1,098, and unless the rule was changed, 732 would be necessary to assure the nomination. There was a good deal of talk about the possibility of making the change—an idea favored by the McAdoo supporters in opposition to practically everyone else—and many observers forecast a deadlock if the rule remained in force. Because of this and other difficulties that had arisen, the New York *Times,* on June 19—five days before the convention opened—published the following headline:

> Longest Convention on Record Forecast

Madison Square Garden had been chosen for the convention—old Madison Square Garden, that is, which occupied the block between Twenty-sixth and Twenty-seventh streets and between Madison and Fourth avenues. It is gone now—a change that brought with it certain practical advantages, no doubt, but which, in destroying the Garden's graceful tower, deprived New York of an architectural accent mark of unusual grace and beauty. The tower was attracting little attention in the days just preceding the opening of the convention. Delegates were arriving from every part of the country, getting settled in hotel rooms, meeting and conferring. Father, the only potential candidate whose actions came under my personal observation, was almost overwhelmed by callers, many of whom, in some way or another, managed to let it be known that they were individuals "of the very greatest importance." Frequently some of these callers had requests to make, or political trades to suggest.

The convention was to open on Tuesday, June 24, and Father, well ahead of time, established his personal headquarters on the top floor of the Manhattan Club, which still stands at the corner of Twenty-sixth and Madison Avenue, directly across the street from where the convention was held. Our whole family was still at the Biltmore, a mile or so uptown, but we saw very little of Father there. Still, we saw him when he returned each evening, though sometimes he was late in reaching the hotel, and we had breakfast with him almost every morning. Now and again we also saw him at other times, but those were busy days and he had no leisure.

Experienced though Father was in politics, he did not have an adequate understanding of the enormous, half-hidden power of the Ku Klux Klan. Throughout his public life he had had political opponents, many of whom had opposed everything he favored. But, with very few exceptions, these had been merely *political* opponents—not personal ones. He had fought Hearst on more than merely political grounds, and there had been other lesser experiences of the kind, but he was utterly unprepared when he found himself confronted by the bitter, unreasoning hatred which lay behind the power and influence of the Ku Klux Klan. Everyone knew, for instance, that the first test of strength between Father and McAdoo would involve prohibition and the Klan. It was even understood that these two issues would be hard to separate. But I do not believe that Father had any idea of the enmity his contest with McAdoo was to arouse. I have never thought of Father as a naïve man, but insofar as his idea of the reason for the Klan's opposition to him was concerned, that word, in my opinion, is most appropriate. Certainly he had not guessed how acrimonious the contest was about to become when he was interviewed by a reporter from the New York *Times* four days before the convention opened. Instead he was cheerful, assured, and more or less unaware of the extent and bitterness of the Klan's opposition to him.

"I believe I will be nominated," the *Times* quoted him as saying, "when the delegates get down to selecting the real man after distributing the complimentary votes."

I do not remember that he ever said just that to me, but I am sure my own feelings reflected his, and I was eager for the convention to open, for I was confident of the outcome.

National political conventions as we know them in the United States are huge, noisy, and hard to follow. Even the most capable presiding officer is often unable to maintain order, and with the best will in the world the average observer is certain to miss much of what goes on. When the Democratic Convention of 1924 met in Madison Square Garden, there were almost three thousand delegates and alternates on the floor, in addition to nearly nine thousand spectators, who filled all the available seats, some of which were so high in the balconies as almost to interfere with the bunting that was draped just beneath the steel rafters supporting the roof.

The decorations of the enormous hall consisted almost entirely of flags and bunting. High above the extensive platform on which the speaker's rostrum stood was a large picture of Woodrow Wilson, while pictures of Jefferson and Jackson hung above the crowded floor a long way off to the right and left.

Early on the morning of June 24 Mother and I, unwilling to run the risk of missing anything, arrived well before the hour that had been set for the official opening and found thousands of people already there. The seats we had were in a box almost directly across the huge hall from the speaker's platform, but for an hour or more no attempt was made to bring any order out of the chaos. On the floor itself thousands of delegates and alternates milled about in apparent aimlessness, and even in the galleries, where the crowding spectators filled every seat, there was almost constant movement.

Finally a beginning was made on the preliminaries. Little by little the delegates found their seats and straightened up the signs that bore the names of the states they represented. The galleries settled down to watch, and, after much going, coming, and conferring on the speaker's platform, the gavel fell and a voice that seemed strangely small and strained called the convention to order.

Mother and I were as eager as anyone to hear and understand what was going on, but by now our box was filled with friends and acquaintances. There were greetings and remarks, questions and explanations. There was considerable shifting about and a good deal of conversation that could be carried on only by leaning sideways or by talking backward across one's shoulder. But gradually a kind of semiorder began to prevail, and Senator Pat Harrison of Mississippi, the temporary chairman, began the keynote speech.

The New York *Times* had carried a headline that morning which read:

McAdoo on the Defensive

but nothing I saw in the convention bore out that statement. The crowded hall exhibited no particular enthusiasm for anything. There were cheers for Wilson when Senator Harrison mentioned him, but there was much less enthusiasm than had been expected.

After the passage of so much time I do not recall the order of events. I remember only that Senator Harrison's speech was not easy to hear, for the enormous crowd in the auditorium gave off a kind of uninterrupted hum. The sound of the speaker's voice always succeeded in reaching my ears, but many of the words did not.

There were committee reports on that first day, but I recall only the one announcing that the proposed change in the two-thirds rule had been rejected. There was a burst of applause when the announcement was made, though it was obvious that the decision did not please everyone.

No person with any understanding of American political methods could possibly fail to be interested in such a convention. But I must admit that these preliminaries were not what I had most looked forward to. I was impatient to hear the speech nominating Father. Literally everything that preceded that was a preliminary to me, and two full days of convention activities passed before I sat forward tensely on the edge of my seat to hear that particular speech.

It has always been customary in American conventions to call on the states alphabetically when the time comes for nominations to be offered. Alabama, therefore, is always the first to be called, and in 1924 Senator Oscar W. Underwood of that state was the first to have his name placed before the convention. Arkansas then nominated Senator Joseph T. Robinson, and after Arizona "passed," Ex-Senator James D. Phelan of California nominated William Gibbs McAdoo.

The nominations of both Senator Underwood and Senator Robinson had started the usual displays of enthusiasm, and on each occasion the convention had been compelled to halt its official activities while groups of shouting, flag-waving, and banner-bearing delegates milled up and down the aisles to the loud music of bands. Senator Phelan had no sooner brought his speech to a conclusion than pandemonium broke loose, and for a solid hour hordes of McAdoo supporters marched up and down and back and forth. Bands blared, sometimes in competition with each other. Banners waved. Pictures of McAdoo appeared "spontaneously," and Senator Walsh, the permanent chairman, wisely left the rostrum and sat down, realizing that with all the gavels in the world he could not quiet that combination of natural and artificial enthusiasm; in its own good time it would wear itself out.

Such activities are time-consuming, and with these and other interruptions the delegates did not get around to what interested me most until Thursday, the third day of the convention.

If one were to look over the entire list of men who were well known in politics in 1924, it would be impossible to find any among them more distinguished or striking in appearance than Franklin Roosevelt. He was tall, clean-cut, and had an excellent speaking voice—even the tragic illness he had undergone three years before had not lessened his great platform appeal. To walk he needed help, but he had already trained himself so well that few observers noticed his affliction once he began to speak. However, I believe it is correct to say that he never—or at least very rarely—spoke extemporaneously.

In order that Father might be most effectively nominated, the nominating speech had to be prepared with great care and with much thought. That is almost always the case. Extemporaneous remarks are hardly in order for such an occasion. But just as those who made up the staff of the New York State Smith Committee had not felt free to ask Franklin Roosevelt to do much work despite his title as chairman, so they were unwilling to ask him to labor over the preparation of the speech he was to give in nominating Father. Since he was used to reading his speeches, no one doubted his ability to perform that task effectively. But the arduous task of writing the speech was another matter, and Judge Joseph M. Proskauer assumed that responsibility, though many conferences were held to decide what the speech should contain. Because of his long and intimate acquaintance with Father and with Father's political accomplishments Judge Proskauer was entirely at home in outlining many high lights, but the speech he wrote was much more than an account of Father as a politician. It was a masterpiece of its kind, and the judge wrote every word of it, crossed every *t* and dotted every *i*. Then he, Herbert Bayard Swope, and Roosevelt went over the speech together. It was at this meeting that the speech was finally accepted, though Roosevelt at first objected to the use of a quotation from Wordsworth in which a reference was made to the "Happy Warrior," a phrase by which, more than any other, the speech came to be remembered. Roosevelt's objection to the expression "Happy Warrior" was that it was too poetic for use in an assembly of hardheaded delegates.

Nevertheless, it was Franklin D. Roosevelt who delivered that speech, and I shall never forget the thrill I felt as I sat on the edge of my chair and watched him grip the rostrum firmly with both hands and begin to speak.

This is no place to reprint the whole of that speech. I still remember passages from it, however: ". . . On our Governor for over twenty years in public office the white light of publicity has pitilessly beaten, and revealed only spotless integrity. . . . Here in this state, through the leadership of this Governor, governmental efficiency has so increased that the executives of other states have done us the honor of seeking to copy our model. . . . He has been elected to office seventeen times. Chosen Governor of this state first in 1918, he suffered the only defeat of his long career in 1920. But it was a defeat more glorious than victory. . . . When our national ticket in the state of New York went down to defeat under a plurality of 1,100,000 votes, he lost this state by only 74,000. He got a million votes more than I did, and I take off my hat to him . . . and in 1922 . . . the people of this state rose again in their might and re-elected him Governor by . . . the largest plurality ever given any candidate for Governor in the history of the United States."

Even there in the crowded and never silent auditorium I heard every word of that impressive address. And finally the speaker, his head held high, concluded with a wonderfully effective quotation from William Wordsworth:

> This is the Happy Warrior; this is he
> Whom every man in arms should wish to be.

Pandemonium had broken loose in Madison Square Garden at the conclusion of Senator Phelan's speech nominating McAdoo. Now, however, enthusiasm that seemed to have no bounds swept through the auditorium. Every aisle on the crowded floor was filled with Father's shouting admirers. Bands burst forth with "The Sidewalks of New York," with "Sweet Rosie O'Grady," "The Bowery," and other songs. The galleries, which for the most part were naturally filled by New Yorkers, stamped and shrieked and shouted, and for seventy-three minutes, so the papers later said, that unequaled demonstration continued.

Again and again tears were in my eyes and my heart was in my throat, but "Fifteen states and territories mustering 424 votes," I later learned from the papers, took part in that demonstration.

As a matter of practical politics it may be that the demonstration was somewhat too enthusiastic, especially where the galleries were concerned. Many Southern and Western delegates had been suspicious from the first, fearing that the galleries would be "packed" in Father's favor. I doubt that that was consciously done. Still, the New York *Times*, in an editorial that appeared the following morning, urged the Smith supporters "to take it easier," pointing out that everyone knew of Father's popularity in New York City.

On the following day, Friday, the twenty-seventh, the final names were offered. John W. Davis, oddly enough, was the last to be nominated.

It had been long apparent—had even been in the headlines—that the Klan was a major issue in the convention, and the very first important test of strength made that point clear. Large numbers of delegates wished to condemn the Klan by name, but many others did not. Father was the Klan's most important target, and he might have been expected to join with those who wished to condemn it by name. That was not his point of view, however.

"I don't feel," he said at the time, "that anything will be gained by the passage of such a resolution. It would denounce too large a group of delegates."

But the resolution did come before the convention. After an angry contest it lost by a single vote—541 3/20 to 542 3/20.

And now the balloting began, with twenty-one candidates to consider.

It is the balloting, in a convention like that of 1924, that surpasses everything else in interest, and I have never forgotten how eagerly I kept my record despite the fact that official figures were almost constantly available.

Earlier in June the McAdoo forces claimed they would be able to poll more than five hundred votes on the first ballot. Father's supporters, even then, said that any such figure was at least fifty votes too high. And they were right. When the vote was finally totaled, the major contenders stood as follows:

MCADOO	431½
SMITH	241
COX	59
HARRISON	43½
UNDERWOOD	42½
DAVIS	31

There was little change on the second ballot, and even on the next no trend appeared. The first day of balloting ended and the second began without bringing any vital changes.

Usually political conventions are concluded in the same week in which they begin, but that did not happen now. The week ended and the next week began, still without bringing anyone into the lead.

From the first the fight was between Father and McAdoo. Others, of course, had their followers, though the votes they were given were never numerous. As ballot after ballot was taken, one voice in particular came to be better known than almost any other.

"Alabama," the presiding official on the rostrum would cry out.

A Southern voice always made the reply—the same Southern voice, it seemed to me. I can still hear it in my memory.

"Alabama," it always said, "casts 24 votes for Oscar W. Underwood."

When the fifteenth ballot had been taken, McAdoo had 479—a gain of 47½ over the first—and Father, with 305½, had gained 64½.

On the thirtieth ballot McAdoo had dropped sharply to 415½. Father had advanced a little, to 323½.

On the forty-second ballot it was McAdoo, 503.4; Smith, 318.6.

That vote frightened me, for McAdoo had leaped ahead, but other ballots followed rapidly, and the sixty-first gave McAdoo 469½; Father, 335½.

The votes were still shifting, but it was evident the deadlock could not be broken. Father, in fact, had long since realized he could not win. He felt sure, though, that McAdoo was in the same position, and when we were later able to examine all the figures we learned that McAdoo reached his greatest strength on the sixty-ninth ballot, when he was given 530 votes—19 less than a majority and 202 less than the two thirds that were necessary for victory. Father, on the other hand, reached 368 votes—his greatest strength—on the seventy-sixth ballot.

Never before had so determined a contest been fought in any American convention. Plainly the Democratic party was being hurt by it. With every additional ballot the bitterness grew. Consequently a conference between Father and Mr. McAdoo was arranged by mutual friends. It was held at the Ritz-Carlton Hotel in the apartment of former Ambassador Hugh Wallace, and in addition to Father, Mr. McAdoo, and the Ambassador it was attended only by Herbert Bayard Swope of the New York *World* and Thomas L. Chadbourne and Stuart Gibboney, both well-known New York attorneys who were prominent in the Democratic party.

Father said later he admitted at this meeting that he could not be nominated, but that he was equally certain Mr. McAdoo could not be. With party harmony in mind he therefore suggested that both should withdraw their names. Mr. McAdoo suggested that, in withdrawing, both he and Father throw their strength to E. T. Meredith of Iowa. Father did not feel free to accept that suggestion, and replied that he had no control of the delegates who were supporting him. They parted on that note, "shaking hands," Father said, "like old-time friends."

The next day Father sent word to his supporters that he was withdrawing his name, though Mr. McAdoo did not. Nevertheless, the end was now in sight. On the hundredth ballot McAdoo was given 190 votes; Father, 351½; John W. Davis, 203½, and on July 9, in the third week of the convention, 839 votes—and the nomination—went to Mr. Davis on the 103rd ballot. Even then McAdoo was given 12; Father, 12½; and Oscar W. Underwood of Alabama, 102½.

It had been a bitter struggle, and I know Father was a disappointed man. Nevertheless, he appeared on the speaker's platform and gave his promise of support to Mr. Davis and to Charles W. Bryan, who had been hurriedly nominated for the Vice-Presidency.

"What are you going to do now?" I asked him late that evening.

"Run for Governor again," he replied, but he spoke without his usual enthusiasm.

"I thought you didn't want to," I said.

"I asked John W. Davis," he explained, "what I could do for him that would make the biggest contribution for his success, and he said 'Run for Governor again,' so I told him I would."

In all probability 1924 would not have been "a Democratic year" in the national election even without that bitter convention fight. Because of it, however, the party was badly split and Mr. Davis, despite his great ability and other admirable qualities, was defeated in November. Father, on the other hand, was re-elected and we remained in Albany. Even yet I cannot think of the convention of 1924 with any pleasure. Traits that I do not like to think of as American played too great a part that year at the old Madison Square Garden, and unfortunately they remained even when the Garden was torn down.

CHAPTER TEN

Re-elected Governor—Challenged as a Catholic

THE LONG-DRAWN-OUT BATTLE at Madison Square Garden had weakened the Democratic party, but Father, who was renominated for Governor without opposition, was confident of the outcome of his contest in New York State. His Republican opponent was Theodore Roosevelt, Jr., whose campaign was an energetic one, but Father's assurance was justified. Though Calvin Coolidge was re-elected President by a total national vote of more than fifteen and a half million, to eight million for Davis, and carried New York State with a plurality of 870,000, Father reversed the trend and defeated Colonel Roosevelt by 108,000. This was clearly a personal and not a party victory, for he was the only Democrat on the state ticket who was elected, and both the Senate and the Assembly went Republican as well.

Any careful examination of Father's career as Governor will show that it was in his third and fourth terms that he succeeded in accomplishing most of what is usually put down to his credit. I think it fair to add that these accomplishments—or most of them—would not have materialized when they did had it not been for what he accomplished during his first two terms and even earlier.

Father's years in the Assembly had given him a comprehensive understanding of the state government, and many proposals he made for its improvement can be traced to ideas he expressed and proposals he favored in the Constitutional Convention of 1915. Now and again events aided him in dramatizing the need for certain developments. Less than two weeks after his second inauguration—in January 1923 —a fire broke out in an old and badly overcrowded state hospital and twenty-five inmates and employees lost their lives.

"I seized upon that fire," he once told me, "in order to awaken the public to the necessity of getting rid of such old firetraps, and also to dramatize the need for new hospital construction to meet the constantly growing need."

In other words, this tragic fire alerted him to an immensely greater need than merely the replacement of the structure that had been burned. By way of his reaction to it, it resulted in a great program for the improvement of the state hospitals generally—a program that won the approval of the people for a fifty-million-dollar bond issue which they voted for that purpose.

This was only one of many programs he initiated. He had long been conscious of the waste and inefficiency that accompanied much public construction. Piecemeal appropriations were often wasteful and usually unbusinesslike. The more Father saw of such methods the more he felt the need for adequate planning in the state's work of construction. The state needed office buildings. It needed prisons. It needed bridges, improved highways, parkways, and more besides. Father saw very clearly not only that public improvements of this nature cannot be accomplished by piecemeal appropriations, but also that current revenue is rarely equal to the task of carrying all needed work to real completion.

"Many public improvements," he explained to me, "outlive the generation which pays for them if they are paid for out of current revenues."

It was with this thought in mind that he proposed an amendment to the state constitution that would permit the Legislature to issue bonds for ten million dollars a year over a period of ten years—a hundred million dollars in all—to cover work of this kind. He was opposed by those who wanted to "pay as you go," but Father insisted that under such a plan "you don't pay, so you don't go," and he made his point so well that though both houses were Republican the amendment was passed in 1924 and again in 1925. There were many Republican leaders who still opposed the amendment when it was submitted to the electorate in 1925, but the public supported it and a great program of construction was actually begun in 1926.

In 1923 Father supported Robert Moses' suggestion for the creation of the "State Council of Parks." This organization, set up by law in 1924, was composed of the chairmen of the state's various park regions, which, up to this time, had never been considered on a unified, state-wide basis. Under the new arrangement the council submitted an idea for a fifteen-million-dollar bond issue for the purchase of land for state parks and for the construction of parkways. Submitted to the electorate in 1924, the proposal was accepted, and the remarkable system of parks and parkways that the state now enjoys began to take form.

Fortunately, so far as this idea was concerned, Robert Moses was chosen to be chairman of the State Council of Parks, and this enormously energetic man was also made president of the Long Island State Park Commission. Already thoroughly familiar with Long Island and convinced of the need for state parks and parkways there, he soon came up with the suggestion that a fortunately located fifteen-hundred-acre estate on Great South Bay be purchased by the state. In fact, he even secured an option on the property, the terms of which made the property available to the state for $250,000 when funds from the pending bond issue became available.

Opposition to this action of the Park Commission promptly developed among some wealthy landowners in the vicinity, and Moses' plea for the park ran into a series of difficulties. The Park Bond Law was approved on November 4, 1924, however, and Moses proposed that the estate in question be taken over by the state by right of eminent domain. To accomplish this Father had to sign certain papers, and before doing so he decided to hold a hearing.

The objections that were offered to the Park Commission's plan were not especially impressive. For example, Father found it easy to laugh when Horace Havemeyer asked—perhaps more in earnest than in jest —"Where can a poor millionaire go?" He did not laugh, though, when someone else objected to the establishment of the park because it would permit the "city rabble" to overrun so select an area.

"Rabble?" he repeated. "Why, that's me."

And in the end he signed the papers.

Now, however, the contest was carried to the courts, the contention being that the action to take the property had been illegal because no appropriation had been made to pay for it. Even the Legislature attempted to interfere, and actually passed a bill which, while it allocated the necessary money, also deprived the Park Commission of the power to acquire land "by entry and appropriation."

Father vetoed this bill, and because the Legislature had adjourned, he called it back in special session so that a bill might be passed to provide the necessary funds without lessening the powers of the Park

Commission. The Legislature was not co-operative. In fact, it passed the old bill over again, and it had to be vetoed once more. But now Father decided on another move. He called August Heckscher, who was not only a personal friend, but was also a philanthropist deeply interested in parks and playgrounds.

"August," Father began when he got Mr. Heckscher on the phone, "I want $250,000 to buy a park."

There was a little more to the conversation than that, but that was the essence of it, and Mr. Heckscher agreed. When the matter had been explained to him, he made out a check for $262,000, for there were some interest charges over and above the original option price.

Once more the Park Commission took possession of the land, but once more the matter was taken to the court. Father himself, along with others, appeared before Judge James Dunne and a jury at River-head, Long Island, and in the end the Park Commission won its case, thus clearing the way for what has ever since been known as Heckscher State Park, an invaluable public playground on the south shore of Long Island.

"What chance did we have?" a member of the opposition asked when the outcome became known. "Al Smith came down here, made a speech to the jury, and then took the judge out to lunch."

It is not surprising, perhaps, that politics and local self-interest should have entered into this particular affair. Yet, it is remarkable, in view of the widespread approval of this and other park developments, how often comparable difficulties developed as the state's great system of parks and parkways expanded. It would be unfair to Robert Moses and to his dedicated sense of public service not to recognize the many battles he has had to fight. Opposition to the various ideas as they were advanced has sometimes appeared to be the rule rather than the excep-tion despite the fact that all the way from Montauk Point to the St. Lawrence River and Niagara Falls the state has been benefited and beautified by the work of the State Park Commission. Here is a mag-nificent monument to Father's interest in the welfare of the people of New York and to Robert Moses' immense energy and originality. Yet neither one of them ever thought of these parks and parkways in those terms.

"I feel fully compensated for all the work and anxiety," Father wrote after he had retired from public life, "when I see breathing spaces in beautifully wooded countrysides and on lakes and beaches for the women and children of today and for countless generations to come."

And I am sure that though Robert Moses, whom I know well, might express his feelings differently, he would agree with Father's sentiment.

Father first came to know New York State as he traveled over it by rail. Later, when he campaigned in almost every corner of it by motor, he came to be troubled by what he once called "the menace of railroad crossings at grade."

"I determined," he said, "that I would do what I could to get rid of them."

Merely to gather the necessary information about grade crossings was an arduous task, but once the data had been compiled, along with a report of deaths and accidents, it became clear that a real program for their elimination had to be worked out. But even before this information had been completely assembled, Father had arrived at an important conclusion.

"I decided," he said, "that if the state was to eliminate dangerous grade crossings within a single lifetime it would necessitate a basic change in policy."

In New York State one half the costs of such work are assessed against the railroads, with the state and the affected localities evenly dividing the other half. But the costs became so gigantic as to pose a serious problem. Having studied the costs, Father recommended an amendment to the state constitution that would permit the Legislature to bond the state for three hundred million dollars for the purpose, this amount being required so that the state could pay its own 25 per cent share of the cost and could lend money to the railroads and the localities when they would otherwise be unable to advance the sums properly chargeable to them.

There was some opposition but the amendment was passed, first in 1924, and for the second time in 1925. And finally it was approved by a vote of the people, as was necessary under the law. The work was far from complete when Father finally left Albany three years later, but nowadays we are hardly aware that such a problem ever existed. Even yet grade crossings exist here and there, and occasionally accidents occur because of them. The worst of these deathtraps, however, have long since been eliminated, and many an individual is alive today because of a constitutional amendment and a bond issue that Father proposed a generation ago.

Throughout all four of Father's terms in Albany he found himself confronted by Republican control of the Legislature. From year to year the Democratic minority shifted up and down and the Legislative support Father was given by the Republicans shifted also. Opposition was forever in order as long as he remained Governor, and his accomplishments, it seems to me, are more remarkable on that account.

The Legislature was usually in session only three and a half or four months each year. For the remainder of the year—except when special sessions were necessary—Father's problems were apt to be administrative rather than legislative. On the other hand, the Governor's term had not yet been lengthened, and therefore he was confronted every second year by those problems which always attend renomination and re-election. Then, too, in 1925, with his third term only well begun, a very special problem arose.

Father, as I have said, had never been favorably impressed by the ability of John F. Hylan who had been elected Mayor of New York City in 1917 and re-elected in 1921. In the 1917 campaign, it is true, Father had worked harder for Hylan's election as Mayor than for his own election as President of the Board of Aldermen. But Hylan had not been Mayor very long before the influence of William Randolph Hearst began to be apparent, and when it became clear that Hylan was being considered by Tammany Hall for a third term, some opposition to the idea arose. In fact, it became so widespread that an astonishing number of individuals talked to Father about the need for a change.

It was one matter to oppose the renomination of Hylan and quite another to find a new candidate on whom the various Tammany leaders would agree. In the end our old friend Jimmy Walker—Senator James J. Walker, as he was at that time—was the one selected.

No one, I believe, knew better than Father just what abilities and weaknesses played their contradictory parts in Jimmy Walker's character, but it may be that Judge Proskauer was right when he said of Father that "he trusted overmuch the integrity of those with whom he dealt." At any rate, when the leaders decided to support Walker for the nomination, Father took him for an automobile ride in Central Park and "for hours" he drove up and down and around the park while he painted a dramatic picture of the great opportunities that would come to Jimmy with the nomination. Father knew that Jimmy was a "playboy," and that he had never found it difficult to shrug off responsibility. In fact, Father had proposed that auto ride in Central

Park so as to have a real opportunity to impress his own sense of duty on his much less responsible friend.

"I talked to him like a Dutch uncle," he explained, and said that Jimmy—with momentary sincerity, I am sure—swore by the memory of his mother that he would give up his playboy ways and devote himself sincerely and wholeheartedly to the welfare of the city of New York.

Everyone who knew Father will understand how inconceivable it would have been for him personally to make so solemn a promise and then fail to live up to it. Even without the oath his sense of duty would have been enough, and it may be, as Judge Proskauer suggests, that he was more or less inclined to credit those he trusted with the same sincerity that always guided him. Certainly he took Jimmy Walker at his word and was convinced that the Central Park ride had led the coming candidate for Mayor to turn over a new leaf. He now looked forward eagerly to seeing his friend in City Hall.

It must not be supposed that Jimmy Walker's nomination was a foregone conclusion. In the eight years Hylan had served as Mayor he had built up a formidable political machine of his own—a machine which was very strongly based on the city-wide patronage the Mayor controlled. Furthermore, there were political leaders who still backed him, especially in his home borough of Brooklyn. Thus the primary campaign was a very determined one, bitter beyond most contests of the kind. Father was right, however, in believing that "the rank and file" were opposed to Hylan. Despite the support that the Hearst papers and the Brooklyn leaders gave him, the primary went against him. He was defeated even in his home borough, and Jimmy Walker, as the Democratic nominee, easily won the election that followed.

Father and all the rest of us were naturally elated on the evening of Election Day. As usual, we were at the Democratic headquarters in the Biltmore Hotel, and Jimmy Walker was there with his wife, Allie. None of us had any doubt about the outcome of the election. The Republicans had not made much of a fight, and when the returns began to come in they promptly indicated a Walker victory. Thus there was nothing to keep us up so very late, and the evening was still young— by Jimmy Walker's definition, anyway—when he and Allie, having been joyously congratulated by everyone at headquarters, left for home.

The following morning soon after breakfast Frank Farrell arrived and asked to see Father. He was not in politics but he was a friend of

Father's, and as a onetime part owner of the New York Yankees he had some knowledge of Jimmy Walker and of Jimmy's more intimate nonpolitical acquaintances.

I did not learn until later what was on Mr. Farrell's mind. It was obvious that something was bothering him, for he was unwilling to say a word except to Father privately. Father consequently led the way to his bedroom, but even there, he later told me, Mr. Farrell was not content. He actually led Father on into the bathroom and even closed *that* door before explaining what had brought him.

Despite the fact that he was not in politics, Mr. Farrell knew of Father's long "Dutch uncle" talk with Jimmy Walker and of the solemn promise Jimmy had made to turn over a new leaf. What he had to report concerned that very promise.

"When Jimmy left the Biltmore last night," Mr. Farrell began, "his wife went home. But Jimmy went to a party at the apartment of his reigning girl friend."

That, I recall, is about the way Father later reported the matter to me. I never learned what else Mr. Farrell may have said, for Father, in talking to me, confined himself from that point on to a troubled expression of his disappointment in Jimmy—disappointment that was to grow, unfortunately, until it reached its climax in Jimmy's political ruin seven years later.

I am quite unable to give any accurate measure of Jimmy Walker. Where his actual ability stopped and mere cleverness began I do not know, and where his cleverness then gave way to utter irresponsibility I cannot guess. Robert Moses, who knew him well, had objected to Walker as a candidate for Mayor.

"He is incapable of sustained effort," he had told Father.

"What does that mean?" Father asked.

"For one thing," Mr. Moses replied, "he cannot bring himself to read and digest as much as a single page of printed matter. His mind rebels. He has admitted as much to me. Even if he is elected he won't last out his term."

I am forced to the conclusion that that measure of Jimmy Walker was not far wrong. Despite his undeniable charm, which I, for one, cannot forget, his political career ended badly. It is true that he lasted out his first term and was re-elected to a second. Fundamentally, however, Robert Moses was right. Jimmy Walker was not a man upon whom heavy responsibility should have been placed, and Father, I believe, never got over his disappointment in his friend's failure. I cannot resist adding that despite Jimmy Walker's many weaknesses he had his full share of delightful qualities. Father, I am sure—and even Robert Moses—would agree with me about that.

The relative importance of Father's various accomplishments as Governor can hardly be set down positively. In his own belief the work he did in reorganizing the state government stood first. Merely to point out that 187 governmental agencies were modified and re-arranged in nineteen distinct governmental departments is enough to dramatize this particular accomplishment, but there was much more to the problem than that.

Because the changes Father wished to make could not be carried out until the state constitution had been amended, the whole process was a slow one. The amendment to consolidate the departments was first passed in 1924, and, as was required by the constitution, would have to be passed again in 1925. Even then it would have to be approved by a popular referendum, so that from first to last a considerable delay was certain. In the meantime some of the work of combining the departments could have been done by special enactments, and because the Legislature, in passing the amendment for the first time, had accepted the basic idea, Father wrote a special message in which several such changes were suggested. The Senate promptly adopted his suggestion, but the Assembly refused, and the task of simplifying the government and improving its efficiency was consequently delayed for two more years.

It is difficult to say just what reasoning lay behind this opposition. But it was Father's opinion—and the evidence seemed to bear him out —that his opponents were merely marking time in the hope that he would be succeeded by some other Governor—preferably Republican —before final action became necessary. Father's re-election in 1924, however, eliminated that Republican hope, and the battle for reorganization was renewed in 1925.

The amendment that had already been passed once and now had to be passed again dealt with the consolidation of the state's many departments and with the so-called "short ballot." This short ballot idea was of especial interest to Father, who had long been convinced that the electorate could hardly be expected to judge intelligently when it came to the election of certain of the state's lesser officials. On one occasion, for example, when he was addressing a combined meeting of the City Club of New York and the Women's City Club, he made the statement that if he were to stop the first thousand people he met in Times Square and ask them the name of the state engineer for whom they had voted at the last election not one of them could give it.

"And I wouldn't have needed to go to Times Square," he remarked afterward. "I could tell from the way those people looked at each other that they didn't know either."

This proposed change, as well as the one that would consolidate the state departments, formed a part of the amendment that now had to be passed for a second time. Many of the members of the Legislature were still inclined to oppose the whole matter, but popular support was behind Father and the amendment went through. It was accepted by vote of the people in the election of 1925, and the task of making the changes began—a complicated procedure that necessitated the passage of dozens of specific statutes concerning all the affected agencies and departments.

When it became apparent that the amendment would pass, Father suggested the organization of a joint commission to be made up of members of the Legislature and additional individuals to be appointed by the Governor. This commission, he suggested, should be given the task of preparing a detailed program of consolidation for presentation to the 1926 Legislature so that the necessary enactments could be expedited. The Legislature refused to accept the idea, though it set up a committee of its own—a committee, incidentally, that was not authorized by any law and for which no appropriation was made. Finally Father was permitted to appoint Addison B. Colvin and Robert Moses to the committee, and after an attempt was made by the Legislature to give the committee chairmanship to Speaker of the Assembly H. Edmund Machold, who had all along been the most energetic opponent of reorganization, Charles Evans Hughes was chosen, though only after Father had suggested his name in a newspaper interview. It was the "Hughes Committee," therefore, that made the recommendations which were adopted by the 1926 Legislature.

The necessary legislation was passed promptly enough and the consolidations could have been put into effect by July 1, 1926—the beginning of the state's fiscal year. A state election was to be held that fall, and in the hope—perhaps even the expectation—that Father would not be re-elected to a fourth term the Legislature insisted on delaying the authorization of the changes until January 1, 1927.

As events turned out, Father disappointed the Republicans by being re-elected for a fourth term and the delay gained them nothing. It merely handicapped the state government for an additional period of time, and it was not for a full five years after Father first proposed the idea that the changes went into effect.

While this complicated struggle was being carried on, another that was comparable was also under way. It had to do with budget reform—a subject that had been considered in much detail even during the Constitutional Convention of 1915.

Under the system that had long been in effect, the budget had to originate in the Assembly, where the chairman of the Ways and Means Committee was the person chiefly responsible for it. Having been prepared by him and passed by the Assembly, it then went to the Senate, where, almost always, it underwent much change and was affected by many compromises. During all this time it was subject to all sorts of changes as each Assemblyman and Senator strove to have his own pet ideas included. Changes and amendments were so numerous and so little understood even by those who were responsible for the bill in its final form that Father once told me of a case in which one of the clerks of the Assembly who was given the task of carrying the Assembly's version of an appropriation bill to the Senate was said to have paused along the way to insert an "amendment" of his own.

It can be seen from these few facts that, so far as appropriations were concerned, a good many improvements were in order. The changes proposed by the Constitutional Convention of 1915 had never gone into effect because the amended constitution was defeated, and for years the method remained as it had been. Both Governor Whitman and Governor Miller had tried to improve the situation by statute, but they failed, and when Father was re-elected in 1922 he decided to ask for a constitutional amendment that would establish an executive budget, which, in this connection, was the change he had in mind.

Here again Speaker Machold was Father's chief opponent. Though in 1923 the Senate passed the proposed bill, the Assembly, under Machold's leadership, defeated it. The same thing happened in 1924, and in 1925 the proposal was defeated in both houses. When the Hughes Committee was formed in 1926, Father's idea was finally accepted. Mr.

Machold himself, who was a member of that committee but was no longer Speaker of the Assembly, signed the committee's report favoring the proposed budgetary change. Despite this action the executive budget was not yet to succeed. The arguments by which it was opposed were carried to exaggerated lengths. For example, when Father agreed to debate the matter with Lieutenant Governor Seymour Lowman at the Women's City Club of New York, the Lieutenant Governor actually went so far as to declare that Father was "attempting to make a King of himself!"

"Behold the King!" Father cried when he was called upon to reply. "The King from Oliver Street!"

The silly charge evaporated before Father's ridicule, but the ridiculous statement was repeated in the Assembly Chamber by Assemblyman Edmund P. Jenks on the day the amendment came up for consideration, and the bill supporting it was defeated.

Father was still not prepared to give up. Elected to his fourth term in 1926, he urged the adoption of the executive budget amendment on the Legislature of 1927. It passed, and because this was its second victory in the Legislature, it was submitted to the people in the 1927 election and was adopted. Here again, after years of unnecessary delay, another important governmental improvement was adopted because of Father's determined interest in it.

Always interested though I was in Father's career as Governor, I must admit that my attention was now and then given to other matters. For reasons that will appear, this was especially true during Father's third term, throughout which he was very busily engaged in attempting—to use his own phrase—to "remake the state."

I have already told how Major John A. Warner came to be appointed superintendent of the state police to succeed Colonel Chandler, and of how, not long before that appointment was made, I had met him for the first time. I have made no mention of the frequency of our later meetings, which led, in 1926, to our marriage. Neither have I referred to the fact that Father's appointee and my husband was—and still remains—a Republican, who, on at least two occasions prior to our marriage, had voted against Father for Governor.

I do not know just when Father began to realize that John's visits to the Executive Mansion had come to be quite frequent. As he later admitted, he was probably the last member of the family to see what was happening. He had learned in the meantime not only that John was a Republican, but also that he was a Harvard graduate, and had studied music—piano and organ—in Paris and in Italy. The son of Mr. and Mrs. J. Foster Warner of Rochester, John had also been interested in a Rochester cavalry troop, and he had joined the state police in 1917, when the force was formed, in the belief that the organization was to become a part of the state's military forces. That did not occur, and thus he had been an officer of the state police for six years by the time Father appointed him to head the force.

John and I were married on June 5, 1926, at the Cathedral of the Immaculate Conception in Albany, and the wedding was a large one. Under the circumstances, and in view of Father's great popularity, it simply had to be, unless we were prepared—which I personally was not—to limit it only to our families and our very closest friends. Once we decided to go beyond that very restricted list, it was hard to draw any line at all, and Father's remark that "it was the biggest crowd since *Ben Hur*," despite its humorous exaggeration, had at least a suggestion of truth about it.

The wedding presents we received were more than I can adequately describe even after thirty years, and when they began to arrive at the Executive Mansion they formed a display the newspaper reporters and photographers were interested in. Father, however, put his foot down.

"I won't have these things publicized," he insisted. "The papers won't talk about anything at all but the spectacular things that have come, and it means just as much that there are a lot of modest presents from old friends who can't afford any more."

He was right, and we attempted to do as he wished, though in the end he permitted some mention of presents that came from organizations and other groups.

With so many presents arriving some plan for their arrangement had to be worked out; and the third-floor hall, which served as the mansion's billiard room, was set aside for the china. It arrived in surprising quantities—seventy-two dozen plates, among other items. The billiard table was soon stacked high, and other tables were filled as well.

"Emily," Father remarked when I showed him all this, "you and John can throw china at each other for twenty-five years and still have enough left over to serve a seven-course dinner to a lot of people."

On the second floor of the mansion the hall directly beneath the third-floor billiard room was a favorite sitting room for the family. We often spent our evenings there, and not long after Father had been shown the china, he noticed a crack in the second-floor ceiling. The house was old, and ceiling cracks were not unknown, but this crack was a new one.

"Do you suppose," he asked, "that the wedding presents are going to come through?"

It seemed possible, and Father asked the state engineer to see what was wrong.

A careful inspection followed, and a report assured us that the ceiling was in no immediate danger of falling, though the combined weight of the billiard table and the china was obviously a bit too much. So the china was piled elsewhere, and the billiard table, which now was serving no purpose, was carefully pushed over alongside a wall.

Father's friends were naturally numerous among our wedding guests, and the Lower East Side was amply represented.

"Even Louis Fook was there," Father explained to a friend, and I am sure that he was as pleased by the presence of this "Mayor of Chinatown" as by the presence of greater and more influential figures in the affairs of the Empire State. But that was typical of Father.

After the wedding reception John and I left on our honeymoon, returning after several weeks to our first home in Albany—a house on Hudson Avenue, from which we moved a year later to another at 52 South Swan Street, just two blocks from the state capitol. Throughout this period I was busy with the important task of mastering my new household duties. Still, I never for a moment overlooked the fact that the Democratic leaders in the state wanted Father to run for Governor again. Even before John and I had been married, many of the leaders had let their hopes be known. Father had put them off at the time, but now his decision could no longer be delayed. Though he repeatedly insisted that the time for his retirement from public life had come, no natural successor was available, and he agreed to run for a fourth term.

It was Ogden Mills, a Republican member of Congress, who ran against him, and the campaign gave Father an excellent opportunity to explain in detail his whole program for the state, for Mills had been an active opponent of many—and perhaps most—of Father's plans. Father, however, said that in the matter of the bond issue for the rehabilitation of the state hospitals Congressman Mills had been "of great help."

When it became clear that Congressman Mills was to be the Republican candidate, Father expressed himself as believing that the campaign would be conducted on a high level. But it turned out otherwise. Mills did not talk about pressing state problems, as he was so widely expected to do, he accepted the support of the Hearst papers and, more strangely still, actually unearthed what Father called "the ridiculous milk-bugaboo campaign started by Hearst in 1919."

"Well," Father remarked when this Mills-Hearst alliance became evident, "Hearst has given him the kiss of death too."

And that proved to be the case, for Father won with a plurality of 257,000 votes, and the Democratic candidates for Lieutenant Governor and for State Comptroller won as well. The only Republican candidate on the newly shortened state ticket who was elected was Albert Ottinger of New York City, who was elected as Attorney-General.

It was on January 1, 1927, that Father took the oath as Governor of New York for the fourth time. Not since the days of George Clinton had anyone been re-elected so often, and with that in mind those who were in charge of the details of the inauguration arranged to have Father seated on the inaugural platform in a chair that had been used more than a hundred and thirty years earlier by Governor Clinton.

Even before Father's fourth term began he had come to be the outstanding leader of the Democratic party in the Empire State, but under the reorganization amendment he now found himself in a much more advantageous position as the state's chief executive. For the first time a Governor of New York was to have a cabinet made up of the heads of the state's newly organized departments—a change that was to prove beneficial in the administration of the state's affairs.

As a result of Father's insistence a number of amendments to the state constitution had already been adopted, but others were still under consideration. One of these provided for lengthening the term of Governor from two years to four. Another provided for an extension of the debt limit of the cities in the state—a move that was planned in order to aid subway construction in New York City and public works elsewhere. And, third, the final moves now had to be made in the adoption of the amendment establishing the executive budget—an administrative improvement of the greatest importance in Father's mind, and one for which he had labored ceaselessly for years.

These three amendments, along with six lesser ones, having been finally approved by the 1927 Legislature, were submitted to the people of the state. The amendment concerning the lengthened term of the Governor, however, did not satisfy Father, for though it would have lengthened the term as he had recommended, it would also have provided for Gubernatorial elections to coincide with those for President. Experience had shown that when national and state elections coincided the state interests and state problems were apt to be lost sight of, and because of this the amendment as it was written did not meet with the approval of the thoughtful people of the state. It was widely debated, but in the end it was defeated—the only one of nine submitted to the people that they failed to accept.

The increased costs of education confronted the state with another problem. Even during Father's first term as Governor it began to be clear that teachers' salaries would have to be increased if adequate numbers of competent schoolteachers were to be maintained, and Father was determined to see this done.

"To do it required two things," he later explained, "Money and nerve."

Despite the fact that he was soon to enter a campaign for re-election in which he was certain to be criticized because of the increased cost of government, he recommended a bill, which he signed when it was passed, increasing by twenty-two million dollars the state's contribution to the salaries of teachers. He also favored the consolidation of rural schools. Many of these were one-room structures that had been built to serve small areas in the "horse and buggy days." Because of improved roads and better transportation larger and better schools serving greater areas were now feasible, and Father constantly favored state aid in the establishment of such schools. Here again he was stubbornly opposed in the Legislature, but with the invaluable assistance of Michael Friedsam, President of B. Altman and Company, who served as chairman of a commission that was organized to study the state's educational problems, great strides were made. Between 1919 and 1929 the state—largely because of Father's urging—increased the annual appropriation for public education from seven million dollars to seventy million.

"You cannot serve the cause of education," Father insisted, "without spending money."

Father would have retired from public life when his term as Governor expired in 1924 had it not been that John W. Davis asked him to run again. The long-drawn-out struggle at Madison Square Garden had been a discouraging experience, and only his loyalty to the party and his desire to be of assistance to the Presidential nominee kept him from leaving the political arena. Even two years later when he entered the 1926 campaign he did so with little enthusiasm. John and I, who were with him at Binghamton when he made the first speech of that campaign, were both struck by the absence of his usual campaign ardor. It was only after he had been campaigning for several days that his normal eagerness and political aggressiveness returned. Once the 1926 campaign was over and his victory was assured, an entirely new situation arose. Even before his fourth inauguration took place, visitors from other states began to appear in rapidly increasing numbers, and Father's mail, which had always arrived in considerable quantities, grew to astonishing proportions. Early in his fourth term he decided to find a new way to handle his growing correspondence and his increasing list of callers.

"Can't your office force take care of it?" I asked when he mentioned the matter to me.

"They could if I told them to," he replied, "but I don't think it's right. They are state employees, but these callers and this mail are not state business. I've got to make some other arrangement."

It was perfectly obvious by now that a nationwide interest was developing in Father as the Democratic nominee for the Presidency in 1928, but as yet he was unwilling to acknowledge such a possibility. However, he felt compelled to permit the organization of an unofficial volunteer committee of New York City friends, and these were to do the best they could in caring for the great volume of correspondence that was now arriving in every mail and the visitors from other states who were already busy measuring the political trends.

Obviously—and with no move whatever having been made by Father —he had developed into a very important potential Democratic Presidential nominee, and because this was evident everywhere, he was forced—though much against his will—to consider seriously a letter he received from Ellery Sedgwick, the editor of the *Atlantic Monthly*.

This communication arrived early in March 1927, and it enclosed an advance proof of an "open letter" to Father from a certain Charles C. Marshall. It also explained that Mr. Marshall was "an experienced attorney of New York City who has throughout his active life been closely associated with the Anglican Church and has made himself an authority upon canon law." Mr. Sedgwick's letter also said that though Mr. Marshall's "open letter" was scheduled for publication in the April number of the *Atlantic,* the forms were being held open for a time on the supposition that Father might wish to prepare an answer.

The Marshall letter was a long one, and very learnedly expressed what many non-Catholics were said to be feeling "as to certain conceptions which your fellow citizens attribute to you as a loyal and conscientious Roman Catholic, which in their minds are irreconcilable with that Constitution which as President you must support and defend, and with the principles of civil and religious liberty on which American institutions are based."

There was much more, including references to and quotations from papal encyclicals and other Catholic literature, of which, up to that moment, Father had never so much as heard. Furthermore, Mr. Marshall's letter asked whether, in case of a conflict between the civil power and the ecclesiastical, Father would accept the idea that the jurisdiction of the Roman Catholic Church should prevail or the decision of the Supreme Court of the United States "that, in matters of religious practice which in the opinion of the State are inconsistent with its peace and safety, the jurisdiction of the State shall prevail." The open letter then wished to know, "if you accept both teachings, how you will reconcile them." It also went on to discuss many problems that involved alleged conflicts in such Catholic institutions as the parochial schools and the marriage sacrament.

I was not with Father when this communication arrived, and therefore cannot give any detailed report of his immediate reaction, but knowing him and knowing how simple and uncomplicated—how almost childlike—his acceptance of the teachings of the Roman Catholic Church had always been, I can believe that this involved and ostensibly learned challenge, based as it appeared to be on a scholarly study of papal encyclicals and other important Catholic declarations and pronouncements, all but overwhelmed him. And I was not surprised when Mrs. Moskowitz, who was working at Father's Biltmore Hotel headquarters at the time, later told me that Father's first reaction seemed to be made up in more or less equal parts of resentment, frustration, and hurt.

Mrs. Moskowitz, to whom I have so far given scant credit, was a woman of extraordinary ability and understanding. Already her important contributions to Father's career had led someone to refer to her, with Woodrow Wilson's closest adviser in mind, as Father's "Colonel House," and the moment her eyes fell on the "open letter," she realized how essential it was that a thoughtful and convincing reply be prepared. But Father, despite her urging, absolutely refused, and Mrs. Moskowitz, realizing that she had to find an ally, called Judge Proskauer on the telephone and urged him to come to the Biltmore at once. It was Judge Proskauer himself who later told me what occurred.

Mrs. Moskowitz had given the judge no explanation over the telephone. When he arrived, however, she showed him the advance proof of the Marshall letter and told him that Father had refused to do anything about it. The judge read the communication carefully and recognized the basic nature of the problem it presented. He agreed with Mrs. Moskowitz that a reply by Father was essential, and with the proof of the Marshall letter in his hand he opened the door of Father's adjoining office.

"When," he asked, holding the Marshall proof out before him, "are you going to start work on your answer to this?"

Father knew instantly what the judge was talking about.

"I'm not going to answer the damn thing," he replied angrily.

"You *have* to answer it, Al," Judge Proskauer insisted. "Here's a man who throws down the challenge to you that your religion makes it impossible for you honestly to be sworn in as President of the United States. You owe it to yourself, to your party, and to your religion to answer it."

"Joe," Father replied, and even though I was not there I know how helpless and hurt he felt, "to tell you the truth, I've read it. But I don't know what the words mean. I've been a Catholic all my life—a devout Catholic, I believe—and I never heard of these encyclicals and papal bulls and books that he writes about. They have nothing to do with being a Catholic, and I just don't know how to answer such a thing."

He paused at that, and I can visualize him as he sat there in his discouragement. But Father was not one to be discouraged long. Presently, so Judge Proskauer told me, a little light came into his eyes and he half smiled.

"You answer it, Joe," he said.

Judge Proskauer, as everyone who knows him must realize, has his own sense of humor.

"Well," he replied, "that would make it perfect. A Protestant lawyer challenges a Catholic candidate on his religion, and the challenge is answered by a Jewish judge."

Father's momentary lightness dropped away.

"You're right, Joe," he admitted. "I've got to answer it, but I need help. Will you study all this for me and help me get up a reply?"

Judge Proskauer agreed.

"But I need help, too," he remarked. "I need the help of a Catholic priest, and it isn't just any Catholic priest who will do. I want one with a record of Americanism and patriotism that no person in the world can possibly question."

Father saw the point, and they decided on Father Francis P. Duffy, the heroic chaplain of the 165th Regiment in the World War I whose statue stands today in New York City's Longacre Square.

Judge Prokauer later told me that it was only after having spent many hours with Father Duffy that he prepared a draft of the answer Father was now quite determined to make.

"But remember," he added, "as was always the case when any document was drafted for your father, this one I handed him was revised and revised again until it bore the unique imprint of his own personality."

Judge Proskauer spent a Sunday in Albany going over the final version of that reply with Father and Mrs. Moskowitz, and finally Father approved it.

"OK," he said at last, "that's done. Send it along."

Judge Proskauer shook his head.

"Not yet," he insisted. "This destroys Mr. Marshall's contention so thoroughly that I'm wondering if we may not have unintentionally included something that is offensive to Catholic dogma. I think it would be wise to submit it first to Cardinal Hayes[1] to check it for points of doctrine."

Father agreed, and Judge Proskauer called on the cardinal that same evening in New York City.

"I would give almost anything to see Al Smith President of the United States," the cardinal remarked when the judge had explained his mission, "but I can take no part in a political campaign or give any advice on a political question. Before I even read this"—he indicated the still unopened reply Judge Proskauer had brought—"I must make

---

[1] Patrick Cardinal Hayes, Archbishop of New York.

clear to you that I consider it my duty to answer one question, and one only. That question is, 'Does this document contain anything offensive to the dogma of the Roman Catholic Church?' If you understand that clearly, I will read it. Otherwise I prefer not to."

Judge Proskauer naturally agreed, and after reading the reply carefully Cardinal Hayes concluded, as Judge Proskauer told me, "that it was both good Catholicism and good Americanism."

CHAPTER ELEVEN

Nominated for the Presidency

FATHER'S REPLY to Mr. Marshall's "open letter" was sent to Mr. Ellery Sedgwick late in March or early in April, and it appeared as follows in the May 1927 number of the *Atlantic Monthly,* the title and the foreword having been prepared by Mr. Sedgwick.

CATHOLIC AND PATRIOT: GOVERNOR SMITH REPLIES

This is an historic incident, historic for the country and for the Church. Now for the first time in the republic's history, under a constitution which forever forbids religious tests as qualifications for office, a candidate for the Presidency has been subjected to public questioning as to how he can give undivided allegiance to his country when his church restricts the freedom of his choice; and the candidate has answered—answered not deviously and with indirection, but straightforwardly, bravely, with the clear ring of candor.

It is an issue of infinite possibilities. Is the principle of religious tolerance, universal and complete, which every schoolboy has repeated for one hundred and fifty years, mere platitudinous vaporing? Can men worshiping God in their differing ways believe without reservation of conscience in a common political ideal? Is the United States of America based on a delusion? Can the vast experiment of the Republic, Protestant and Catholic, churched and unchurched, succeed?

And this is the converse of the question: Will the churches suffer their members to be really free? "Thou shalt have none other gods but me," thundered the Jewish Jehovah from Sinai, and ever since the gods of the churches have demanded that their control be not abridged nor diminished. But as the creeds clash about us, we remember that not in political programmes only may religion have its place separate and apart from politics, from public discussion, and from the laws of society. Quite elsewhere it is written, "Render therefore unto Caesar the things that are Caesar's; and unto God the things that are God's."

The discussion has served its purpose. Not in this campaign will whispering and innuendoes, shruggings and hunchings, usurp the place of reason and of argument. The thoughts rising almost unbidden in the minds of the least bigoted of us when we watch a Roman Catholic aspire to the Presidency of the United States have become matters of high, serious, and eloquent debate.

THE EDITOR

Charles C. Marshall, Esq.
Dear Sir:—

In your open letter to me in the April *Atlantic Monthly* you "impute" to American Catholics views which, if held by them, would leave open to question the loyalty and devotion to this country and its Constitution of more than twenty million American Catholic citizens. I am grateful to you for defining this issue in the open and for your courteous expression of the satisfaction it will bring to my fellow citizens for me to give "a disclaimer of the convictions" thus imputed. Without mental reservation I can and do make that disclaimer. These convictions are held neither by me nor by any other American Catholic, as far as I know. Before answering the argument of your letter, however, I must dispose of one of its implications. You put your questions to me in connection with my candidacy for the office of President of the United States. My attitude with respect to that candidacy was fully stated in my last inaugural address as Governor when, on January 1, 1927, I said:—

"I have no idea what the future has in store for me. Everyone else in the United States has some notion about it except myself. No man could stand before this intelligent gathering and say that he was not receptive to the greatest position the world has to give anyone. But I can say this, that I will do nothing to achieve it except to give to the people of the State the kind and character of service that will make me deserve it."

I should be a poor American and a poor Catholic alike if I injected religious discussion into a political campaign. Therefore I would ask you to accept this answer from me not as a candidate for any public office but as an American citizen, honored with high elective office, meeting a challenge to his patriotism and his intellectual integrity. Moreover, I call your attention to the fact that I am only a layman. The *Atlantic Monthly* describes you as "an experienced attorney" who "has made himself an authority upon canon law." I am neither a lawyer nor a theologian. What knowledge of law I have was gained in the course of my long experience in the Legislature and as Chief Executive of New York State. I had no such opportunity to study theology.

My first thought was to answer you with just the faith that is in me. But I knew instinctively that your conclusions could be logically proved false. It seemed right, therefore, to take counsel with someone schooled in the Church law, from whom I learned whatever is hereafter set forth in definite answer to the theological questions you raise. I selected one whose patriotism neither you nor any other man will question. He wears upon his breast the Distinguished Service Cross of our country, its Distinguished Service Medal, the Ribbon of the Legion of Honor, and the Croix de Guerre with Palm of the French Republic. He was the Catholic Chaplain of the almost wholly Catholic 165th Regiment in the World War—Father Francis P. Duffy, now in the military service of my own State.

Taking your letter as a whole and reducing it to commonplace English, you imply that there is conflict between religious loyalty to the Catholic faith and patriotic loyalty to the United States. Everything that has actually happened to me during my long public career leads me to know that no such thing as that is true. I have taken an oath of office in this State nineteen times. Each time I swore to defend and maintain the Constitution of the United States. All this represents a period of public service in elective office almost continuous since 1903. I have never known any conflict between my official duties and my religious belief. No such conflict could exist. Certainly the people of this State recognize no such conflict. They have testified to my devotion to public duty by electing me to the highest office within their gift four times. You yourself do me the honor, in addressing me, to refer to "your fidelity to the morality you have advocated in public and private life and to the religion you have revered; your great record of public trusts successfully and honestly discharged." During the years I have discharged these trusts I have been a communicant of the Roman Catholic Church. If there were conflict, I, of all men, could not have escaped it, because I have not been a silent man, but a battler for social and political reform. These battles would in their very nature disclose this conflict if there were any.

I regard public education as one of the foremost functions of government and I have supported to the last degree the State Department of Education in every effort to promote our public-school system. The largest single item of increased appropriations under my administration appears in the educational group for the support of common schools. Since 1919, when I first became Governor, this item has grown from $9,000,000 to $82,500,000. My aim—and I may say I have succeeded in achieving it—has been legislation for child welfare, the protection of working men, women, and children, the modernization of the State's institutions for the care of helpless or unfortunate wards, the preservation of freedom of speech and opinion against the attack of war-time hysteria, and the complete reorganization of the structure of the government of the State.

I did not struggle for these things for any single element, but in the interest of all of the eleven million people who make up the State. In all of this work I had the support of churches of all denominations. I probably know as many ecclesiastics of my Church as any other layman. During my long and active public career I never received from any of them anything except cooperation and encouragement in the full and complete discharge of my duty to the State. Moreover, I am unable to understand how anything that I was taught to believe as a Catholic could possibly be in conflict with what is good citizenship. The essence of my faith is built upon the Commandments of God. The law of the land is built upon the Commandments of God. There can be no conflict between them.

Instead of quarreling among ourselves over dogmatic principles, it would be infinitely better if we joined together in inculcating obedience to these Commandments in the hearts and minds of the youth of the country as the surest and best road to happiness on this earth and to peace in the world to come. This is the common ideal of all religions. What we need is more religion for our young people, not less; and the way to get more religion is to stop the bickering among our sects which can only have for its effect the creation of doubt in the minds of our youth as to whether or not it is necessary to pay attention to religion at all.

Then I know your imputations are false when I recall the long list of other public servants of my faith who have loyally served the State. You as a lawyer will probably agree that the office of Chief Justice of the United States is second not even to that of the President in its influence on the national development and policy. That court by its interpretation of the Federal Constitution is a check not only upon the President himself but upon Congress as well. During one fourth of its history it has been presided over by two Catholics, Roger Brooke Taney and Edward Douglass White. No one has suggested that the official conduct of either of these men was affected by any unwarranted religious influence or that religion played with them any part other than it should play in the life of every God-fearing man.

And I know your imputations are false when I recall the tens of thousands of young Catholics who have risked and sacrificed their lives in defense of our country. These fundamentals of life could not be true unless your imputations were false.

But, wishing to meet you on your own ground, I address myself to your definite questions, against which I have thus far made only general statements. I must first call attention to the fact that you often divorce sentences from their context in such a way as to give them something other than their real meaning. I will specify. You refer to the Apostolic Letter of Pope Leo XIII as "declaring to the world that the orders of the Church of England were void, her priests not priests," and so forth. You say that this was the "strange fruit" of the toleration of England to the Catholics. You imply that the Pope gratuitously issued an affront to the Anglican Church. In fact, this Apostolic Letter was an answer to a request made at the instance of priests of the Anglican Church for recognition by the Roman Catholic Church of the validity of their priestly orders. The request was based on the ground that they had been ordained in succession from the Roman Catholic priests who became the first priests of the Anglican Church. The Apostolic Letter was a mere adverse answer to this request, ruling that Anglican priests were not Roman Catholic priests, and was in no sense the gratuitous insult which you suggest it to be. It was not directed against England or citizens of that Empire.

Again, you quote from the Catholic Encyclopedia that my Church "regards dogmatic intolerance, not alone as her incontestable right, but as her sacred duty." And you say that these words show that Catholics are taught to be politically, socially, and intellectually intolerant of all other people. If you read the whole of that article in the Catholic Encyclopedia, you would know that the real meaning of these words is that for Catholics alone the Church recognizes no deviation from complete acceptance of its dogma. These words are used in a chapter dealing with that subject only. The very same article in another chapter dealing with toleration toward non-Catholics contains these words: "The intolerant man is avoided as much as possible by every high-minded person. . . . The man who is tolerant in every emergency is alone lovable." The phrase "dogmatic intolerance" does not mean that Catholics are to be dogmatically intolerant of other people, but merely that inside the Catholic Church they are to be intolerant of any variance from the dogma of the Church.

Similar criticism can be made of many of your quotations. But, beyond this, by what right do you ask me to assume responsibility for every statement that may be made in any encyclical letter? As you will find in the Catholic Encyclopedia (Vol. V, p. 414), these encyclicals are not articles of our faith. The Syllabus of Pope Pius IX, which you quote on the possible conflict between Church and State, is declared by Cardinal Newman to have "no dogmatic force." You seem to think that Catholics must be all alike in mind and in heart, as though they had been poured into and taken out of the same mould. You have no more right to ask me to defend as part of my faith every statement coming from a prelate than I should have to ask you to accept as an article of your religious faith every statement of an Episcopal bishop, or of your political faith every statement of a President of the United States. So little are these matters of the essence of my faith that I, a devout Catholic since childhood, never heard of them until I read your letter. Nor can you quote from the canons of our faith a syllable that would make us less good citizens than non-Catholics. In fact and in truth, I have been taught the spirit of tolerance, and when you, Mr. Marshall, as a Protestant Episcopalian, join me in saying the Lord's Prayer, we both pray, not to "My Father," but to "Our Father."

But I go further to demonstrate that the true construction of your quotations by the leaders of Catholic thought is diametrically opposite of what you suggest it to be.

I

Your first proposition is that Catholics believe that other religions should, in the United States, be tolerated only as a matter of favor and that there should be an established church. You may find some dream of an ideal of a Catholic State, having no relation whatever to actuality, somewhere described. But, voicing the best Catholic thought on this subject, Dr. John A. Ryan, Professor of Moral Theology at the Catholic University of America, writes in *The State and the Church* of the encyclical of Pope Leo XIII, quoted by you:—

"In practice, however, the foregoing propositions have full application only to the completely Catholic State. . . . The propositions of Pope Pius IX condemning the toleration of non-Catholic sects do not now, says Father Pohle, 'apply even to Spain or the South American republics, to say nothing of countries possessing a greatly mixed population.' He lays down the following general rule: 'When several religions have firmly established themselves and taken root in the same territory, nothing else remains for the State than to exercise tolerance toward them all, or, as conditions exist to-day, to make complete religious liberty for individual and religious bodies a principle of government.' "

That is good Americanism and good Catholicism. And Father Pohle, one of the great writers of the Catholic Church, says further:—

"If religious freedom has been accepted and sworn to as a fundamental law in a constitution, the obligation to show this tolerance is binding in conscience."

The American prelates of our Church stoutly defend our constitutional declaration of equality of all religions before the law. Cardinal O'Connell has said: "Thus to every American citizen has come the blessed inheritance of civil, political, and religious liberty safeguarded by the American Constitution . . . the right to worship God according to the dictates of his conscience."

Archbishop Dowling, referring to any conceivable union of Church and State, says: "So many conditions for its accomplishment are lacking in every government of the world that the thesis may well be relegated to the limbo of defunct controversies."

I think you have taken your thesis from this limbo of defunct controversies.

Archbishop Ireland again said: "Religious freedom is the basic life of America, the cement running through all its walls and battlements, the safeguard of its peace and prosperity. Violate religious freedom against Catholics, our swords are at once unsheathed. Violate it in favor of Catholics, against non-Catholics, no less readily do they leap from the scabbard."

Cardinal Gibbons has said: "American Catholics rejoice in our separation of Church and State, and I can conceive no combination of circumstances likely to arise which would make a union desirable to either Church or State. . . . For ourselves we thank God that we live in America, 'in this happy country of ours,' to quote Mr. Roosevelt, where 'religion and liberty are natural allies.' "

And referring particularly to your quotation from Pope Pius IX, Dr. Ryan, in *The State and the Church,* says: "Pope Pius IX did not intend to declare that separation is always inadvisable, for he had more than once expressed his satisfaction with the arrangement obtaining in the United States."

The President of New York City's Board of Aldermen and his family in 1918. The children, left to right, are Walter, Emily, Alfred, Catherine, and Arthur.

Alfred E. Smith in 1930. Two years after the Presidential election of 1928, and while the Empire State Building was being erected.

Governor Smith meets his daughter and son-in-law, Major and Mrs. John A. Warner, on their return from Europe in May 1928, a couple of months before the Governor was nominated for the Presidency by the Democratic Convention at Houston, Texas.

Governor Smith and his two younger sons, Walter (left) and Arthur. This photograph was taken beside the Executive Mansion greenhouse in Albany about 1923.

The Executive Mansion as it appeared during the years of Governor Smith's incumbency.

Fishing continued to be one of the Governor's favorite sports in the years after he left Albany.

Campaigning for the Presidenc
in North Carolina during 1928

Boating on Peconic Bay, near
Canoe Place Inn, in 1930.

With these great Catholics I stand squarely in support of the provisions of the Constitution which guarantee religious freedom and equality.

II

I come now to the speculation with which theorists have played for generations as to the respective functions of Church and State. You claim that the Roman Catholic Church holds that, if conflict arises, the Church must prevail over the State. You write as though there were some Catholic authority or tribunal to decide with respect to such conflict. Of course there is no such thing. As Dr. Ryan writes: "The Catholic doctrine concedes, nay, maintains, that the State is coordinate with the Church and equally independent and supreme in its own distinct sphere."

What is the Protestant position? The Articles of Religion of your Protestant Episcopal Church (XXXVII) declare: "The Power of the Civil Magistrate extendeth to all men, as well Clergy as Laity, in all things temporal; but hath no authority in things purely spiritual."

Your Church, just as mine, is voicing the injunction of our common Saviour to render unto Caesar the things that are Caesar's, and unto God the things that are God's.

What is this conflict about which you talk? It may exist in some lands which do not guarantee religious freedom. But in the wildest dreams of your imagination you cannot conjure up a possible conflict between religious principle and political duty in the United States, except on the unthinkable hypothesis that some law were to be passed which violated the common morality of all God-fearing men. And if you can conjure up such a conflict, how would a Protestant resolve it? Obviously by the dictates of his conscience. That is exactly what a Catholic would do. There is no ecclesiastical tribunal which would have the slightest claim upon the obedience of Catholic communicants in the resolution of such a conflict. As Cardinal Gibbons said of the supposition that "the Pope were to issue commands in purely civil matters":—

"He would be offending not only against civil society, but against God, and violating an authority as truly from God as his own. Any Catholic who clearly recognized this would not be bound to obey the Pope; or rather his conscience would bind him absolutely to disobey, because with Catholics conscience is the supreme law which under no circumstances can we ever lawfully disobey."

Archbishop Ireland said: "To priest, to Bishop, or to Pope [I am willing to consider the hypothesis] who should attempt to rule in matters civil and political, to influence the citizen beyond the range of their own orbit of jurisdiction that are the things of God, the answer is quickly made: 'Back to your own sphere of rights and duties, back to the things of God.'"

Bishop England, referring to our Constitution, said: "Let the Pope and the Cardinals and all the powers of the Catholic world united make the least encroachment on that Constitution, we will protect it with our lives. Summon a General Council—let that Council interfere in the mode of our electing but an assistant to a turnkey of a prison—we deny the right, we reject the usurpation."

Our Supreme Court has marked out the spheres of influence of Church and State in a case from which you quote copiously, *Watson v. Jones,* 13 Wall. 729; but you refrain from quoting this statement:—

"The right to organize voluntary religious associations, to assist in the expression and dissemination of any religious doctrine, and to create tribunals for the decision of controverted questions of faith within the association, and for the ecclesiastical government of all the individual members, the congregation and officers within the general association, is unquestioned. . . . It is of the essence of these religious unions and of their right to establish tribunals for the decision of questions arising among themselves that those decisions could be binding in all cases of ecclesiastical cognizance, subject only to such appeal as the organism itself provides for."

That is the State's attitude toward the Church. Archbishop Ireland thus puts the Church's attitude toward the State:—

"To the Catholic obedience to law is a religious obligation, binding in God's name the conscience of the citizen. . . . Both Americanism and Catholicism bow to the sway of personal conscience."

Under our system of government the electorate entrusts to its officers of every faith the solemn duty of action according to the dictates of conscience. I may fairly refer once more to my own record to support these truths. No man, cleric or lay, has ever directly or indirectly attempted to exercise Church influence on my administration of any office I have ever held, nor asked me to show special favor to Catholics or exercise discrimination against non-Catholics.

It is a well-known fact that I have made all of my appointments to public office on the basis of merit and have never asked any man about his religious belief. In the first month of this year there gathered in the Capitol at Albany the first Governor's cabinet that ever sat in this State. It was composed, under my appointment, of two Catholics, thirteen Protestants, and one Jew. The man closest to me in the administration of the government of the

State of New York is he who bears the title of Assistant to the Governor. He had been connected with the Governor's office for thirty years, in subordinate capacities, until I promoted him to the position which makes him the sharer with me of my every thought and hope and ambition in the administration of the State. He is a Protestant, a Republican, and a thirty-second-degree Mason. In my public life I have exemplified that complete separation of Church from State which is the faith of American Catholics to-day.

III

I next come to education. You admit that the Supreme Court guaranteed to Catholics the right to maintain their parochial schools; and you ask me whether they would have so ruled if it had been shown that children in parochial schools were taught that the State should show discriminations between religions, that Protestants should be recognized only as a matter of favor, that they should be intolerant to non-Catholics, and that the laws of the State could be flouted on the ground of the imaginary conflict. My summary answer is: I and all my children went to a parochial school. I never heard of any such stuff being taught or of anybody who claimed that it was. That any group of Catholics would teach it is unthinkable.

IV

You next challenge the action of the Rota in annulling the Marlborough marriage. You suggest that the Rota by annulling the marriage (where the civil courts recognized it, but granted only a divorce) is interfering with the civil jurisdiction. That might be so if anybody claimed that the decree of the Rota had any effect under the laws of America, or any other nation of the world. But you must know that it has no such effect and that nobody claims it has. The decree merely defined the status of the parties as communicants of the Church. Your Church refuses to recognize the ecclesiastical validity of divorces granted by the civil tribunals. Your Church has its tribunals to administer its law for the government of its members as communicants of your Church. But their decrees have no bearing upon the status of your members as citizens of the United States. There is no difference in that respect between your tribunals and the Rota.

V

Finally you come to Mexico. By inference from the brief of a distinguished lawyer you intimate that it is the purpose of organized Catholics to seek intervention by the United States. Now I never read Mr. Guthrie's brief. I do not have to read it to reply to you, because the Pastoral Letter of the Catholic Episcopate of the United States in unmistakable words disclaimed any such intention. I do not see how, with complete candor, you could write me about Mexico without quoting the following from that Pastoral Letter:—

"What, therefore, we have written is no call on the faithful here or elsewhere to purely human action. It is no interposition of our influence either as Bishops or as citizens to reach those who possess political power anywhere on earth, and least of all in our own country, to the end that they should intervene with armed force in the internal affairs of Mexico for the protection of the Church. Our duty is done when, by telling the story, we sound a warning to Christian civilization that its foundations are again being attacked and undermined. For the rest, God will bring His will to pass in His own good time and in His own good way.'

My personal attitude, wholly consistent with that of my Church, is that I believe in peace on earth, good will to men, and that no country has a right to interfere in the internal affairs of any other country. I recognize the right of no church to ask armed intervention by this country in the affairs of another, merely for the defense of the rights of a church. But I do recognize the propriety of Church action to request the good offices of this country to help the oppressed of any land, as those good offices have been so often used for the protection of Protestant missionaries in the Orient and the persecuted Jews of eastern Europe.

VI

I summarize my creed as an American Catholic. I believe in the worship of God according to the faith and practice of the Roman Catholic Church. I recognize no power in the institutions of my Church to interfere with the operations of the Constitution of the United States or the enforcement of the law of the land. I believe in absolute freedom of conscience for all men and in equality of all churches, all sects, and all beliefs before the law as a matter of right and not as a matter of favor. I believe in the absolute separation of Church and State and in the strict enforcement of the provisions of the Constitution that Congress shall make no law respecting an establishment of religion or prohibiting the free exercise thereof. I believe that no tribunal of any church has any power to make any decree of any force in the law of the land, other than to establish the status of its own communicants within its own church. I believe in the support of the public school as one of the corner stones of American liberty. I believe in the right of every parent to choose whether his child shall be educated in the public school or in a religious school supported by those of his own faith. I believe in the principle of noninterference by this country in the internal affairs of other nations and that we should stand steadfastly against any such interference by whomsoever it may be urged. And I believe in the common brotherhood of man under the common fatherhood of God.

In this spirit I join with fellow Americans of all creeds in a fervent prayer that never again in this land will any public servant be challenged because of the faith in which he has tried to walk humbly with his God.

Very truly yours,

ALFRED E. SMITH

The publication of this reply undoubtedly made, as Judge Proskauer has said, "a profound impression." Certainly Ellery Sedgwick himself seems to have been deeply impressed by it. Otherwise how could he have said in his introductory note that Father had answered "with the clear ring of candor," and that "whispering and innuendoes" would not now "usurp the place of reason and of argument" in the campaign that lay ahead? And it is possible that the reply helped to convince some of the doubting leaders of the Democratic party. But unfortunately bigotry is most frequently an attribute of shallow minds, and throughout the nation such minds either failed to interest themselves in what Ellery Sedgwick called a "matter of high, serious, and eloquent debate" or remained in Judge Proskauer's words "utterly impervious" to Father's "inexorable logic."

The Marshall letter and Father's reply, it should be remembered, appeared in print some eighteen months before the Presidential election of 1928, and more than a year before the Democratic National Convention convened in Houston, Texas. Even then it was clear to observers everywhere that Father would be a serious contender for the Presidential nomination, though he was still rigidly adhering to the promise he had made in his inaugural address on January 1, 1927, to do nothing to further his nomination "except to give the people of the state the kind and character of service that will make me deserve it." As July approached, however, Robert Moses, who was now Secretary of State, as well as Mrs. Moskowitz and Father's other close advisers, began to hope that he would attend the 1927 "Governors' Conference" which was to be held on Mackinac Island, Michigan.

All of us who were close to Father knew he had never been willing, in all his years as Governor, to leave the state for any purpose not clearly connected with the affairs of the state. For him it was unthinkable that he should take any time from his official duties in order to further his own personal political ends. This attitude was so well known to everyone around him that the time had long passed since any close adviser had made any such suggestion.

The conference at Mackinac Island, however, was quite another matter. The program and the discussions were certain to be of value to the Governors of all the forty-eight states, and if, in Father's case, the conference would also seem to dramatize him as a potential Presidential candidate, that could be justified as being no more than incidental to an official journey taken in order to further the legitimate interests of New York State.

It was Mrs. Moskowitz who especially urged Father to attend, arguing that it was a matter of official business.

He shook his head.

"I'm too busy," he replied.

"But it's only for a week," Mrs. Moskowitz argued. "Bob Moses can handle things while you're away."

"Sure. Sure he could," Father agreed. "But I'm not going."

Mrs. Moskowitz was not a person to give up easily, and she returned to the attack again and again. She urged Bob Moses and Judge Proskauer to help her, but to no effect. Father not only insisted that he was not going, but failed—which was unusual for him—to give a good reason for his refusal.

Once more Mrs. Moskowitz pointed out that during the week of the Governors' Conference nothing was likely to come up that Bob Moses could not handle, and Father somewhat impatiently agreed.

"Then won't you go?" Mrs. Moskowitz asked.

"No," he replied, "I won't."

"But, Governor," Mrs. Moskowitz insisted, "this is important. You really should go. And you haven't given a single good reason for not going."

He leaned back in his chair and raised his brows.

"Listen," he said, "I'm not going, and this is the reason why. Emily's going to have a baby this month, and I've got to be here."

"But, Governor——" Mrs. Moskowitz began.

"Never mind," he interrupted. "I'm not going. I won't leave Emily at such a time."

I knew nothing of this then, but later that same day, having gone to the Capitol to see Father, I met Mrs. Moskowitz in one of the corridors.

"We could *kill* you!" she remarked in mock anger.

I was astonished.

"Who could kill me?" I asked.

She shook her head.

"Judge Proskauer, Bob Moses, and I," she replied.

"But what have I done?" I asked.

"Well, you know," she began, "that it would be a wonderful idea for your father to go to the Governors' Conference in Michigan. But he will not do it."

"Why not?" I asked.

"Don't you know?" she demanded.

I shook my head.

"It's because you're going to have your baby this month," she told me.

I nodded. It was the first I had heard of Father's attitude in the matter, but it sounded like him.

"You know Father," I remarked. And there was nothing else to say. The Governors' Conference and the Presidential nomination were important matters, but Father stayed in Albany, where our first daughter, Mary, was born on July 25. The Governors' Conference was in session on Mackinac Island at the time but to Father the Albany event was the more important of the two.

The 1928 session of the Legislature had accomplished nothing of great moment. For one thing the national political situation was in the minds of the members of both houses, and the Republicans among them—who were in the majority as usual—had no desire to add to Father's prestige. But even under these circumstances great accumulations of bills were sent to Father, who, in the thirty days following the adjournment, had to consider and act upon them all. After that, however, he was able to turn his attention to administrative problems, and before the Democratic National Convention met, his desk was almost clear.

After the Legislature has adjourned, Albany is always a much less busy city, and even the Governor's office is under lessened pressure.

But in 1928 the executive offices had little opportunity to quiet down. The state affairs that required attention diminished, as usual, but visitors from almost every state in the Union more than made up the difference.

But Father was never so busy that the gentler things of life were neglected. Thus, many years after the 1928 election, Eddie Corning, son of Lieutenant Governor Edwin Corning, showed me a letter Father had written to him when he was a boy—dated February 15, 1928. It was Father's acknowledgment of a valentine Eddie had sent, and the wording of the letter made it plain that Father had dictated it personally.

"I note on your valentine," Father said in part, "that you say you love me. I am pleased to hear it and the feeling is entirely mutual." And then Father went on to express his hope that Eddie would continue to do well in school.

The "unofficial" office that had for a long time been open in New York City to handle Father's swollen correspondence had been of great help, and now it broadened its activities to attend to the endless matters that required attention during what had become a very active preconvention campaign. So far as the Democratic party was concerned, the preconvention political situation in 1928 bore little resemblance to that of 1924. Father had grown in stature and in political appeal in the intervening four years and, at the same time, the number of potential candidates that had existed in 1924 had greatly decreased. Everyone around Father—and even Father himself—expected other potential candidates to appear. No one expected another such "battle of ballots" as had marred the 1924 convention, but opposition is usually part and parcel of politics, and though all of us about Father were confident of the outcome, we anticipated a struggle.

I find myself tempted, after the passage of so many years, to simplify my account of what occurred, for it is possible, in retrospect, to brush aside thought of all but the major developments, but as the time for the convention approached, it seemed to me that the activities of the whole Smith family had become extremely complicated.

Four years before—in 1924—my eldest brother, Alfred, had been married. Three years before Arthur, my "middle" brother, had followed suit. Two years before, my wedding had taken place, and now, on June 9, only two weeks before the Democratic National Convention was to open in Houston, my sister Catherine was married to Francis J.

Quillinan in the Cathedral of the Immaculate Conception in Albany. It was a very large wedding—larger than my own wedding had been, but it was no sooner over than the Houston convention once more began to dominate the actions of the other members of our family.

I had been selected as one of the New York State delegates to the convention and was looking forward to the part I hoped to play in Father's nomination. Father, however, decided to remain in Albany while the convention was in session, and though Mother, Aunt Mamie, and my three brothers, as well as Catherine and her husband, were all planning to be in Houston, where, during the convention, they were to be the guests of our old family friend William F. Kenny, I suddenly had a change of heart. Though I was a delegate, I decided to remain in Albany with Father, for his reaction—not that of the convention—was my primary concern.

It was not difficult to have an alternate act for me in Houston, and when, on June 26, 1928, the convention met, my husband and I, together with Dr. and Mrs. Moskowitz, my daughter, and my brother Arthur's two young sons, were with Father at the Executive Mansion.

It would be hard to imagine two conventions more dissimilar than the Democratic National conventions of 1924 and 1928. Where, in 1924, more than thirty potential candidates were more or less actively in the running, and two among them were each able, from the first, to block the aspirations of the other, in 1928 no name but Father's attracted more than fractional support.

I have heard much talk in the years since then of "deals" of various kinds which, in some way or another, assured Father in advance of the nomination, but the simple truth is that there were no advance "deals" of any kind. Nor had any arrangements been made for the preparation of such a platform as Father, left to himself, would have written. For example, his stand on prohibition was well known, but the "plank" that referred to that troublesome problem included neither his ideas nor those of the New York delegation.

Throughout the convention Father was in almost constant touch with Houston, and when the wording of the prohibition plank was read to him over the telephone, he reacted instantly.

"That isn't on the level," he told his political advisers in Albany. "It doesn't *say* anything. It only dodges and ducks."

But he did not stop there. Unwilling to leave the convention in any doubt as to his views, he insisted on writing out a telegram that outlined in the clearest possible language his attitude toward prohibition.

"Listen," he was told, "if you send that telegram you may not be nominated."

"I don't care," he replied, and I am setting this statement down as Father himself later recorded it in a memorandum. "I'd just as lieve *not* be nominated as to stand for something that I don't believe in. Let them read the telegram before they call the roll, and if the convention nominates me after that, I have put them on notice as to what I am going to say in the campaign. On the other hand, if they don't want to nominate me after reading the telegram, that's all right with me too."

So the telegram was sent.

In it he agreed to the rigid enforcement of the prohibition amendment and the Volstead Act as long as they remained the law of the land, but he made it clear that he was determined, whatever the outcome of the convention, to work for their repeal.

"Great as the distinction might be to be called upon to lead the forces of the Democratic party in a Presidential contest," he pointed out in his autobiography, which was published the following year, "I was unwilling to accept it if I had to pay as the price the abandonment of any conviction that I entertained or if I had in any way to compromise with the principle involved."

Though so many members of the family were in Houston while the convention was in session, the Executive Mansion was far from empty. In addition to those of us who were actually staying with Father, members of his cabinet and other state officials, as well as neighbors, were in and out of the house almost constantly.

Franklin Roosevelt had once more been chosen to deliver the address nominating Father, though he had not accepted with much confidence or enthusiasm. Four years before he had been very effective in delivering the nominating speech, but he realized that a second attempt might prove to be an anticlimax. However, he was prevailed upon to give it when Judge Proskauer agreed to write it, and when the time came, he gave it effectively. If it was less dramatic than his 1924 speech had been, it must be remembered that the Houston convention itself was much less dramatic than the one that had been held in Madison Square Garden.

Throughout the time the convention was in session, the Executive

Mansion in Albany was a busy place. In addition to the visitors I have mentioned, newspapermen were always there, and when, early in the evening in Houston but late in Albany, the balloting for President began, not only the mansion itself, but also the porches, the grounds, and even the nearby streets were filled with thousands of people.

Four years before, radio had played only a minor part in reporting the convention. Now every detail reached us by way of a receiving set, and in the Executive Mansion there was utter silence when the loud-speaker, clearing its throat of static, announced that the roll call by states was about to begin.

George Van Namee, Father's very good friend and former secretary, had long since established the necessary Al Smith headquarters in Houston, and the work he had gone there to perform had been done well. Because of that, as well as because no other strong contender had come before the convention, the votes cast for Father mounted rapidly from the start.

Alabama! Arizona! Arkansas!

One by one those states were called, and one by one their delegations answered. Those of us who were gathered about Father in the mansion's crowded drawing room listened closely in our attempts to separate the facts we wished to hear from the occasional rasping static. Even Jeff, the great Dane, pricked up his ears now and then as he lay at Father's feet, and as each state answered, excited murmurs, and even shouts, ran through the mansion and out across the porch and the grounds.

California! Colorado! Connecticut!

I was sitting close beside Father, taking down as best I could every figure that the sometimes unclear radio gave out. All about us the very air seemed charged with excitement, and I—because of some strange mixture of great confidence and hesitant uncertainty—found myself keyed to an even greater pitch of excitement than I had felt in 1924. Others were tense in much the same way, but Father, whatever he felt within, seemed quite the calmest of us all. Occasionally his cigar would go out and he would light it again or replace it with another. Now and then he would reach over and turn the radio dial a little, or smile and make some passing remark, or answer a question. So far as I could see, he was relaxed and surprisingly at ease.

Delaware! Florida! Georgia!

The names were called and the votes of the delegations were reported while murmurs or muted shouts of approval or surprise ran across the drawing room and out across the hall.

It was very late by now—getting late even in Houston. The Executive Mansion was a blaze of light. I glanced out the window and saw the crowded porch and grounds—saw motion picture operators with their tripod-mounted cameras and with their batteries of floodlights that had been mounted on temporary supports and in the trees.

Sometimes the reports from Houston were delayed, but now and then they speeded up—Idaho! Illinois! Indiana! Iowa! Then a pause— to straighten out some misunderstanding, apparently—before the roll call was resumed again.

Kansas! Kentucky! Louisiana! Maine!

The total was mounting well into the hundreds by now, and Father was far in the lead.

Maryland!

Excited voices in the drawing room were echoed in the hall.

Massachusetts!

A cheer rippled across the drawing room and hall and then, as the news of the Massachusetts vote was called to the crowd outside, a wave of cheers swept down the driveway and out into the street.

Michigan! Minnesota! Mississippi! Missouri! Montana!

More votes for Father. More cheers. Out beneath the trees photographic flashlight powder flared, puffing clouds of white smoke up among the overhanging branches.

Nebraska! Nevada! New Hampshire! New Jersey!

More than half the votes had been cast by now, and Father's lead had become impressive.

New Mexico!

Six votes, but those of us gathered about Father hardly heard that addition to the total. We were waiting tensely for the next state on the list.

New York!

Without exception we had known what that vote would be. There was no surprise about it. Nevertheless, when it was announced by the blaring loudspeaker we cheered, and cheered again. Even Jeff stood up and barked, and Father was about the only person there who did not leap to his feet. With his cigar well over to one side of his mouth he said nothing. There was a smile on his face, and he nodded as some-one spoke to him.

North Carolina! North Dakota!

The figures were mounting higher and Father's lead was growing. Ohio!

Here was another great block of votes, and we all fell silent as word came over the radio that they would be cast for the Ohio delegation by Senator Atlee Pomerene.

There was a pause, and the loudspeaker chattered raucously with static. Then came the Senator's voice announcing that forty-five of Ohio's votes were being cast for Father, three for Pomerene.

From the time the vote had begun, Father's lead had grown. Long since it had exceeded the maximum he had received four years earlier, and as his total passed the halfway mark and continued to mount toward the necessary two thirds, I found myself growing tenser as each additional delegation was polled. And now, as Senator Pomerene's voice reached us on the radio, that vital two-thirds mark was reached.

More votes were still to be cast, and the convention had more duties to perform. But the peak of its interest for me had been reached when Senator Pomerene spoke, and in the sudden realization that the Democratic Presidential nomination had been decided in Father's favor, I leaped to my feet and threw my arms about his neck.

Those about us in the drawing room, having heard the report of the Ohio vote, were as quick as I to catch its great significance, and instantly Father was almost inundated as a wave of happy friends pushed forward to congratulate him. Those who were outside had to guess what had occurred, but I had no sooner thrown my arms about Father's neck than they guessed right. They could see us clearly through the unshaded windows of the drawing room, and as if my action had been a signal, they swept abruptly up the steps, across the porch, and into the house itself. Cheering, laughing, and shouting their congratulations, they poured into room after room. Suddenly the hall was solidly packed, and as more and more people pushed in, those already inside moved on into the drawing room, the music room, the dining room, and library. They were even thrust, despite themselves, up the broad stairway to the second-floor hall, and beyond it to the third-floor billiard room.

It was almost three o'clock in the morning in Albany by the time the Ohio vote was announced, and the crowd in and about the Executive Mansion had been there since early the evening before. Now they knew

Father had been nominated but they showed no inclination to go home. They wanted him to speak to them. They wanted to greet him—to shake his hand. And they stayed until he did as they demanded, though the eastern sky was light and the morning papers were coming off the presses before the last of them had left.

John brought me one of those morning papers before I went to bed, and the headline of its leading story is still vividly imprinted on my memory:

DEMOCRATS NOMINATE

SMITH FOR PRESIDENT

ON FIRST BALLOT

Tears came to my eyes as I read and reread those words. Everyone, it seemed to me, was being told at last what I had known for years—that Father had come a long, long way from Oliver Street.

CHAPTER TWELVE

Religious Bigotry and Political Defeat

THE DAYS immediately following Father's nomination were crowded with activities and filled with excitement. Telegrams of congratulations began to arrive within an hour or two of the time the vote had been announced, and within another twenty-four hours a veritable flood of them was pouring into Albany. Letters too—mail pouches filled with them. The first came from nearby, but as the days passed, letters from farther and farther away were received. Many were from friends and acquaintances, but the greatest portion were from admirers and well-wishers who were not only strangers to Father, but, for the most part, were also quite without self-interest.

Father could be reasonably well protected from telephone calls, for these were largely handled by his office staff. However, when a telephone operator announced that Denmark was calling and Father was told that someone in Copenhagen wished to speak to him, he took the call himself. To his surprise—though naturally to his gratification—the caller was a man he hardly knew, and the call, though I remember it because transatlantic telephone calls were new to me in those days, was merely another message of congratulation.

Unlike the Madison Square Garden convention of 1924 the Houston convention performed its duties in a most expeditious manner. First called to order on Tuesday, June 26, it adopted the party platform, nominated Father for President and Senator Joseph T. Robinson of Arkansas for Vice-President, and completed its other tasks all within three days. By the end of the week Mother and the rest of the family were back in Albany, bringing with them a very special gift that had been sent to Father—an amusing little burro which, as a native of Texas, had been named Sam Houston. This living symbol of the

Democratic party was given the run of the Executive Mansion grounds, and he seemed to thrive in his new surroundings, though he did not remain a resident of Albany very long. Sometime that autumn while Father and Mother were away, a cold spell for which his Texas birth had apparently not prepared him put him on the sick list, and Harry Whitehead called me from the Executive Mansion. The veterinarian, he reported, had decided that the burro should be given some brandy, but where to get it was a problem. Prohibition was in effect, and there was none to be had in the Executive Mansion, so he had called to ask if John and I had any.

Brandy, it seemed to me, was odd medicine to be prescribed for a burro, but I knew little of burros and less of brandy, so I was in no position to argue the point. And vaguely I remembered that Father, a couple of years before, had given John and me a bottle of brandy. Just why he had given it to us I did not recall, except that it had been a gift to him that had already been about the place for years and was not likely to serve any useful purpose. Perhaps he thought we could find some use for it. There was something else about it, too—something rather special, I thought, though I couldn't remember what it was. But poor Sam Houston apparently needed the stuff, so I told Harry Whitehead that I was sure I could find it and that he had better send over for it right away. He did so, and in half an hour or less the brandy was at the Executive Mansion and, except for a large portion of it that was spilled on the floor of Sam Houston's stall, for burros, it seems, do not take readily to brandy, the whole bottle of "medicine" was given to the patient in the next forty-eight hours.

I thought very little about the matter until a few days later when I was told that the poor little burro had died. But then, somewhat distressed at the news, I told John about it when he came home from the office and even told him of the bottle of brandy I had sent in response to Harry Whitehead's call.

"Brandy?" John asked suspiciously.

"Yes." I nodded, explaining where I had found it.

Just why John seemed so little interested in the burro's untimely end was not clear to me, nor did I understand why, the moment I stopped talking, he hurried away. But presently he was back and I was given the explanation.

"Just what I was afraid of," he remarked, half to himself, I believe.

"What do you mean?" I asked.

"That bottle of brandy," he replied slowly and with disappointment very obvious in his voice. "Don't you remember," he went on, "what your father told you about it when he gave it to us?"

I could only shake my head, though I began to wonder if I had done something wrong.

"Well, it was this," he explained. "When prohibition went into effect, the Biltmore Hotel had to get rid of its stock of liquor, some of which was very fine. And Mr. Bowman put aside a few of the choicest bottles for his close friends. One of these was a very old bottle of Courvoisier cognac."

He paused for a moment.

"I take it," he went on presently, "that this irreplaceable stuff means nothing whatever to you. And I suspect that it meant very little more to your father. But to connoisseurs it is known as 'Napoleon brandy,' for Napoleon himself was very fond of it. And the particular bottle Mr. Bowman gave your father, and that your father gave to us, was *1810 vintage* Napoleon brandy of the very finest."

I do not recall that he said anything more. In a way, of course, he didn't need to, for I now understood that I may have played a part in poor Sam Houston's precipitate demise. Texas burro though he was, that bottle of vintage Napoleon brandy must have been too rich for his blood.

Even before Sam Houston left us, the Presidential campaign was making very heavy demands on Father. Herbert Hoover and Senator Charles Curtis had been nominated for President and Vice-President by the Republican Convention, which had met in Kansas City on June 12, and though the active campaign would not begin for some time, preliminary demands connected with it began at once.

One of the first important decisions Father made had to do with the selection of a national chairman. The candidates themselves almost always decide this matter, and Father selected John J. Raskob, a very successful businessman who was an official of the Du Pont Company, General Motors, and many other organizations. Mr. Raskob had had no political experience, but his other qualities were unusual, and Father, who knew him well, chose him with this in mind.

"I have confidence in his ability," he told me when I asked him why he had not selected someone with more knowledge of politics, "and I believe that it is good political strategy to let businessmen of the country know that one of the country's most important industrial leaders has confidence in the Democratic party as well as in its platform and in me."

It was only a few days after the Houston convention had adjourned that the Democratic National Committee, at a meeting in New York, accepted Mr. Raskob as its new chairman and chose Mrs. Nellie Tayloe Ross to be vice-chairman. Formerly Governor of Wyoming, Mrs. Ross was one of the outstanding Democratic women of the day. She and Father were well acquainted, and on at least one occasion she had been a guest at the Executive Mansion, where the rest of the family had met her also.

With these appointments made, and with the committee's general plan of action outlined, Father returned to Albany and went to work on his speech of acceptance. He was interrupted frequently, for many duties devolved upon him, and as Presidential candidate he was constantly subject to call when campaign issues came up for discussion. Political leaders from one end of the country to the other were constantly arriving in Albany to confer with him. He was still Governor of New York, and the administration of the state's affairs was a responsibility he still insisted on shouldering. Robert Moses, as Secretary of State, was invaluable to him, and relieved him of many administrative duties, but it was not in Father's character to make any attempt to escape his own duties. Despite the growing demands made upon him by the campaign he insisted on attending to the tasks he faced as the state's chief executive.

Though he had been nominated before the end of June, his "address of acceptance" was not delivered until August 22. Of all the speeches a candidate for public office is called upon to make, this first address is the most difficult to prepare. In the very nature of things it is a kind of keynote address. Properly prepared it can serve as a foundation upon which all the rest of the campaign may be erected, but many pitfalls are almost certain to surround every phase of it.

"One of the chief dangers to look out for in a speech of acceptance," Father explained in a moment of relaxation at this stage of the campaign, "is that if you say too little on any given subject you may give the impression that you are trying to minimize that topic."

He went on to point out that there are some subjects which must be treated at length because otherwise they cannot be adequately explained, and that there is danger in saying only a little about a lot of things, for this may suggest the candidate is playing down some subjects that are important. But there is danger, too, in speaking at length on so few subjects as to overemphasize them. To do this is likely to throw the speech out of proportion. Though it is easy to say that a speaker should cover every subject thoroughly, it is not an easy thing to do. Even if it could be managed, it would tire the speaker's audience and wear out those who tried to follow what was said.

He was talking after years of experience, and it was with many of these ideas in mind that he undertook the preparation of his acceptance speech. Written out in full detail, it was actually read when the time came for its delivery. But that was not Father's usual way, and it was the only speech he read during the whole campaign.

"I have never been able to give a good set speech," I heard him say later during the campaign. "I've never been able to write them, and am never able to read them effectively."

The date for Father's "notification" and his speech of acceptance was set far in advance. Because a huge crowd was certain to be present, the ceremony was to take place on the steps of the Capitol in Albany. The city was crowded far beyond its normal capacity when the day arrived. The Chamber of Commerce, conscious of the fact that Albany would be in the national limelight when the ceremony was held, saw to it that the city was effectively decorated. A platform was erected on the Capitol steps. Special arrangements were made to handle the traffic and the crowds. Loudspeakers were installed so that Father's words would be clear to the expected multitude, and when the morning of the great day dawned with all the work of preparation completed, it began to rain.

Hurried inquiry at the local weather bureau brought out a report that the rain was only local—that the skies were clear almost everywhere around at a distance of thirty miles—and because the ceremony had been planned for the evening, it seemed likely that the rain would stop before the ceremonies began. But all day long the rain fell without letup. The handsome decorations that had been put up at such cost and effort were sodden. The gutters were full. The trees were dripping. The awnings, unaccustomed to so much rain in August, now and then saturated pedestrians with sudden deluges of accumulated rain water.

By late afternoon even the most optimistic observers had given up all hope of better weather, and finally—by five o'clock—a corps of workmen began to transfer the radio transmitters to the Assembly Chamber while newspapers all across the country began setting in type their more or less humorous references to the wetness of the weather and the candidate.

Promptly at seven-thirty—for now that radio was so important in such affairs, promptness was essential—John J. Raskob, chairman of the Democratic National Committee, called the Assembly Chamber to order. The speech he gave was short, and was followed by "The Star-Spangled Banner" and by the Invocation. Chairman Raskob then introduced Mayor Thacher of Albany, and when he had spoken, Senator Pittman of Nevada, the chairman of the Committee of Notification, was presented. It was only after Senator Pittman had formally notified him of his nomination that Father rose to speak, and for the first time his voice was broadcast nationally by radio.

Father's speech was a long and thoughtful one, and although I had read it carefully before, I felt even more keenly his great sincerity as I sat listening in the crowded and familiar Assembly Chamber.

"While this is a government of laws and not of men," he concluded, "laws do not execute themselves. We must have people of character and outstanding ability to serve the nation. To me one of the greatest elements of satisfaction in my nomination is the fact that I owe it to no one man or set of men. I can with complete honesty make the statement that my nomination was brought about by no promise given or implied by me or anyone in my behalf. I will not be influenced in appointments by the question of a person's wet or dry attitude, by whether he is rich or poor, whether he comes from the north, south, east, or west, or by what church he attends in the worship of God. The sole standard of my appointments will be the same as they have been in my Governorship—integrity of the man or woman and his or her ability to give me the greatest possible aid in devoted service to the people.

"In this spirit I enter upon the campaign. During its progress I shall talk at length on many of the issues to which I have referred in this acceptance address, as well as other important questions. I shall endeavor to conduct this campaign on the high plane that befits the intelligence of our citizens.

"Victory, simply for the sake of achieving it, is empty. I am entirely satisfied of our success in November because I am sure that our victory means progress for our nation. I am convinced of the wisdom of our platform. I pledge a complete devotion to the welfare of our country and our people. I place that welfare above every other consideration and I am satisfied that our party is in a position to promote it. To that end I here and now declare to my fellow countrymen from one end of the United States to the other that I will dedicate myself with all the power and energy that I possess to the service of our great Republic."

The better part of another month was to pass before the campaign actually began. In the meantime I had a part to play in it myself.

Just as Father had been "notified" in Albany of his nomination for the Presidency, so Senator Robinson was to be "notified" in Arkansas of his nomination for the Vice-Presidency. Unfortunately, however, Father had long before agreed to appear at the state fair in Syracuse on the date now set for the ceremony in Arkansas, and because of that he asked me to go to Hot Springs as his representative. Two days after the Albany ceremony, therefore, I left for St. Louis with Mr. Raskob, Senator and Mrs. Peter Gerry of Rhode Island, and Mrs. Franklin D. Roosevelt, who was head of the Democratic Advisory Committee on Women's Activities. I took part in a series of conferences held by Democratic women from the Middle West before going on with the party to Hot Springs and the notification ceremony.

Senator Robinson's speech attracted a good deal of attention and aroused much comment, for though he devoted himself primarily to a discussion of farm problems he defended Father's stand on prohibition —which was already playing an important part in the campaign—and did not hesitate to condemn what he called "the poisons of slander and libel."

The stand Senator Robinson took was a strong one. He did not hesitate to refer to opponents who "with venomous malice seek to poison the thoughts and arouse the prejudice of those who will decide issues of such far-reaching consequence."

Even at the time Senator Robinson was speaking, which was nearly three weeks before Father opened the campaign with a speech in Omaha, it was clear that the bitterest and most unreasoning opposition to Father was based upon the fact that he was a member of the Roman Catholic Church. And I had no more than arrived home again when I read a report of a speech Senator Robinson had made in Texas only three days after the Hot Springs ceremony.

"I am a Protestant," Senator Robinson "almost shouted," according to the New York *Times,* "but I would deem myself unworthy if I repudiated the principle upon which Thomas Jefferson stood and asked you to vote against him"—against Father, that is—"because he is a Catholic.

"Times come and men pass but it is upon the principle of equality of the individual, the freedom of action, of the press and of religion that the nation is based."

More than a year had passed since Father had replied in the pages of the *Atlantic Monthly* to the "open letter" that had been addressed to him by Charles C. Marshall, and at that time Mr. Ellery Sedgwick, the editor of the *Atlantic,* had written, "The discussion has served its purpose. Not in this campaign will whispering and innuendoes, shruggings and hunchings, usurp the place of reason and of argument."

But now, even before the campaign had actually begun, Mr. Sedgwick's confident belief was being shown to be without foundation. Even after the passage of twenty-eight years it is difficult for me to discuss this deplorable development in the otherwise happy and constructive story of Father's career. To ignore it, however, would be to ignore the deepest shadow in his life—the greatest sorrow, I am sure, that ever came to him—a sorrow all the deeper for having been caused by fellow countrymen, who, had they really known him for what he was, could never in honesty have opposed him on the grounds they chose.

With the active weeks of the campaign in mind Democratic leaders all over the country began writing to the Democratic National Committee asking that their particular areas be placed prominently on the itinerary that would be prepared for Father. Each request was made in perfectly good faith, but too few of those who wrote seemed to have any real understanding, first, of the fundamental necessities of any Presidential campaign or, second, of the almost unbelievable number of requests that were being made for Father's appearance all about the country. It was from Father himself after he had returned from one of his visits to Democratic national headquarters that I first learned of this particular problem.

"I looked over the requests that have come in," he told me, "and it seemed to me that if the Committee consented to 1 per cent of them the campaign would have to run for the rest of the year."

From the very first, in other words, it was necessary to limit what

Father was to do, and in order to do that, some estimate had to be made of what he *could* do.

It had always been Father's campaign policy to go thoroughly and accurately into any subject he decided to discuss. Little, inconsequential speeches made no appeal to him, and he was opposed to the idea of repeating his arguments very often. But thorough, accurate speeches cannot be given except at length, and with the best of help much time must be expended in preparing them—even for the kind of extemporaneous presentation that Father always favored. While Father's speeches were always extemporaneous, the ground to be covered, and even the order in which it was covered, was a matter of careful preparation. And the facts he used had to be checked and double-checked before he would consent to use them.

Because of these time-consuming methods it was finally decided that he would confine himself to a maximum of three speeches a week. But that meant three *different* speeches on three different subjects. And each speech would be designed with a particular and important campaign issue in mind. Even before the days of radio Father had found this method productive of excellent results in the state of New York, and now, with every major speech broadcast nationally by radio, it was theoretically possible to reach almost every person in the country with every speech he gave.

With all these and many more ideas in mind Father's first campaign tour was planned, and arrangements were made for his special campaign train. From first to last the number of people aboard varied from a low, perhaps, of sixty to a high of seventy-five. The largest single group, naturally, consisted of the newpapermen. Most of them remained aboard for the entire trip. A few appeared for special assignments, so that there were new faces from time to time. The group next in size consisted of stenographers, mimeograph operators, and other "office" workers, who almost literally found that their work was never done. And finally there was Father's personal party, which, in addition to Mother and Father, included William F. Kenny, a businessman and financier of New York City who had long been an intimate friend of Father's; our cousin, John Glynn, and me. This personal party from time to time also included my sister Catherine; my brother Alfred; my husband; Mrs. Charles Dana Gibson; Mrs. Caroline O'Day; General Charles W. Berry, and General William N. Haskell of the New York

National Guard; Norman H. Davis, former Acting Secretary of State under President Wilson; Bruce Kremer of the Democratic National Committee; Judge Bernard L. Shientag of the City Court of New York, and Justice Joseph M. Proskauer of the Supreme Court of New York. A number of friends, acquaintances, and political leaders also came aboard for short trips as we passed through their particular areas.

It was on Sunday evening, September 16, that we left Albany on that first fifteen-day trip. Before returning to New York again we were to travel through more than a dozen states and Father was to give seven major speeches in seven carefully selected cities.

Only those who have some knowledge of the methods of campaign committees will be able to guess at the complexity of the problems they must solve in preparing for the kind of campaign tour that had now begun. We were traveling aboard an elaborately equipped special train that was made up of eleven cars. With only one exception the states through which we were to travel had been lost by the Democrats in the campaign of 1924, and it was important to gain their support if possible. In many of these areas the balance of political power four years before had actually been held by the forces of Senator La Follette, and a part of Father's task on the present trip was to win over those former La Follette supporters if he could.

His first speech was given in Omaha on the evening of September 19. We arrived in the city that morning, and all day long, in a large suite that had been reserved at the Fontenelle Hotel, Father and his advisers met and conferred with Democratic leaders and supporters from widely scattered portions of the Middle West. Omaha had not been chosen merely as a place for a series of conferences. It had been selected as an important city in the politically unhappy "farm belt"— an ideal place for a speech on the Democratic party's plans for farm relief.

Father spoke that evening in a crowded auditorium throughout which every seat seemed to be occupied. Rows and rows of seats had been placed even on the extensive stage, and the total number of people present may have reached ten thousand—an excellent attendance, we felt, for Father's first campaign speech, especially as it bore out the promise the cheering crowds had given us when we had arrived that morning.

Father, I thought, was at his best when he rose to speak, and the crowd was with him. The friendliness that had been apparent in the streets of Omaha earlier in the day, and that was just as evident as he spoke, was something all of us had hoped to see. Here was political America as everyone would wish it to be—friendly and willing to listen. Many people were partisan, but there were many others who were willing to weigh each candidate's arguments and to judge his character before deciding finally either in his favor or against him.

Unfortunately it was already apparent that very widely in the shadows Father was being attacked because of his religion. Hardly a meeting with local political leaders took place without someone remaining behind when it was over to warn against the hidden but extensive presence of bitter, determined bigotry.

As yet, it is true, we had not reached the areas most affected by this blight. In reporting Father's Omaha speech the New York *World* pointed out that "Even correspondents frankly opposed to his election were astonished at the way in which he carried his audience with him." But as we left Omaha and journeyed southward to Kansas and Oklahoma, ominous signs of bigotry appeared.

Judge Proskauer, who was with us, has referred to this phase of the campaign in his autobiography, *A Segment of My Times,* and has pointed out that what had begun as a whispering campaign had by now developed into a "campaign of bigotry almost unbelievable in its intensity."

"We encountered circulars, hand-sheets and placards," his book points out, "that screamed the most dastardly canards against the integrity and the morality of the Catholic Church and its adherents."

Having left Omaha on the morning after Father spoke there, we made a daylight run across southern Nebraska and Kansas, with Oklahoma City as the next place at which Father was to speak. The train made a number of stops along the way, and each time this occurred, Father was called to the rear platform to greet the crowds that had assembled. And when, the following morning, we reached the capital of Oklahoma, an enormous crowd—a hundred thousand people, so the papers said—was there to greet him. By now, it was perfectly clear, as Father himself said, that "the foremost issue, so far as this portion of the country is concerned, is religion."

Because of that he decided not to give the speech he had planned but to speak, instead, on the subject of religious tolerance.

During that day in Oklahoma City, Father talked with many political leaders and found considerable opposition to the speech he had in mind. Nevertheless, in the end, he adhered to his decision.

"I listened to both sides of the argument," he wrote some months later, "and concluded that inasmuch as I had personal knowledge of the underhand attacks and the undercurrent of the whispering campaign that was being conducted against me and my family, and as I personally had knowledge of the scurrilous, blasphemous literature being circulated throughout the country against me and my people, I felt deep in my heart that I would be a coward and probably unfit to be President if I were to permit it to go further unchallenged."

In the city's colosseum that evening, before an audience that Father later said was the largest he had ever addressed, he made a speech that is undoubtedly unique in the history of American politics.

"In this campaign," he said, "an effort has been made to distract the attention of the electorate . . . and to fasten it on malicious and un-American propaganda.

"I shall discuss tonight and denounce that wicked attempt. I shall speak openly on the things about which people have been whispering to you."

In some detail he outlined his political record in New York, returning then to the attacks that had been made upon him in the campaign.

"I know what lies behind all this and I shall tell you," he continued. "I specifically refer to the question of my religion. Ordinarily that word should never be used in a political campaign. The necessity for using it is forced on me . . . and I feel that at least once in this campaign I, as the candidate of the Democratic party, owe it to the people of this country to discuss frankly and openly with them this attempt . . . to inject bigotry, hatred, intolerance, and un-American sectarian division into a campaign which should be an intelligent debate of the important issues which confront the American people."

For almost an hour he gave instance after instance of bigoted, untruthful accounts that had been circulated about him.

"I single out these few incidents," he said, "as typical of hundreds. I well know that I am not the first public man who has been made the object of such baseless slander. It was poured forth on Grover Cleveland and upon Theodore Roosevelt, as well as upon myself. But, as to me, the wicked motive of religious intolerance has driven bigots to attempt to inject these slanders into a political campaign. I here and now drag them into the open and I denounce them as a treasonable attack upon the very foundations of American liberty.

"I have been told that politically it might be expedient for me to remain silent upon this subject, but so far as I am concerned no political expediency will keep me from speaking out in an endeavor to destroy these evil attacks."

"The absolute separation of state and church is part of the fundamental basis of our Constitution," he said in his conclusion. "I believe in that separation and all that it implies. That belief must be a part of the fundamental faith of every true American.

"Let the people of this country decide this election upon the great and real issues of the campaign and nothing else. . . . If the contest is fought on these lines, as I shall insist it must be, I am confident of the outcome in November."

Broadcast over a national hookup, the speech was heard in New York by Mrs. Moskowitz and members of her staff. The microphones, however, had inadequately reproduced the sounds and voices of the audience. Father's voice came through with almost perfect clarity, and the daring that had impelled him to speak so frankly on so emotional a subject was evident. The sounds that originated in the audience, however, seemed, as the loudspeakers reproduced them, to be a fluctuating hum of anger, and a telephone call from Mrs. Moskowitz was waiting when we had returned to our hotel.

"Where are you?" she demanded when Father took the phone.

"Back at the hotel," he told her.

"Thank God for that," she replied, and only then was he able to tell her that the "angry" sounds she had heard had been no more than badly reproduced cheers of approval and shouts of "Pour it on 'em, Al!"

No one as experienced in politics as Father could have expected to bring so extensive and so bitter a campaign of vilification to an end with a single speech, and during the remaining ten days of that campaign trip additional evidence of its continuation was constantly before us. Four days after the Oklahoma City speech, while our train was on its way to Helena, Montana, and paused for half an hour at Billings, a newspaper report told us of a fiery cross that had burned for almost an hour the evening before. Erected high on the strangely level Rim Rock that overlooks the city, it had been visible, we were told, in almost every part of that area. Despite this and other signs that the campaign of bigotry was continuing, Father confined his speeches to the subjects that had originally been decided on—water power in Denver, the oil scandal of the Harding administration in Helena, leadership in government in St. Paul, and prohibition in Milwaukee.

It would be impossible, in recalling Father's part in the campaign, to overlook the endlessly repeated renditions of "The Sidewalks of New York." Wherever we went that tune was in the air. It was played and replayed and played again, morning, noon, and night. It was played well and it was played badly by soloists, bands, and orchestras. It was sung and hummed and shouted. Little bands that were a bit unsure of their notes tackled it with energy and confidence. Big bands played it more accurately and sometimes with more variations, but with no more assurance or determination. Now and then more than one band could be heard playing it simultaneously, but not in real collaboration, and when that happened, one might sometimes wonder if the nearer rendition were the original and the farther one the somewhat discordant echo.

Other music frequently interrupted this endless repetition of Father's "theme song." "The Star-Spangled Banner," "America," and many resounding renditions of Sousa's marches were a part of almost every day, while Irving Berlin's "Good Times with Hoover, Better Times with Al," which was written especially for that campaign, and his earlier song, "We'll All Go Voting for Al," were second (if I may measure their positions by their reiteration) only to "The Sidewalks of New York" itself.

While Father was completing this speaking trip in the West, the Democratic leaders of New York State were preparing for their biennial convention in Rochester—a gathering that faced the necessity of deciding on a new candidate for Governor. For ten years no one but Father had been seriously considered for the nomination, but now that he was running for President, some promising candidate had to be found to succeed him.

Those who are familiar with politics will recognize the fact that, from the point of view of a political party, both an advantage and a disadvantage attend the long continuance in office of any especially popular elected official. The advantage lies in the fact that his renomination and re-election are usually easy. The disadvantage derives from the fact that his popularity and frequent re-election usually prevent the development of any natural successor, and this was the situation which had arisen in New York, where, now that Father was running for the Presidency, it was necessary for the Democratic party to decide upon a candidate for the governorship.

Therefore, as our campaign train returned to New York, it took us not to Albany, but to Rochester, where the convention was in session and where Father was certain to play a vital role in the selection of the candidate who, with good fortune, would succeed him as Governor of New York.

In view of what occurred, it may seem strange that no one, when the convention opened, had any clear idea whom the party leaders might select. It was generally recognized that good political judgment dictated the choice of a candidate not connected with the city of New York, if only to show that the Democratic party in the state was not subservient to Tammany. At that point, however, the leaders were forced to admit that no potential candidate existed who had the required exeperience and was widely and favorably known by the electorate. It was not that ability was lacking in the Democratic party. It was, instead, that during Father's long dominance conditions had not favored the development of any other very popular figure.

Names were suggested, but most of them were discarded as soon as they were offered. Townsend Scudder, a prominent Mason and a justice of the New York State Supreme Court, was seriously considered, not only by Father but also by other leaders. Those who knew the justice well recognized his ability, but the unusual austerity that characterized the man stood in his disfavor as a candidate for Governor.

"You can't talk to him," was the typical reaction among the practical politicians, and they insisted on looking elsewhere, though no other likely candidate appeared with the exception of Franklin D. Roosevelt. But he had not held any political office for eight years—had never held any elective office except for his short service in the New York State Senate which had ended fifteen years before. Furthermore, he had been seriously ill, and when the idea of running for Governor had been suggested to him, he had expressed himself as being hesitant to accept the nomination.

"I need another year or two at Warm Springs," he had replied, and that was where he was while the convention was in session in Rochester.

The Democratic party of New York State has rarely been so lacking in potential Gubernatorial candidates as it was in 1928. When too little support developed for Townsend Scudder, those who were meeting at Rochester were unable to find any other promising name but that of Franklin Roosevelt, and "practically every leader of the party," as Father later had occasion to say, was opposed to him. Because of Mr. Roosevelt's physical condition Father was hesitant to bring any pressure to bear on him, especially as the two were in no sense intimate. Mr. Roosevelt had never been one of Father's close political associates or advisers, but now, in the absence of anyone more acceptable to the party leaders, Father decided to support him for the nomination. Because Mrs. Roosevelt was there in Rochester, Father had a talk with her. Primarily he wished to learn whether or not she felt that her husband's health would make it possible for him to run and, if so, whether she favored the idea and would be willing to urge him to accept the nomination.

He found that Mrs. Roosevelt was entirely willing to have her husband nominated, and the day after she and Father had discussed the matter, she called Mr. Roosevelt at Warm Springs from one of the rooms of the hotel suite that Father and George Van Namee had reserved for the duration of the convention. She and Father, in turn, were on the wire. As a result of that call Franklin Roosevelt agreed to run, and because of Father's influence with the Democratic leaders he was nominated. No one opposed him in the primary, so his candidacy was certain.

With the Rochester convention over, Father was compelled to return to Albany to attend to state budgetary matters and to clear his desk of other accumulated business. Within ten days of our return from the West, however, we were on our way again—through the South, this time, in parts of which the bitterest attacks of all were being directed against Father.

"These ferocious and senseless assaults," as the New York *Times* of October 3, 1928, called them, could, for the most part, be divided into three categories. "The primary objection to Smith is his Catholicism," the *Times* explained. "His wet views come second; his Tammany affiliations third. But it is hard to tell where one leaves off and the other begins. The simple truth is that there would be only a negligible amount of bolting among Democrats if Smith were not a Catholic, regardless of his Tammany affiliations and his opposition to prohibition."

However, Father did not return to the subject of his Oklahoma City speech. Even when Senator Tom Heflin of Alabama, one of his most bigoted opponents, spoke against him in the outskirts of Albany to the usual Ku Klux Klan accompaniments of sheeted figures and a burning cross, Father made no reply. Instead he called in the superintendent of the state police—John Warner, my husband—and gave him specific orders to see that Heflin was protected against the possibility of any attack by angered citizens of Albany. And John, who had not ridden a motorcycle for years, rode one that day so as constantly to oversee the scattered members of his force who had been carefully posted to guard Tom Heflin while he made his attack on the Governor of the state he had invaded and the Presidential candidate of the party of which he was a member.

Going south through Virginia, Father paid his respects to Governor Harry Byrd in Richmond before going on to Nashville, Tennessee, where he spoke on the farm problem, water power, and prohibition. In Louisville he attacked the Republican tariff policy and at Sedalia, Missouri, he devoted his attention to the fiscal policies of the Republican administration.

"Governor Smith's genius for dealing with questions of public finance in simple and understandable terms," said the New York *World,* "is well known in this State. He turned it upon an exposition of the Nation's fiscal affairs in his speech last evening at Sedalia, Mo., and very decidedly did something to make it known to the whole country.

"His major text was Coolidge economy and the Republican boast thereby to have cut down Federal expenditures by $2,000,000,000 annually in recent years. Never was a campaign fiction so completely and mercilessly riddled."

I remember the conditions that surrounded the Sedalia speech because of an amusing incident that occurred there.

Sedalia is a small city located about halfway between Jefferson City, the capital of the state, and Kansas City. It had been chosen because the area of which it is the center was more heavily Democratic than either St. Louis or Kansas City, and Father addressed a very large audience in the local fairgrounds.

Not long before we had left New York, Mrs. Charles Dana Gibson, wife of the nationally known artist, sister of Lady Astor, and one of the famous "Langhorne sisters" of Virginia, had asked Father if she might go along on that campaign trip. The two had been friends for years, and Father, along with all the rest of us, was happy to have her as a member of our party. She joined the train at Baltimore, and from that point on was a most delightful addition to our group.

Virginian that she was, she constantly called Father "Cousin," and she followed his speeches and activities with great interest.

Just what Mrs. Gibson may have expected to encounter on a campaign trip I do not know, but she had apparently expected to be under some expense, and was carrying several hundred dollars in her purse—a sum which did not become much smaller along the way for the expenses of the party were paid by the campaign fund. Therefore when we reached Sedalia, she still had most of the money she had started out with, and when we were joined in the Missouri town by Norman H. Davis, formerly Acting Secretary of State under Woodrow Wilson and an old friend of Mrs. Gibson, she mentioned the fact that she was carrying more money in her purse than she liked to have with her.

"Give it to me," he said. "I'll take care of it for you."

She handed it over to him, and we all went off to the fairgrounds, where Father spoke so effectively about "Coolidge economy."

Mrs. Gibson, along with Mother and most of the rest of our immediate party, were with Father on the platform for the next hour, but Mr. Davis, interested in learning at first hand what impression Father was making on the audience, decided to mingle with the crowd. I never heard what he learned about the impression Father made, for while he did his mingling, some member of that crowd very successfully picked his pocket, getting away not only with his own money, but also with the sum he was "guarding" for Mrs. Gibson.

We did not learn of this until we had returned to the hotel, and even then we didn't hear about it until our whole party gathered in Father's room to discuss the fairgrounds speech and Sedalia's reaction to it. Father, incidentally, had found time to take a shower and received us in dressing gown and slippers.

The Sedalia hotel was not the most luxurious in the world, and Father's room was just a hotel room and nothing more. When we gathered there, Father met us with his finger on his lips, and when all of us—Mrs. Gibson and Mr. Davis included—had assembled, he assumed his most mysterious air.

"Sh!" he whispered, after which he silently and solemnly looked under the bed, poked his head into the closet, and even opened the door to the hall in order, his pantomime made clear, to see that no unauthorized person was about to overhear what he had to impart. And finding no one, he turned to us at last.

"Something has happened," he told us slowly and solemnly in a stage whisper, "and it must not get out of this room!"

He paused for a moment.

"Norman Davis's pocket has been picked," he announced in a tone that was intended to portray the shock he felt. "But we must keep it a secret or the campaign will be ruined and the country hicks will get the idea that they can take over all of us New York City slickers!"

We burst into laughter, the more readily, perhaps, because Father's nonsense was so far removed from the bitterness that had permeated large sections of the South and West.

Father's next speech was in Chicago, but I remember it less clearly than I might because of the almost unbelievable reception he received in that city's Union Station when we arrived. At no other time, I believe, have I ever encountered so vast a throng. The station, which is a large one, seemed jammed far beyond its capacity, and even the streets that surround it were filled. As we left the train, I was beside General Charles W. Berry, but we had no sooner entered the station itself than we found ourselves separated from our party and practically lost in that enormous but good-natured crowd. How we would catch up with Father again we didn't know but General Berry felt sure we could get help from the almost overwhelmed policemen who were themselves half lost in the throng. Little by little we edged our way toward one, and General Berry took him by the arm.

"This is Governor Smith's daughter," the general began, but the policeman was not in the proper mood. It may be that others in the throng had already imposed upon his credulity, but I am sure that General Berry's statement was instantly put down as pure fabrication.

"Forget it!" the officer growled. Then he pulled away, and General Berry and I did not reach our hotel for two hours after the rest of the party—who had first been driven through streets that were lined by hundreds of thousands of people—had arrived and gone to their rooms.

Back in Albany on October 21 Father barely found time to clear his desk again before leaving to speak in Boston, Philadelphia, Baltimore, and Newark. And finally, after a speech in Brooklyn on November 2, one in New York's Madison Square Garden on the third, and one over the radio from a studio in Carnegie Hall on the fifth, the campaign ended.

"I am about to utter my last spoken word before the American people start in the morning to make their decision," Father said in conclusion in that final radio address, "and it is this: At no time during my long public career in elective office did I ever trade a promise for a vote. I have made no promises to any man or to any group of men. Nobody was authorized to make any promises for me and, in fact, none has been made. I can enter upon the duties of the greatest office in the world without commitment to anybody except the American people. I can enter upon the duties of that great office with a mind single to the best interests of this country, and I promise you that in return for your vote of confidence tomorrow I shall give this country the best that is in me to bring about a constructive, progressive, and forward-looking administration."

But twenty-four hours later we had all learned that it was not to be. From the time the returns began to come in, Republican victory was in the air, and I recall no other time in my many experiences at Democratic headquarters when the atmosphere was so heavy with forebodings of defeat.

But defeat was one matter and some of the details of that defeat were quite another. As I sat there amid the discouraged confusion that surrounded us I found it impossible to believe the reports. How was it possible for states in the "solid" South to go Republican? It was unthinkable—inconceivable. The reports and figures *must* be wrong.

I went to a telephone and called the New York *World,* and when the call went through, I identified myself and asked to speak to Herbert Bayard Swope, the executive editor of the paper—a friend of Father and one of his most enthusiastic supporters.

"Herbert," I replied when he had answered, "this is Emily. Tell me, is it possible that these reports we are getting from down South are right? That Virginia and North Carolina and Florida are going Republican? It isn't possible. It simply cannot be."

He paused before he replied.

"I'm sorry, Emily," he said in effect, though the language he used was more sulphurous than anything I can put in print, "but there's no mistake. That's what is happening. But there is something else that bothers me even more."

"What?" I demanded.

"New York State," he replied, adding a few very sturdy epithets. "Your father is going to lose that, too."

After twenty-seven years I find it quite impossible to describe my feelings on the evening of Election Day in 1928, and I never learned in detail how my father felt. I have no hesitation in saying that it was not the defeat itself that struck us hardest. Father had been defeated before and all of us, despite our disappointment, had accepted it for what it was. Now, as I believe we realized even at the time, our feelings were the result of something far more fundamental.

In the years since 1928 I have come to understand that it was not "a Democratic year." Even had no bigotry appeared—even had the Democratic candidate been anti-Tammany, a Protestant, and a dry— the Republicans would still have won. And I am not alone in believing that four years later the reverse was true, for just as 1928 was not a Democratic year, 1932 was not a Republican one.

Anterior to all such reasoning as this, however, lay the essential cause of Father's deepest disappointment. Neither he nor those who were close to him found it easy to accept the defeat, but that was secondary. Far more profound, and far more bruising to his spirit, though the actual outcome had been only in part affected by it, was the melancholy fact that many a vote had been cast not for his opponent but against him, on grounds quite unacceptable by those who fully grasp the meaning of America.

Election Day that year was on November 6, which was Mother's birthday, and the evening before, Father had arranged for a birthday cake, for he was determined that we would celebrate the event. Early on the evening of Election Day he went to the 69th Regiment Armory, where members of the Tammany Society had assembled to hear the returns. He had been there only a short time when the outcome began to be evident. He soon returned to the Biltmore Hotel and came to the apartment, where Mother, Aunt Mamie, my brothers, my sister, and I, along with a group of friends, were waiting for him. But when he came he called the immediate family into his bedroom.

I wish I could remember just what he said, but I cannot. I know he tried to prepare us for the news that even we, by now, had begun to expect, and he said later that all of us took it "like good soldiers." I personally was stunned rather than philosophical, and just what my brothers, my sister, and I may have said I do not now recall, though Mother's words recur to me.

"It's God's will," I remember her saying, and there were tears in her eyes. "It's all for the best."

Then she spoke of the threats that had been made against Father during the campaign.

"But aside from all that," she went on, "we'll see more of you now." Father smiled and put his arm over her shoulder.

"Now you mustn't forget," he said to the rest of us, "that today is your mother's birthday. So come along. We'll join our friends and cut the cake."

Within the hour Father sent a telegram of congratulation to Mr. Hoover, and he promptly congratulated Franklin Roosevelt, for though the Republican candidate for President had been elected by a vote of 21,392,190 to 15,016,443 and had carried New York State by 103,481 votes, Roosevelt had defeated Albert Ottinger with a plurality of 25,564, and was now to succeed Father as Governor before another two months had passed.

With the campaign over we all returned to Albany, where a great welcome awaited Father. As he himself said later, he could not have been received with more friendliness and enthusiasm if he had been elected President. All the way from the Union Station to the Executive Mansion the streets were lined by Albany's police reserves, and Father marched the whole distance with the men and women paraders who had come to meet him.

A large amount of work had accumulated on his desk, and it took him some time to clear it away. That accomplished, he went to Biloxi, Mississippi, for a vacation. With Mr. Kenny, Mr. Raskob, and several other friends he went South in Mr. Kenny's private car, and the train to which it was attached was met almost everywhere it stopped by friendly, enthusiastic crowds reminiscent of the campaign itself.

Returning from Biloxi to Albany again, Father gave his attention to two tasks that especially interested him. The first had to do with the installation of an elevator and a number of ramps in the Executive Mansion for the use of Governor Roosevelt. The second was concerned with the very difficult and time-consuming problem of getting together the necessary estimates upon which the new executive budget and the appropriation bill would be based when Governor Roosevelt and the newly elected Legislature were confronted for the first time with the budgetary requirements of the state.

For years, as I have pointed out, Father had favored the establishment of an executive budget, and at last his idea had been accepted by the Legislature and the people. However, it was not actually to go into effect until the next fiscal year, when he himself would no longer be in office. But more serious than that was the fact that the newly elected Governor, though he could not be expected to understand in detail all the many complexities of the state's financial needs immediately, would be required shortly after his inauguration to prepare the state's first executive budget—to list the state's budgetary requirements, and to ask in detail for the appropriations essential to the operation of the state during the ensuing year. In a way Father's work in gathering the basic information for this was his final responsibility as Governor of New York. And it should not be overlooked that this last great task was also of vital importance to the administrative success of the state's new Governor.

Father's last Christmas as Governor saw every member of our family at the Executive Mansion—a gathering that was larger than formerly because of the presence of three grandchildren. It was gay and exciting with the many toys that Santa Claus succeeded in bringing down the mansion's big chimney. I also remember that a day or two later Father once more had a special party for all the little children of the Catholic orphanage that stands close to the Executive Mansion. In the years since Father's first term as Governor this particular party had come to be an annual event, with motion pictures for the children, and with toys and cake and ice cream. I still remember their wide-eyed pleasure, and I can see them yet as Father, his face all smiles, came forward to greet them. I have never forgotten how happily he thrust everything else aside in his effort to please and entertain his little guests.

Just as Governor Whitman, and later, Governor Miller, left the Executive Mansion a day or two before their terms ended so that we might take possession a little ahead of time, so Father reserved rooms at the DeWitt Clinton Hotel for the final two days of his administration, and either on December 28 or 29—two or three days, that is, before Father and Mother were to leave the mansion—John and I were there for dinner.

The conversation that evening naturally dealt, at least in part, with plans for the future, though few ideas were definite as yet. John and I were to remain in Albany, where the superintendent of state police belonged, but Father and Mother had not yet decided where they would live. Two years earlier the church had sold the house we had formerly lived in on Oliver Street, and its furnishings had gone into storage. For the time being, therefore, Father and Mother were going back to the Biltmore before leaving for Florida. When they returned to New York they would make up their minds about their permanent home.

With dinner over, the four of us went to the comfortably furnished second-floor hall which had long served as the family's favorite "living room." A fire was burning in the big fireplace. A lamp was on the table, and as we dropped into the familiar chairs, only one item in our surroundings served to remind us of the change that now confronted us. That item consisted of a large cluster of trunks that had arrived earlier in the day from Hyde Park. They had been brought upstairs and had been placed just around a corner in the hall, there to await the coming of the Roosevelt family.

As I remember that evening I am sure I was quite the most depressed member of our little group. My life, I realized, was certain to undergo many changes. Ever since our daughter had been born, Father had made it his almost daily habit, when he left his office in the Capitol at five or five-thirty, to come to our house for an hour or so. Usually he brought someone with him—Judge Proskauer or Bob Moses or Mrs. Moskowitz. Now and then he brought others along as well—state officials, members of the Senate or the Assembly, political leaders, or out-of-town friends. And for a while, with the responsibilities of office pushed aside, he would sit with Mary—his "girl friend," as he had called her—cuddled in the crook of his arm or bouncing on his knee while he talked of events and people and problems and affairs. And presently Mother would appear, having driven over to call for him and take him back to the Executive Mansion for dinner.

Perhaps I had not realized, until I saw the Roosevelt trunks there in the mansion's second-floor hall, how much Father's daily visits had meant to me. I realized now that they were over, which no doubt explains my deep depression. And Mother, who was concerned more with my feelings than her own, fell silent also, wondering, no doubt, what the future held for all of us.

Something was said about "how different" life was going to be, and Father, who was always able to interpret our various moods, was quick to do so now.

"Well now," he remarked, "we mustn't think about that. You'll come to New York often, and we'll come to see you now and then. So let's not be unhappy."

He paused for just a moment.

"I'll tell you," he went on, "we'll just have a little farewell party."

He rang for Whitehead, who also was rather solemn that evening, and when he arrived, Father asked him to bring a bottle of champagne. The atmosphere was still a good deal less than joyous, and Father decided to lighten it up a bit.

We all knew that Mrs. Roosevelt was quite sincerely a "dry," though none of us knew just what the new Governor's point of view was. Father, however, was concerned at the moment only with lightening the gloom I had brought to the party, and having filled our glasses, he marched solemnly over to the Roosevelt trunks. Then, shaking a little champagne onto his fingers, he bowed to the trunks and lightly "sprinkled" them in humorously solemn welcome. In some way he became an actor for the moment.

"Now, Frank," he said as if the new Governor were actually present, "if you want a drink, you will know where to find it."

We burst into laughter at his nonsense, and the atmosphere of depression I had been responsible for disappeared and did not return that evening.

For some reason that was never clear to me, the state, in authorizing the employment of fifteen servants at the Executive Mansion, made no provision for either a chauffeur or a cook. Those who were employed while Father was Governor were paid by Father himself, their duties at the mansion coming to an end when he completed his final term as Governor.

The cook, who was especially devoted to Father, was a Japanese named Hyda. He was entirely competent in the kitchen and, except for an exaggerated interest in the races, he had no weaknesses that I recall. Each year he arranged to take his vacation while the races were on at Saratoga, and there, no doubt with a "system" of his own to guide him, he placed bet after bet until his savings were exhausted. Even then he could not bring himself to stop, but continued to place more bets until his credit was all gone too. Each year, consequently, it was necessary for Father to advance a greater or a lesser sum in order to rescue the cook from Saratoga. Then, at work in the kitchen again, Hyda would reimburse Father by means of weekly deductions from his pay. Thus he spent a part of each year in debt, though he spent the rest in saving all he could against his next trip to Saratoga where, of course, he was confident of recouping all his losses.

As Father's last term as Governor approached its conclusion, Hyda, loyal and devoted as he was, apparently decided to express his devotion by means of his culinary art, and some three weeks before December 30, which was Father's fifty-fifth birthday, he set about the creation of a confection so elaborate that I still recall many of its details.

It was a birthday cake of mammoth proportions, built up in three heavily iced and intricately decorated tiers, and topped by a donkey made of sugar on which rode a man who was also made of sugar, and who was waving a brown sugar derby.

I suspect that Michaelangelo or Gutzon Borglum or some other really competent sculptor might have improved a little on the modeling of those figures, but I am certain that no one could have surpassed the boldly lettered message on the convoluted scroll which, made of icing in various colors, was draped gracefully around the second story of that breathtaking cake.

"TO HON. GOV. A. E. SMITH," it read, "MANY HAPPY RETURNS OF THE DAY. GOODBYE ALBANY, HELLO NEW YORK."

This wonderful concoction was clearly intended to cap the climax of Hyda's career as cook at the Executive Mansion, and no one could doubt that it did. But it had been weeks in the making and when, at last, with the whole family present for dinner and with Hyda watching from the pantry doorway, it was ceremoniously brought to the table, it proved to be a little less than fresh. Almost spontaneously we greeted it with cheers, and Father was profuse in his thanks to Hyda, but when he cut the cake and served us each a piece, we found it less appetizing than impressive.

When we left the table, the armor of icing on Hyda's work of art was broken where a crumbling cavity had been cut in the lowest and broadest tier. However, the cake was still almost entirely intact, and it may be that when Mrs. Roosevelt, two or three days later, made her first inspection of the mansion as its new mistress, she came upon what was left of that marred but still impressive tribute to Father when she entered the pantry. And if she did, I can believe that this supreme example of Hyda's artistry supplied the evidence upon which, in her book *This I Remember,* she based her statement that the servants at the Executive Mansion, having "always had to make monumental desserts for the Smiths," were "troubled" because they thought the Roosevelts "would expect even grander dishes."

I must admit that this confuses me a little, for Hyda, who made all our desserts, left the mansion when Father and Mother did in order to make way for the cook the Roosevelts brought with them. And anyway, even in Hyda's hands, apple pie, which was the dessert Father usually favored, never quite reached the "monumental" stage, and to use that expression in connection with rice pudding, which was Father's other favorite, is quite impossible.

Father's fifty-fifth birthday party was held on the evening of Sunday, December 30, when all but the very last preparations to leave the mansion had been made. Most of the family's personal belongings had already been taken away, but birthday presents by scores were still arriving—many more than ever before.

"The first year I was here," Father told us, "the presents came from the old Fourth Ward. The second year a few also came from uptown. Then, later, presents came from various parts of the state. But this year they have come from all over the world."

For weeks other preparations for Father's departure had been under way. His zoo, for instance, which, in six years, had grown surprisingly in size, had now been broken up. The birds and animals had been given to various zoos throughout the state, and a new home had been found for Jefferson, Father's great Dane. Both for Father and for Jeff that decision had been a difficult one, but obviously no such animal could be cared for at the Biltmore Hotel. Therefore, after much thought, arrangements were made for Jeff to go to Congressman and Mrs. Parker Corning, whose home, a few miles outside of Albany, provided plenty of space for so large an animal.

I am certain Jeff had an idea that something was up, and for days before he was finally taken away, he was almost constantly at Father's side. He and Father were very unhappy when they parted.

With the birthday party over, and with only one more day to serve as Governor, Father still had several duties to perform. With his and Mother's very last belongings sent to the DeWitt Clinton Hotel on the morning of December 31 both he and she returned to the Executive Mansion to greet the Roosevelts when they arrived at about three-thirty. That duty performed, Father went to the capitol to say good-by to the state officials and the office staff.

Already his personal mementos had been removed from the Governor's office, but it was there, though amid a kind of unaccustomed bareness, that he said good-by to Lieutenant Governor Edwin Corning, to Comptroller Morris S. Tremaine; to Bobby Fitzmaurice, his "special messenger"; to his secretary, George Graves; to Colonel Frederick Stuart Greene, superintendent of public works, and to the many state employees closely associated with his office. It was there, too, that the office staff came to say good-by—secretaries and stenographers, clerks and messengers.

He shook hands with them all, and had a word for each. Then, as he turned to go, his eye fell on the desk that had been his. There was nothing on it now but a pile of letters, newly arrived and addressed to Governor Roosevelt.

He smiled, blew them a kiss, and made his way toward the door with those who had come to say good-by still pressing around him as if they did not wish to let him go.

Out of the corner of his eye he caught a glimpse of Comptroller Tremaine.

"Oh, Morris," he called.

The Comptroller looked up.

"Yes?" he replied.

"Don't forget," Father ordered.

"Don't forget what?" Mr. Tremaine asked.

"Don't forget my pension," Father answered with a grin, and hurried out the door.

Though Father and Mother had by now moved to the hotel, Father was still Governor. Consequently he and Mother were hosts at the Executive Mansion for dinner that evening. Governor-elect Roosevelt and Lieutenant Governor-elect Lehman, together with their wives, were the guests of honor, but their families and ours were included also.

When dinner was over, Governor Roosevelt took the oath of office, after which all of us attended the Inaugural Ball. From there Father and Mother went to the DeWitt Clinton Hotel for their last night in Albany.

Governor Roosevelt's inauguration took place in the Assembly Chamber of the Capitol a little after noon on January 1, 1929, and after attending the new Governor's reception at the Executive Mansion, John and I escorted Mother and Father to the station. There, with thousands to see them off, and with scores of friends who had come to Albany for the inaugural ceremony, they went aboard Mr. Kenny's private car, which had been attached to the two-forty train for New York. And in Grand Central Station, to Father's delight, they were met by a great throng, and they made their way from the train to the nearby Biltmore between two facing columns of New York City's 69th Regiment. Ten years before, this very organization had gone to Albany to play their part in Father's first inauguration as Governor. Now, having attended Governor Roosevelt's inauguration, they had preceded Father back to New York in order to welcome him home. Once more their regimental band played "The Sidewalks of New York," but as Mother and Father reached the Biltmore and turned to wave good-by, that endlessly repeated air gave way to another, and the 69th Regiment gave Father and Mother their final salute to the tune of "Auld Lang Syne."

CHAPTER THIRTEEN

The 1929 Depression and Franklin Delano Roosevelt

FROM THE TIME I had first known Albany as a child, Father had been a public figure of ever increasing importance there. Except for the two-year period following his defeat for re-election in 1920, retrogression had played no part in his political career. Step by step he had advanced, and even during his years as Governor he had gained in stature and in influence. Long before he was nominated for the Presidency he had come to be recognized as the leading member of the Democratic party in the state.

Now he was out of public office—defeated but, according to an editorial in the New York *Times,* "victorious in defeat."

"His unaffected simplicity," the *Times* editorial concluded, "his entire naturalness of bearing, his affability with great or humble equally, the conviction which he so easily conveyed that here was one who 'loveth well both man and bird and beast'—all these things seemed to cast a spell about the Governor as he moved on from one conquest of hearts to another, and left behind the impression of a flashing and fascinating personality which must long endure."

To me, in Albany, the change was of very great proportions. I still knew many people there, but with Father's departure my interest in politics decreased. I understood him well enough to know that he would never lose his interest in public affairs, but I also knew—and others about him knew as well—that he had accepted his defeat for the Presidency, to use Judge Proskauer's words, "as the end of his political career."

"I heaved a deep sigh of relief," he wrote a few months later in reference to his arrival in New York City on the day of Governor Roosevelt's inauguration, "and felt that I was coming into a new freedom it had not been my pleasure to enjoy for a long while."

Soon afterward he and Mother left for a long rest in Florida, and when they returned to New York, he applied himself so energetically to the very considerable task of writing his autobiography that the manuscript was completed and the book was published under the title *Up to Now,* before the year was out.

I mention these particular facts because, in the years since then, it has been said several times that Father, having been succeeded as Governor by Franklin Roosevelt, laid his plans to control the new state administration by indirection. Even the fact that he reserved rooms at the DeWitt Clinton Hotel prior to the arrival of the Roosevelts at the Executive Mansion has been offered as evidence, and I have nowhere seen any explanation that Father's departure for the hotel, like that of earlier Governors, was carried out only with the convenience of the incoming Governor in mind. Far from remaining in Albany after Governor Roosevelt's inauguration Father and Mother left for New York City within less than three hours of the time the inauguration ceremony was held.

Nevertheless, and in spite of these easily ascertainable facts, the imaginary story of Father's plan to control the new Governor of the state of New York frequently recurs, usually in more or less the form Mrs. Franklin Roosevelt gives it in her book *This I Remember*.

". . . I was not greatly surprised," this reference to Father reads, "when after his defeat it became evident that he thought he was going to retain a behind-the-scenes leadership in the state. It would not work; and he soon discovered that it would not work and left Albany for New York City."

Unparalleled world developments in the years since 1928 tend to make us forget that when Governor Roosevelt took the oath of office in Albany he was not especially well known to the people of the state. His family was an old one, but even in New York State many people thought he was a son of former President Theodore Roosevelt. However, the part he had played as Assistant Secretary of the Navy and as Democratic candidate for Vice-President had established him as a

political figure in his own right. His heroic efforts to carry on despite
the physical handicaps with which his illness had afflicted him had
properly aroused extensive admiration—admiration which had grown
as the people, by way of radio, had come to be familiar with his
cultured and pleasantly modulated voice. His campaign, partly obscured though it had been by the Presidential struggle, had been an
energetic one in which he made an excellent impression. His election
had been widely hailed, though observers here and there pointed out
that little was known of his executive ability.

In 1921 Father had been succeeded as Governor by Nathan L. Miller,
a Republican. Despite his successor's political party, however, Father
had then offered to help the new administration if he could be of
service—an offer, incidentally, that was later accepted. And now, in
1929, his attitude was in no way different except that it would naturally be more pleasant to be of service to a Democratic successor than a
Republican one, and that Father had an enthusiastic belief that the
soon-to-be-tried executive budget he had been able to initiate would
prove as successful as he hoped.

None of this was either new or surprising to me. Over and over again
Father had made his point of view entirely clear. He had always felt
that "public office is a public trust," but his belief did not end there. In
or out of office he never hesitated to play his part in the public interest.
Consequently, though there is no foundation whatever for the story
that he remained in Albany in order to influence the new administration, he did make an appointment to come to Albany about the third
week in January to talk to Governor Roosevelt about the executive
budget.

When the appointment was made, he was invited to stay at the
Executive Mansion but he declined so as to stay with John and me.
After dinner on the day he arrived he went to see the Governor at the
mansion.

For the first time in the history of the state this new budgetary
method was about to be confronted by such hurdles as the Republican
Legislature could concoct, and Father was eager to help in confound-
ing its critics and opponents. All this came out at dinner, and when he
left, I assured him I would be waiting for him when he returned,
whatever the time might be.

During the years I had spent in Albany, I had come to be familiar
with most of the political leaders of the state. But I knew very little

about Franklin Roosevelt. I had met him on a number of occasions, and had also met Mrs. Roosevelt. Then, too, there was no member of our family who was not grateful for the very effective way in which, twice, this new Governor had nominated Father for the Presidency. I was still impressed, as I had been in 1920 when I first met him aboard the battleship in San Francisco Bay, by his manner, his voice, and his bearing.

Bob Moses, it is true, had not favored him for Governor. "He'll make a good candidate but a poor Governor," Bob had said in my presence at the Rochester convention. But knowing Bob, and knowing how sturdily he always favored or opposed whatever he was for or against, I had given his remark little thought. And certainly I was not thinking of what he had said as I waited for Father. For along with all the family—except my husband, who never voted for him—I was a strong supporter of Governor Roosevelt.

When Father returned, I went to meet him at the door and helped him with his coat.

"How did it go?" I asked, though for no other reason than to have something to say. Certainly I had no idea that this first meeting with the new Governor since the inauguration would not go well. Father was noncommittal, however, until he had put away his coat and gone to the living room.

"Frank," he said then, "wanted to talk about mending our political fences."

It seemed to me that that was not surprising. After all, those fences were in pretty bad shape as a result of the Hoover landslide. But suddenly I realized that Father had come to Albany for quite another reason. Few things he had accomplished seemed so important to him as the executive budget, and it had been with that in mind that he had made his appointment with the Governor.

"Well"—I hesitated—"what *did* you talk about?"

His face was serious.

"The executive budget," he replied.

That was the first inkling I had that Father and Franklin Roosevelt differed in their points of view. Nothing more was said that evening, and it was some time before I recognized the fact that a rift was developing. But even then a cloud "like a man's hand" had arisen from the sea of politics—a cloud that was hardly visible but that was to grow much larger.

As I look back now I can see that though this was the first incident that made me wonder if Father and Franklin Roosevelt were not seeing eye to eye, earlier incidents might have suggested the same thought had I not been so favorably inclined toward the new Governor. The New York *World* for December 30, 1928, for example, said that "The appointment of organization Democrats to supplant some of the Smith Independents already forecasts a change in the political picture." So far as I was concerned, no serious doubts were aroused by this story or even by what Father now told me. Differences of opinion and of method are forever a part of politics, and I had seen such differences dissipated too often to imagine that these were likely to be of consequence. I had been given a hint, however, and I was more carefully observant from then on. In fact, I even reconsidered a few accounts that had already reached my ear.

After the election but before Governor Roosevelt was inaugurated, Father and he had seen each other on several occasions. The first of these—or the first, at least, that gave them any real opportunity to discuss the problems that would confront the new state administration —was not long after the election when Father called the Governor-elect on the telephone in order to arrange a meeting. Roosevelt was at his Hyde Park home about sixty miles south of Albany, and Father arranged to go there to see him. I can give only a fractional report of their conversation, for Father, in telling me about it, said little except about Robert Moses.

"I told Frank," he assured me, "that I had no desire to pick his appointees for him. Any Governor should do that for himself. He's the one who has to live with them. But I said that Bob Moses had a great record and a lot of ability, and on that account I thought it would be a good idea to keep him on as Secretary of State."

Governor Roosevelt, at that point, leaned back and puffed on his cigarette for a moment.

"No," he replied. "He rubs me the wrong way."

Father made no attempt to argue the point, though he once more said that in his belief it would be a mistake to let the state or the new administration lose the services of a man who had proved so useful. That more or less ended the conversation, and Father left to return to Albany.

I was sorry to hear that Bob was not to be reappointed, but I did not find it hard to understand. Personal likes and dislikes cannot always be explained, though in the particular case of Roosevelt vs. Moses the explanation ultimately came to light. A collision between them had taken place three years before—a collision that had attracted little attention at the time, but the story of which has since been well authenticated.

In 1925, when the New York State park movement was in its early stages, and when those responsible for its development had been provided with only limited resources, the State Council of Parks, headed by Robert Moses, was authorized to include the Taconic State Park Commission, of which Franklin Roosevelt, then in private life, had been appointed chairman. Enthusiastic about the new Taconic Park, Mr. Roosevelt also interested himself in the development of a parkway that would lead north from New York City and across Dutchess County, where his home was, to where Taconic Park was being developed. Robert Moses agreed that there should ultimately be such a parkway, but he insisted that the parkways of Long Island should come first because the need of recreational facilities was very much greater there. In the end, and in order to settle this difference of opinion, Father approved Robert Moses' stand and the Taconic Parkway consequently did not come into existence until later.

It was at about this time that Mr. Roosevelt, as chairman of the Taconic State Park Commission, again came into conflict with Robert Moses. As Franklin Roosevelt grew in political prominence, the story came to be told, and in 1938 *Fortune* magazine recounted it as follows:

"Roosevelt, as head of the Taconic State Park Commission and thus under State Chairman Moses, appointed his political secretary, Louis Howe, as secretary of the commission, at a $5,000 salary. Howe then told Moses that of course he wouldn't be able to devote more than a few hours a week to the job, as he'd be working for Roosevelt personally almost all the time."

"Moses blew up," this account added, and knowing him well, I can believe it. He has also been reported as having said "very forcefully" that if Mr. Roosevelt wanted "a secretary and valet" he would have to provide the salary himself—that no sinecures were to be permitted in the state park system.

"You don't want me to stay on, do you?" Bob Moses asked the first time the two met after Father's visit to Hyde Park. He was given no direct reply, but he nevertheless offered his resignation as Secretary of State. It was accepted, though Roosevelt asked him to remain as head of the State Park Commission, and even offered to appoint him chairman of the Transit Commission. The Park Commission interested Bob Moses immensely, but the Transit Commission did not. Therefore, continuing in the one position but refusing the other, he remained in the service of the state, though he did so, I think I should add, without salary.

Though I do not know the details, I recall that Father also urged Governor Roosevelt to find some use for Belle Moskowitz—Mrs. Henry Moskowitz—in his administration. Father had known her for many years, and throughout his terms as Governor she had been of inestimable value. In the whole field of social service there were few who were her equals, and she certainly contributed enormously to the success of his administration, throughout which her ideas constantly played a part in the social legislation Father favored. However, Governor Roosevelt was unwilling to make use of her, not because he was unaware of the breadth of this dedicated woman's understanding of social problems, but because he assumed that her loyalty was to Father personally and that it could not be transplanted.

So far as I knew—and I am confident that nothing of significance was kept from me in this connection—Father made no other important administrative suggestion to Governor Roosevelt beyond those having to do with Robert Moses, Mrs. Moskowitz, and the executive budget. A lesser suggestion—which actually took the form of a request—had to do with Alexander MacDonald, the state's Commissioner of Conservation.

Commissioner MacDonald had been in the service of the state since long before Father had first been elected Governor, and he would be eligible shortly for a pension. He was a Republican, and since he had been a state employee throughout practically all of his adult life, his pension was of especial importance to him. Because of that Father spoke to Governor Roosevelt about him.

"If you want me to keep him," Governor Roosevelt replied, "I'll be glad to."

"No," Father objected. "I don't want to ask you to do anything of the kind as a favor to me. You have to live with these people, and all I hope is that in this particular case you'll keep MacDonald on until he is due for his pension. And will you tell me, before you announce that he has to go, so I can let him know about it?"

Father clearly understood that Governor Roosevelt had agreed, and several weeks later he and Mother left for Florida, where they spent the month of February. In Miami, Father paid a friendly visit to President-elect Hoover. In Sarasota he was the guest of John Ringling and took almost boyish pleasure in spending two full days with the animals of the Ringling Brothers and Barnum & Bailey Circus. Then, after visiting Havana and returning to New York, he began the task of writing his autobiography, and months later he learned from the newspaper, though no word had come to him from Governor Roosevelt, that Commissioner MacDonald had been replaced by a neighbor of Governor Roosevelt, Mr. Henry Morgenthau, Jr.

I know that any account I have given here is subject to possible misinterpretation, for I have referred to a number of incidents that took place during an extended period of time. As these events occurred, their relationship was less obvious. Many unrelated incidents intervened, and everyone concerned was attempting to adapt himself to new conditions. Father, for instance, now that he was back in private life again, was faced by the very considerable problem of deciding what to do.

Living at the Biltmore Hotel, as he and Mother did for months after their return to New York, Father was confronted every day by reporters. Over and over again the same questions were asked and the same replies were given. And finally, in an effort to save his own time and that of the reporters, he asked them in.

Father's love of birds and animals was evident even there at the Biltmore, although he and Mother had no dog at the time. But they had a parrot in a cage in the living room of their apartment. The parrot could talk, even if what it had to say was seldom relevant.

When the reporters entered, Father received them as he always had. He knew them all, and some were old acquaintances. He talked with them at length, pointing out that daily interviews were certain to be productive of very little now that he was no longer in public office.

"We haven't decided where we are going to live," he told them. "And I haven't decided what I'm going to do. But when anything happens that you would like to hear about, I'll let you know. I'll tell you."

It was his way of suggesting that they bring their daily visits to an end, and it was clear that the interview was now over. And for once the parrot made a perfectly appropriate remark.

"Good-by," he remarked pointedly, before anyone could say another word.

Though Father had not yet decided on his future, it was not for lack of offers and suggestions. He had a number of opportunities to speak commercially on the radio, for example, and some of the fees that were offered astounded the family when he told us about them. The idea of a former Presidential candidate and Governor appearing under commercial sponsorship, however, jarred on his sensibilities.

"Both NBC and CBS have told me," he explained, "that any time I want to speak to the American people they'll arrange a hookup, but I don't want to talk on the radio and then have a 'commercial' tell the world that I've been sponsored by Lydia Pinkham's Pink Pills for Pale People."

It was at about this time that Father was invited to be the guest of honor at a dinner in Boston given by forty Harvard professors who had supported him for President. The invitation came to him from Felix Frankfurter, who is now an Associate Justice of the Supreme Court of the United States, but who was then a professor of law at Harvard, and the address of the evening was to be given by Alfred North Whitehead, a distinguished British philosopher who had joined the Harvard faculty as a professor of philosophy several years earlier. Father had also been invited to speak.

Professor Whitehead's address that evening was an especially scholarly one, and in it he discussed the significance of Father's career in its relationship to world democracy. He was very laudatory, and he spoke at length and very enthusiastically. When he had completed his address, Father was to speak.

Judge Proskauer was a guest at this Harvard dinner, and I have learned what I know of it from him.

"Al Smith," he wrote when he referred to this incident in his autobiography, "had an innate modesty which caused him to exhibit a certain degree of diffidence in the presence of learned scholars."

That, it seems to me, is understandable under the conditions that confronted Father at this dinner. He could hardly have been other than diffident when he got to his feet after having heard himself made the subject of so erudite and eulogistic an address. He actually hesitated and almost fumbled.

"Gentlemen," he began, "I just can't make a speech here tonight. I think the best thing I can do is to tell you how I ran the government of the state of New York and how I think a government should be run."

Then he spoke for half an hour, and when he sat down, Judge Proskauer has told me, it was "to tumultuous applause." And it was then that a professor of civics turned and spoke to Judge Proskauer.

"If I had a transcript of that speech," he said, "I would have the greatest textbook on civics ever written."

Not long after Father had returned from this trip to Boston, he was called by his old friend Bernard Baruch and invited to dinner at Mr. Baruch's home. Mr. Winston Churchill, Mr. Baruch explained, was visiting him from England, and when Mr. Baruch had asked his guest whether there was any particular person he would like to meet, Mr. Churchill had immediately named Father.

Even in 1929 Mr. Churchill's name was familiar to Americans. He had long been a distinguished personage, and Father looked forward to meeting him. On the only day he, Mr. Churchill, and Mr. Baruch would all be free, Father had long since agreed to speak at Tammany Hall, and he explained to Mr. Baruch that, though he was happy to be able to accept, he would, unfortunately, have to leave early.

Mother and I attended the Tammany Hall meeting that evening and, having arrived before Father appeared, we were seated on the stage, where two rows of chairs had been placed back of the speaker's rostrum. We had been there only a few minutes when Father arrived in company with several other men whom I did not clearly see as they took their seats in the second row of chairs behind the speaker.

Father was introduced presently, and shortly after he began his speech there was a burst of applause, in the midst of which I heard a voice behind me.

"Hear! Hear!" it said, and the accent was quite unlike any with which Tammany Hall was normally familiar.

Father told us later that he had remained at Mr. Baruch's until the last possible moment. Finally he had been compelled to leave, and in apologizing had explained where he had to go.

"Would it be possible," Mr. Churchill asked, "for us to come too?"

Father instantly agreed, and having seated them on the platform and given his scheduled talk, he introduced them to several members of Tammany and to Mother and me before suggesting that we go to the Biltmore.

It was late before that fascinating evening ended, and I recall that Mr. Churchill made the point that the English system had at least one great advantage over the American—an advantage derived from the fact that even in defeat a leader is able, as a member of the minority, to continue to represent the point of view of his supporters.

Father agreed. And it is interesting to note that he had made the same point when he had spoken to the Harvard professors, and had even suggested that a candidate running second in a Presidential race might advantageously be sent to the Senate as a Senator at large for the duration of the term for which his opponent had been elected.

Among the many business opportunities that came to Father during the first half of 1929 was one that did not actually make the headlines until the last day of August.

"Smith to Help Build Highest Skyscraper," the New York *Times* announced on August 30, and other papers gave the story equal prominence—a story that told the public for the first time of the plan to build the Empire State Building.

The plan had been originated by Pierre S. du Pont, John J. Raskob, Louis G. Kaufman, and Ellis P. Earle, and Father, who had already accepted the position of chairman of the board of directors of the County Trust Company of New York, now also became president of Empire State, Inc.

This corporation was to erect, at the corner of 34th Street and Fifth Avenue, the world's tallest office building—a 102-story structure capable of housing some twenty-five thousand tenants. Furthermore, the plans had been drawn, and many of the contracts had been let before the first authentic news of it appeared in the papers. The task of demolishing the old Waldorf-Astoria Hotel, which the skyscraper was to replace, was shortly to begin.

It has often been pointed out that had the plan been delayed for only a few more months the Empire State Building would never have been built at all. As it was, the contract for the construction of the building had been let and the demolition of the old Waldorf-Astoria was under way when, on October 29, 1929, the stock market crashed, sixteen million shares changed hands in a single day, and the greatest economic depression in our history began.

The problems confronting the men who were behind the erection of so enormous a structure as the Empire State Building were very complex. Father, as president of the corporation, was gravely concerned, for the building needed tenants, and businessmen were giving up offices rather than taking on new ones.

The depression was a widespread phenomenon. Everyone felt it, and those in politics were no exception to the rule. Rather the contrary, in fact, for the complicated economic situation gave demagogues endless opportunities to urge the adoption of their nostrums while sincere leaders, who were more thoughtfully interested in the national welfare, were confronted with the fact that the remedies most needed at such times are almost certain to be distasteful.

The depression, coming as it did within a year of President Hoover's victory and when the Republicans had been in full control in Washington for nine uninterrupted years, produced the expected political effects. The Republicans lost strength everywhere. This happened even in localities where the only issues were far removed from the national policies of the political parties concerned. And in the midst of this, less than a year after the depression struck, Franklin Roosevelt, with his first term as Governor soon to end, became a candidate to succeed himself.

In view of the fact that so great a rift ultimately came to separate Father and Franklin Roosevelt, I think I should point out that I, who was as close to Father as anyone, was not conscious of its actual beginning. Father's resentment was not easily aroused. Sometimes I found myself resentful for him when he had no such feeling. During Governor Roosevelt's first term, however, I was not aware of anything of the kind either on Father's part or on my own, though gradually I became puzzled and doubtful. And Father, I know, was more surprised than resentful, and more hurt, perhaps, than either, for, as Judge Proskauer has pointed out, "he considered that he and Roosevelt were members of the same team."

Finally Father realized that he and Franklin Roosevelt approached their problems and reached their conclusions in radically different ways. "Let's look at the record" was much more than a mere remark to Father. It was his natural and invariable method of approach. His effectiveness as an executive as well as a campaigner was based primarily on the fact that he not only "looked at the record" but acquainted himself with every important detail of it before he reached his conclusions and made his plans. His critics have often said that he was not a reader of books, and while that is true, it is misleading, for though he was little inclined to get his information from books he was remarkably successful in informing himself in other ways. No one, for example, was more familiar than he with the constitution of the state of New York or with the details of the legislation enacted during his many years in Albany. And his ability, by means of conferences with experts, to grasp and retain a real understanding of their subjects often astonished those who saw him inform himself in this way. The farm policy that Father outlined in his campaign speech in Omaha, for example, has been referred to as "the most rational farm policy ever proposed for this nation," yet Father, after having admitted that "I am wholly ignorant of the farm problem on the national scale," went to work on the subject and evolved that policy with the aid of associates and experts, and after long, detailed conferences with dozens of farm leaders and agricultural specialists from all over the country.

During 1929 and 1930 I never heard Father question Governor Roosevelt's ability to direct the affairs of the state but Governor Roosevelt had not been in office more than a few months before Father began to feel that many decisions were being made instinctively rather than as a result of careful study and thorough understanding. He realized that this method had its advantages when the decisions were sound. Promptness of decision is often an advantage in itself, but when decisions are arrived at in this way, the evidence pro and con has not been carefully weighed, and because of that, serious errors may result. In mere matters of administration such errors can often be corrected, of course. But this is less likely where basic policies are concerned, and Father, who always thought things through, became more and more troubled by what appeared to him to be an innate willingness on the part of Governor Roosevelt to be guided more by intuition than by thoughtful judgment.

Troubled as Father was, it never occurred to him to oppose Governor Roosevelt's renomination. The 1930 Democratic Convention was held in Syracuse, and Father was active among the Roosevelt supporters there. He even succeeded in having the rules of procedure changed so that he, who was not a delegate, might renominate Governor Roosevelt.

The outcome of the election of 1930 was reasonably obvious in advance. No Republican candidate for Governor of New York since 1920 had been victorious, and the depression had made a Democratic victory doubly sure. It was a surprise to no one that Governor Roosevelt won.

Many were astonished, however, when they learned that his plurality had reached the unprecedented figure of 725,107.

Long before the election most political observers were convinced that Franklin Roosevelt hoped to be nominated for President in 1932. Louis Howe, who had been his devoted follower since those remote days when Roosevelt had been in the New York State Senate, had had that idea in mind for years, and James A. Farley, who, along with many others, had urged Father to enter his first campaign for Governor, had apparently been thinking in those same terms at least since 1928. And now, with so enormous a plurality to Roosevelt's credit, Farley gave a statement to the papers in which he announced that he "fully" expected "that the call will come to Governor Roosevelt when the first Presidential primary is held."

Mr. Farley, in writing his book *Jim Farley's Story,* pointed out that Governor Roosevelt "was not in the least surprised by my statement." But it might have been added that no one else was, either.

It must be remembered that though Father had now been out of public office for almost two years his acquaintance among state officials and others connected with political affairs in the state was very broad. He had a natural propensity for friendship, and the fact that he now spent little time in Albany had no real bearing on his knowledge of events there. His interest in state affairs being what it was, he was able to keep himself well informed merely by reading the papers. Beyond that were the reports that reached him from old and intimate friends whose understanding of politics and political trends was rarely handicapped by lack of information.

I believe those who knew Father will agree that during this period no single disagreement that might have arisen between him and Governor Roosevelt would have been enough to cause him to turn against the Governor. Loyalty, both personal and political, was deeply imbedded in Father's character. Many instances, however, suggested that in Governor Roosevelt's mind political considerations were sometimes more controlling than those concerning the public interest, and by the time Governor Roosevelt's second term was half over, Father's opposition to him had definitely taken form.

In the autumn of 1929 Father and Mother left the Biltmore and took an apartment at 51 Fifth Avenue. I often visited them there and they sometimes came to Albany. They were at our home in May 1930 when, on the twelfth, our daughter Emily was born, and this new member of the family served as an additional magnet to draw them back again from time to time. However, Father saw little of Governor Roosevelt during this period. There was hardly an observer of political developments in Albany to whom this was not obvious, but because of Father's energetic support of Roosevelt for renomination and re-election in 1930, no one thought of any coolness between the two. The fact of the matter is that they had never been intimate, and nothing much had changed when, following the election, the Governor made no advances.

Father was still widely recognized as an important influence in the Democratic party, especially in the state of New York. In March 1931, when the Democratic National Committee was about to meet in Washington, Governor Roosevelt, without consulting Father or even informing him, called a meeting of the state committee of the party. The Governor had been re-elected only five months earlier on a platform that had contained a wet plank Father had favored and Roosevelt himself had finally accepted. Now, however, without Father's knowledge, he pushed through the state committee a resolution requesting the New York State members of the national committee to oppose the adoption of a wet plank in the 1932 Democratic national platform, and Robert Moses has told me that there was a very obvious feeling among Governor Roosevelt's supporters even during his first term "to leave Smith out of the picture."

Any examination of Father's relations with Franklin Roosevelt from January 1, 1929, to the end of 1931 can hardly fail to turn up many additional incidents that would show fully as well as those I have chosen how the rift had been widening. From the day he had become Governor, Franklin Roosevelt had clearly been pulling away from the man he had twice nominated for the Presidency. But he may not have been conscious of two powerful influences that were also at work to force them apart. The first of these was Father's growing distrust, which was based in large part on his conviction that the Governor sometimes acted without proper consideration for the public welfare. The second was Father's increasing realization that Franklin Roosevelt's very great personal charm was sometimes marred by what Robert Sherwood, in his book *Roosevelt and Hopkins,* later referred to as "a capacity for vindictiveness." Along with these influences went many specific incidents that were little to Father's liking—"a long series of incidents," as the New York *Sun* put it—and on December 28, 1931, a front-page story in the New York *Times,* somewhat prematurely, announced that Father would be again a candidate for the Presidency in 1932.

About a month after the appearance of this story Mother went to Lake Placid to spend a week with friends, and I went to New York to stay with Father during her absence. By this time Governor Roosevelt had developed much political strength all over the country. As I talked with Father's friends and visitors—Judge Proskauer, Mrs. Moskowitz, and Bob Moses, among the rest—I began to realize that there was a "stop Roosevelt" movement of considerable proportions, and that many of its backers were looking to Father to lead it.

I asked him about it and found him reluctant to head the movement, though he was constantly being assured that he was the logical person about whom it should be formed. More and more he was being discussed as an actual candidate, though he shook his head when I brought the subject up.

"What are your objections?" I asked.

"Well," he began slowly, "in order to build up any great amount of support for me, somebody would have to go all over the country. It would take a lot of money—more than I could put up. And I don't want to ask my friends to do it. I just don't want to do that any more. In 1920 my name was offered to the convention, though it was just a gesture. In 1924 I made a fight for the nomination. In 1928 I was actually nominated. So I don't want to go looking for it again in 1932. I don't want to be the Bryan of the party."

Here was an expression of his personal inclination—an inclination that would have guided him, I believe, had he been left to himself. But he was *not* left to himself. He was being pressed from every side, and before the week was out, he felt compelled to issue the following statement:

Office of Alfred E. Smith
Empire State Building
New York, N. Y.

So many inquiries have come to me from friends throughout the country who worked for and believed in me, as to my attitude in the present political situation that I feel that I owe it to my friends and to the millions of men and women who supported me so loyally in 1928 to make my position clear.

If the Democratic National Convention, after careful consideration, should decide it wants me to lead I will make the fight; but I will not make a pre-convention campaign to secure the support of delegates.

By action of the Democratic Convention of 1928 I am leader of my party in the nation. With a full sense of the responsibility thereby imposed I shall not in advance of the convention either support or oppose the candidacy of any aspirant for the nomination.

ALFRED E. SMITH

It was on February 8, 1932, that this statement appeared in the papers, and from coast to coast it was the story of the day. It was given prominent headlines everywhere, those in the New York *Times* reading as follows:

SMITH WILLING TO ACCEPT NOMINATION

BUT WON'T MAKE FIGHT FOR DELEGATIONS

HIS ANNOUNCEMENT STIRS BOTH PARTIES

"What promised at one time to be a rather tame contest for the Democratic nomination," the New York *Times* commented in an editorial, "will hereafter be bristling with excitement. When one of the contestants is named 'Al' Smith, none of the others can afford for an instant to be off their guard."

It may have been at about this time that Mr. Thomas Cochran, a partner in the firm of J. P. Morgan & Company, came to see Father. The two were old friends, and in the conversation they had, the political situation naturally came up for discussion.

"It is probable," Mr. Cochran remarked, "that I am the only member of the firm of J. P. Morgan who voted for you in 1928. But they are all for you now, and what I'd like to know is what we can do to help."

Father held up his hand in mock alarm.

"Tom," he replied in a stage whisper. "Just don't tell anyone."

From this time on Father's visitors were even more numerous, and one evening before I returned to Albany, Herbert Bayard Swope came in. He was well informed as to the extent of the "stop Roosevelt" movement, and within a few minutes of his arrival several names, including that of William Gibbs McAdoo, had been mentioned in connection with it.

Nothing less than an automatic recording device could catch and retain the details of Herbert Swope's remarks when his pressure is up, and I do not pretend, after more than a score of years, to remember the conversational gambits that followed his arrival. But it began to appear that much evidence suggested that McAdoo was as interested as many others were in stopping Roosevelt. And with that in the air the question arose as to whether Father would object to associating, for that purpose, with his old 1924 opponent.

"Certainly not," Father replied. "I don't oppose men on personal grounds. If McAdoo is willing to go along on this, I'm willing to go with him."

No one but McAdoo could decide that, and he was in California. But a telephone was handy and presently, with Father and me sitting by, Mr. Swope put in a long-distance call. It went through promptly, and once Mr. McAdoo was reached, Mr. Swope explained Father's point of view. In the conversation that followed, it became clear that McAdoo's attitude was what it had been assumed to be. He was glad to go along, though he asked a question that had to be answered—a question which, as Mr. Swope passed it on, was approximately as follows:

If the opposition to Roosevelt were ultimately to necessitate a conference of Democratic leaders in order that some other nominee might be selected, would Father accept Mr. McAdoo as one of the conferees?

"Certainly," Father replied. "And I'll do more than that. Unless he is included, I'll refuse to be a conferee myself."

The telephone conversation ended on that note, with the understanding that Father and Mr. McAdoo would meet in Chicago when the Democratic Convention opened.

Up to this time Governor Roosevelt's progress toward the nomination had encountered few obstacles of consequence but now serious problems were arising. Still, his supporters were well organized and strong, and there was no inclination among them to lessen their efforts. The contrary was true, in fact. With Father an openly avowed contender for the nomination whose every move was news and who, on April 13, would be one of the principal speakers at the Democratic party's much publicized Jefferson Day dinner in Washington, Governor Roosevelt prepared and arranged for the delivery of a speech over the radio on April 7.

This speech, which, among other things, advanced the claims of "the forgotten man" and attacked some of Father's ideas, was given as planned but it was widely criticized. For instance, Frank Kent, of the Baltimore *Sun,* called it an "unfortunate speech," adding that it "so completely clashed with the facts and figures that it found no defenders."

By now the lines were drawn between Father and Governor Roosevelt, but a very much greater event was about to make the headlines.

Six days after Governor Roosevelt's radio speech the Jefferson Day dinner was held in Washington, and though Governor Roosevelt as well as Father had been scheduled to speak, he sent his "special regret" in a last-minute telegram which said that the pressure of his official duties made it impossible for him to attend.

I was at home in Albany on the evening of that dinner, but the speeches were broadcast by radio, and because I knew something of what Father planned to say I listened eagerly. John J. Raskob presided, James M. Cox was toastmaster, and Father, who had been deeply troubled by parts of Franklin Roosevelt's "forgotten man" radio speech, was the last of four speakers.

Even as we heard Father's speech on our radio in Albany we were aware that he was causing a sensation. It was not until we read the next day's papers, however, that we realized just how effective he had been.

"Smith ran away with the Democratic mobilization gathering," the New York *Times* account read the following morning. "Not only did his open fire on Roosevelt provide the dramatics, but his carefully studied plan for relieving the economic situation has started a discussion which is bound to hold attention for weeks to come and perhaps supply a cause of war in the national convention.

"Weighing his words to lend each its full emphasis, Mr. Smith, eyes flashing and face red with anger, hurled his denunciation at demagogic appeal. In a recent radio speech which has been criticized widely, Gov. Roosevelt based his first campaign appeal on his plan for relief of the 'forgotten men at the bottom of the pyramid.' It was in direct answer to that speech that Mr. Smith addressed himself. He said:

" 'This is no time for demagogues. At a time like this, when millions of men and women and children are starving throughout the land, there is always the temptation to some men to stir up class prejudice, to stir up the bitterness of the rich against the poor and the poor against the rich. Against that effort I set myself uncompromisingly.

" 'I protest against the endeavor to delude the poor people of this country to their ruin by trying to make them believe that they can get employment before the people who would ordinarily employ them are also again restored to conditions of normal prosperity. A factory worker cannot get his job back until business conditions enable the factory owner to open up again, and to promise the great masses of working people that they can secure renewed employment by class legislation is treachery to those working people, to the principles of the Democratic party, and to the United States itself.

" 'I have recently stated that while I would accept a nomination for the Presidency if it were tendered me by the convention, that until the convention assembled I would not be for or against any candidate. I announce tonight an exception to that statement. I will take off my coat and vest and fight to the end against any candidate who persists in any demagogic appeal to the masses of the working people of this country to destroy themselves by setting class against class and rich against poor.'

"That was not all," the account in the *Times* continued. "Following up his right-fisted blow, the former Governor delivered a left-hander in quick succession. Again proposing his idea of a big Federal bond issue to speed up public work and provide employment—the plan he put out at the Jackson dinner in January and which did not get a big response—he challenged Gov. Roosevelt's criticism. In his 'forgotten man' speech Mr. Roosevelt spoke slightingly of the Smith venture into high finance as a 'stop-gap.' Smith said:

" 'Exception to this plan has been taken in a nationwide address by a prominent Democrat on the theory that it is a stop-gap. Whoever said it was anything else? It is at least better than nothing and infinitely better than a continuance of the disguised dole in States and municipalities until the localities have given to the point of exhaustion and have reached a point where they are close to the limit of their borrowing and taxing power and at the end of the private resources of their citizens.'

"Calling for constructive suggestions rather than faultfinding, Mr. Smith said it is easy to tear down but hard to build. He pleaded with the Democrats to forget about patronage and partisanship and try to do something for the nation in this time of stress. He ended in this striking phrase which brought the audience to its feet:

" 'If the United States is not going to win, what difference does it make which party wins?' "

Though Governor Roosevelt had not formally announced his candidacy until January 23, 1932, when he had been compelled to do so in order that his name might be entered in the North Dakota preferential primary, his preconvention campaign had been under way ever since his re-election in 1930. Under the management of James A. Farley, and with much behind-the-scenes help from Louis Howe, the task of drumming up Roosevelt support had been actively under way for more than a year when the Democratic Convention opened in Chicago on June 27.

Though no campaign had been made in Father's behalf, ninety-four delegates representing Massachusetts, Rhode Island, Connecticut, and New Jersey had either been instructed or pledged to support him, and when the convention opened, other groups of pledged or instructed delegates were lined up in support of some other candidates.

"A majority," the New York *Times* pointed out, "would be 578, but the Democrats do not nominate by majority. Unless the old rule is changed the successful candidates for President and Vice-President must command a two-thirds vote or 770. Putting it the other way, the 'stop Roosevelt' movement must be able to have and to hold a minimum of 385 votes. The line-up on the eve of the convention is as follows:

ROOSEVELT	(instructed and pledged)	485
	(claimed)	103
SMITH	(instructed and pledged)	94
GARNER	(pledged)	90
LEWIS	(pledged)	58
WHITE	(pledged)	52
REED	(instructed)	36
BYRD	(instructed)	24
MURRAY	(instructed and pledged)	23
RITCHIE	(pledged)	16
Doubtful		173
TOTAL		1,154

". . . It will be seen that at the present moment Governor Roosevelt, while claiming a majority of the delegates, has far less than the requisite two thirds. It is equally obvious that Smith, while hoping to exert a veto, has far less than the minimum one third. For either to succeed in his efforts, he must make recruitments from the ranks of the unpledged or alliances with delegations from States instructed for favorite sons."

Father arranged to reach Chicago several days before the convention opened, and Mother went with him. John and I joined the party, and a large group of friends, including Judge Proskauer, William Kenny, Charles S. Hand, Mr. and Mrs. Daniel Mooney, Mrs. Reginald Fincke, Mrs. Josiah C. Thaw, and Dr. and Mrs. Moskowitz, either accompanied us or joined us in Chicago. Mrs. Charles Dana Gibson, as well as John and I, stayed with friends in Lake Forest. Most of us understood that Father did not expect to win the nomination for himself, and I was not certain I wanted him to.

As had been arranged over the telephone two months before, Father and Mr. McAdoo had a conference, and in it they agreed that they and their followers would stand in opposition to Roosevelt. If, when the balloting began, a deadlock were to develop, they agreed to meet again in the hope of uniting in support of some candidate.

In the meantime Father hoped to see the convention take a strong stand in opposition to prohibition, and even before the convention opened, it was clear that many others felt as he did. Senator Alben Barkley, in his keynote address, recognized that fact and advocated the repeal of the Eighteenth Amendment.

Father, as a member of the Platform Committee, was determined to urge the adoption of a wet plank. The one he wrote, however, failed to get the necessary support in the committee. This was largely due to the fact that Franklin Roosevelt's adherents on the committee refused to accept it. But Father's convictions were involved and he was determined to take the matter to the floor of the convention. He made it clear, therefore, that he was prepared to present a minority report.

The Roosevelt supporters had already been in touch by telephone with the Governor in Albany. In fact, their opposition to Father's plank had resulted from such a conversation. With Father resolved to take his plank to the convention floor, however, they called the Governor again, no doubt giving him some idea of the backing Father's move was likely to get. And just fifteen minutes before Father was scheduled to address the convention, Governor Roosevelt withdrew his objections. The "minority" plank consequently gained enough votes in the committee before Father spoke to make it the "majority" plank, though gossip about Father's headquarters quoted Jim Farley as saying, "Well, don't call Roosevelt about it again or he'll change his mind again."

The opening session of the convention had begun quietly, but Senator Barkley had no sooner recommended repeal than a demonstration in support of the idea followed, and when, at the second session, Father was recognized and rose to speak in support of the prohibition plank, "a thunder of applause, unparalleled in this convention," a report in the New York *Journal* put it, "rocked the huge stadium. . . . At times Smith had to speak piecemeal, wedging in his phrases between the intermittent outbursts of his admirers' plaudits."

During these first two days a move by Roosevelt supporters to change the two-thirds rule had come to nothing, and a plan to defer consideration of the platform until the nominations for President and Vice-President had been made was also defeated. A fight over the permanent chairmanship had resulted in the selection of Senator Walsh of Montana, and on the third day the wet plank in favor of which Father had spoken was adopted by a vote of 934¾ to 213¾. It was still too early to say who the nominee would be, but Father had at least won this victory though the fight had been a long one and had been begun against heavy odds.

It was on June 30—the fourth day of the convention—that the platform was adopted and the nominating speeches for candidates for President began. There had been an attempt on the part of some of Roosevelt's opponents to delay matters in the hope of strengthening their opposition to him, but in the end the chairman was able to clear away the complications and the nominating speeches began.

Though I was familiar with the ways of political conventions, I was entirely unprepared for what took place before that session finally adjourned. The nominations began with no surprises. Roosevelt was nominated and an enthusiastic "demonstration" brought hundreds upon hundreds of milling delegates into the aisles for almost three quarters of an hour. Father was nominated by Governor Joseph B. Ely of Massachusetts, and was accorded a demonstration that lasted well over an hour—a concentrated bit of political enthusiasm that Margaret Lane of the International News Service called "the convention's real emotional storm."

Mother, John, and I were in our seats in the convention hall when Governor Ely spoke, and we remained there even after the wildly enthusiastic demonstration finally wore itself out. But we had no idea that we were to remain where we were all night long, or that the convention would continue in session until nine-thirty the following morning.

There had been all-night sessions at Democratic conventions before. In 1912 there was an all-night session in Baltimore during which Champ Clark attained a majority of the vote, only to be defeated in the end by Woodrow Wilson. Now most of the night was spent in nominating additional candidates, and that task was not completed until four o'clock in the morning.

The names of ten nominees had by now been placed before the convention—Roosevelt, Smith, Garner, Ritchie, Byrd, Traylor, Reed, White, Murray, and Baker—and one might have imagined that the delegates, sleepy and bedraggled after so many noisy hours, would have been willing to adjourn in order to get breakfast and a little rest. But instead, with the final nominating speech completed and the last candidate's name offered, the actual balloting began.

Incessant wrangling marked the hours that followed, and several large delegations, as well as a number of small ones, had to be polled one vote at a time—a slow and discouraging process when such states as New York, Pennsylvania, and Ohio are concerned. Finally as the summer sun rose above Lake Michigan, the first ballot was completed, the vote standing as follows:

ROOSEVELT	666¼
SMITH	201¾
GARNER	90¼
WHITE	52
TRAYLOR	42¼
BYRD	25
REED	24

MURRAY	23
RITCHIE	21
BAKER	8½

A move to adjourn was now offered by those who opposed Roosevelt, but the Governor's supporters were so confident that on a second ballot they could turn their comfortable majority into the necessary two thirds that they voted adjournment down, demanding a second ballot instead. Once again the balloting process was repeated. State after state voted. Delegation after delegation was individually polled. And once again scenes as turbulent as any Madison Square Garden had known eight years before angered the delegates and tried the patience of the chairman. Finally the second ballot was completed, though the vote had been changed but little. It now stood as follows:

ROOSEVELT	677¾
SMITH	194¼
GARNER	90¼

The others had hardly changed at all except that Murray's votes, with one exception, had gone to Will Rogers.

Now a move to adjourn was offered by the Roosevelt supporters. Apparently their six-o'clock confidence had weakened in the succeeding two hours, and they may have felt that some further effort would be required to find the additional support they still needed. This time the Roosevelt opponents opposed adjournment, and the third ballot began.

Once more the whole slow process was repeated, and once more the delegates of several states were individually polled. And finally the totals were recorded:

ROOSEVELT	682 79/100
SMITH	190¼
GARNER	101¼

Except that neither Rogers nor Murray now had any votes at all, no vital changes affected the other candidates.

But the sun was high in the sky, and the delegates, hungry and disheveled, were unable to keep the session going longer.

"We did little more than hold our own on that ballot," Mr. Farley wrote in *Jim Farley's Story* some sixteen years later. "Our situation was desperate. There were indications that we could not hold our delegates through the fourth ballot. . . . The crisis was at hand."

It was nine-fifteen on the morning of July 1, 1932, and the motion to adjourn which the delegates now accepted may very well have made possible the final outcome of that convention.

Most of the delegates naturally dragged themselves to their hotels and went to bed. But many were still intent on the problem that had confronted them all night.

Garner's strength rested primarily on forty-six votes from his own state of Texas, and forty-four votes from California. If these two blocks could be diverted to Franklin Roosevelt, his nomination would be certain. In fact, though neither block alone would raise his total to the necessary two thirds, any dramatic shift would surely set the ball rolling and others would follow. This was plain to every experienced observer. Father and Mr. McAdoo, however, had considered various possibilities and had agreed to hold another conference in the event a deadlock materialized. But that conference was never held. Within little more than an hour of the time the all-night session had adjourned, newspapermen somehow obtained reports that the California delegation, which Mr. McAdoo headed and with which William Randolph Hearst was very influential, was in caucus where, obviously, their next move was being decided.

Word of this had no sooner reached Father than he asked Herbert Bayard Swope to call McAdoo on the telephone to learn why he had not called Father. But McAdoo would not answer, so Father asked Judge Proskauer to call Speaker Garner in Washington. The call was put in, but the judge found it impossible to reach Garner. Mrs. Moskowitz knew the manager of the Washington hotel at which Mr. Garner was staying, so she telephoned him and explained that it was Father who wanted to speak to Mr. Garner.

" 'You may tell Governor Smith from me,' " Mrs. Moskowitz quoted the manager as saying, " 'that Speaker Garner is here. The reason you can't get him is that he refuses to answer the telephone.' "

When the convention was called to order again that evening, Father was at his headquarters, but John and I were in the convention hall and saw Mr. McAdoo as he rose when California's name was called.

"Louder!" someone shouted when he began to speak.

"I'll make it loud enough," he shouted into the microphone. "California came to this convention to nominate a President of the United States. We did not come to take part in another deadlock or to enter another contest like the one of 1924."

For once the convention was actually listening, for it was obvious that something dramatic was about to happen.

"California," McAdoo cried as he leaned closer to the microphone, "casts forty-four votes for Franklin D. Roosevelt."

Franklin Roosevelt, I hardly need add, was nominated on that fourth ballot, though the betting odds even in Chicago had been 5 to 1 against him that morning. The final vote was 945 for Roosevelt, 190½ for Father, and 12 for three other candidates.

Governor Roosevelt immediately arranged to fly to Chicago to address the convention that had nominated him. But before he arrived, Father sent him a telegram of congratulation and without waiting for the Vice-Presidential nomination to be made, left for New York with Mother and others of his group, though John and I remained until the convention adjourned.

That Father was concerned for the future of the country was perfectly clear. On the other hand, the Democratic platform followed his ideas very closely, and the second day after he reached New York he issued a statement of his position.

"We are living under a system of two major political parties," this statement concluded. "The party out of power should constitute the necessary check on the party in power. The question before us today for decision is, shall the record of the last twelve years of Republican administration be approved at the polls in November? As far as I am concerned, I am totally dissatisfied with that record and shall do nothing to lend it countenance. I shall therefore support the Democratic party."

CHAPTER FOURTEEN

The New Deal—Father Takes a Walk

FATHER, as a member of the Platform Committee at the Democratic National Convention, had played an important and, in a way, even a controlling part in the writing of the platform. He had opposed the nomination of Franklin Roosevelt, but Mr. Roosevelt, in accepting the nomination, had also accepted—to use his own words—"that admirable document, the platform." "I accept it 100 per cent," he had announced.

Thus, in the campaign, both the party and the candidate based their claims for support on a statement of principles that very accurately reflected Father's point of view, and because of that he was willing to give them his aid. He made no apology for having opposed Roosevelt. In fact, he made few, if any, references to him. In the speeches he gave he confined himself almost exclusively to attacks on the Republican record and to clear and forceful expositions of Democratic principles as those were presented in the party platform.

Since he was not the party's candidate, his schedule of speeches was limited, but he was enthusiastically welcomed wherever he spoke. I joined him in New York, and though I missed the speech he gave in Boston I went with him to Chicago, Pittsburgh, and Albany, where he was as forceful, I thought, as ever, and where he was received with heart-warming enthusiasm.

The outcome of the election, except perhaps for its landslide proportions, was no surprise. Political observers had widely predicted a Roosevelt victory, though much time had to elapse before the new administration could take office. No change had yet been made in the long-established date for the inauguration, and President Hoover had four months to serve even after his defeat—an especially prolonged period under the circumstances, for economic conditions, despite the fact that the great depression had now existed for almost three and a half years, had shown no signs of any considerable improvement.

President Hoover's position was exceedingly difficult and very weak. Nothing could be accomplished in the time that still remained to him, and though he suggested that he and the President-elect co-operate in the public interest, Roosevelt, perhaps for a mixture of reasons, declined. Even if he had agreed, the situation might not have improved, but as it was, a nationwide banking panic developed by the time Inauguration Day had come and the country was confronted with an economic crisis of the first magnitude.

During this period, and even during seven or eight weeks that followed the inauguration, I had little opportunity to learn at first hand just what Father's feelings were so far as the new administration was concerned. In May, some two months after the inauguration, he came to Albany for a visit, and bit by bit his concern for the country's welfare became apparent.

His attitude first revealed itself as he referred to a long list of President Roosevelt's advisers and appointees, many of whom seemed to Father to be too radical in outlook, too lacking in practical experience, or too limited in ability. He was doubtful of the wisdom of the so-called "brain trust," distrustful of Roosevelt's frankly stated willingness to experiment, and very much troubled by what appeared to him to be the "New Deal's" somewhat lighthearted ideas for remodeling the national economy.

"In many ways," he said, "conditions are as serious as if we were at war. The Administration should call upon the ablest, the soundest, and the most experienced men we have. But that is not being done. I know that at times there seems to be a dearth of ability in one party or the other, but that's not the situation now. The Democratic party has many men of exceptional ability, but judging from Roosevelt's appointments so far he isn't going to use many of them."

"What about yourself?" I asked. "Would you accept an appointment?"

"What else could I do?" he asked in reply. "Under conditions as serious as they are now it would be any person's duty to serve if he were called upon."

The New Deal had hardly more than started. Many of its plans had not even been evolved as yet. Nevertheless, the air was filled with ideas for inflating the currency, for governmental guarantees of interest on mortgages, for paying farmers not to produce, and for doles and assistance plans of endless different kinds.

"This is the greatest country in the world," Father remarked when these and other economic cure-alls were mentioned. "Our energy, our ingenuity, and our natural resources would seem to make almost anything possible. But Franklin Roosevelt and these 'brain trusters' of his are giving people the idea that the government *owes* them something. And that is *wrong*. No government can support its people. They must support the government. Not even this country of ours can foot the bill if everybody who wants a dole is given one. But that is what Roosevelt and his New Deal brain trusters seem to be heading for, and unless they are stopped, you and I may never live to see the time when this country will get back to the fundamental principles it was founded on."

In later years the opinions Father was expressing came to be very extensively held. In May 1933, however, such thoughts were new and Father was the first to point them out to me.

By now Father had been in private life for more than four years, though he was still widely thought of as a public figure. And this was not merely a popular reaction. Because of the work he had done he received many honors from universities and other institutions. In 1929 he was awarded the Laetare Medal by the University of Notre Dame. In 1930 the National University of Ireland awarded him an honorary degree of Doctor of Laws. In 1933 he received another such honorary degree from Columbia University, and in the same year one from Fordham. And about a month after his visit to me in Albany, he was awarded still another honorary LL.D—this time by Harvard University.

"Harvard is to bestow the degree of Doctor of Laws on an alumnus of the Fulton Fish Market," said the Republican New York *Herald-Tribune,* "because, in the estimation of its authorities, it fits him. And so it does. It is open to question whether any man living is a greater authority on state government than our former Governor."

The Boston Daily *Globe,* under a headline reading, "Al Smith—a Real Doctor of Laws," expressed the opinion that "By bestowing the honorary degree of doctor of laws upon Alfred E. Smith today Harvard University is honoring itself . . ."

These honors, and others that were yet to come, were given him in recognition of his accomplishments as a public official. But his reputation was growing as a businessman as well. The Empire State Building, it is true, had been completed at a most unfortunate moment in our economic history, and now stood half empty at a time when city, state, and nation were confronted with problems for which no one had found the answer. But even here, as well as in the County Trust Company, of which he was chairman of the board of directors, Father's reputation as a level-headed man of business was growing. It was growing because of his membership on other boards of directors as well, and less than three weeks after he had been awarded Harvard's honorary degree he was elected a member of the board of directors of the New York Life Insurance Company.

His interests were just as wide as they had ever been. Though he was no longer in public office, public affairs never failed to hold his attention, and when, in 1932, he was offered the editorship of the *Outlook* magazine, which had established its national reputation under the editorship of Dr. Lyman Abbott a generation earlier, he seized the opportunity. Under the business direction of Frank A. Tichenor the *New Outlook* gave Father an opportunity to keep his views before the public.

On October 12, 1933, the University of the State of New York awarded Father an honorary degree as Doctor of Laws, and President Graves, in conferring it, pointed out that the university "wishes especially to emphasize your constant encouragement and support of the state school system and your consistent efforts to afford equal educational opportunities to every boy and girl in the state."

This recognition on the part of a great university of Father's aid to public education was very gratifying to him. The great breadth of his accomplishments, however, may appear in a new light when I add that Columbia University had awarded him its honorary degree "as a distinguished legislator, constitutionalist, and Governor," while Harvard's honorary degree had come to him "for your clear thinking on economic, political, and social questions and for independence and courage in urging your conclusions." And differing from these, St. Bonaventure's College in December 1933, awarded the Catholic Action Medal to Father for the part he had played in "humanitarian statecraft" and his aid to Catholic Charities.

Father was very greatly troubled by most of the New Deal's early legislation, and was particularly discouraged by the fact that President Roosevelt and the Democratic majority in Congress had plainly cast the party platform aside. But there was one legislative development with which he was in hearty accord, for he, more than any other single person, had brought it about.

Early in 1933 both the Senate and the House of Representatives had passed the Twenty-first Amendment to the Constitution, which, once it had been accepted by the necessary number of states, would repeal the Eighteenth Amendment and bring to an end the disastrous attempt to legislate liquor out of existence. Thus even before President Roosevelt had been inaugurated, and before the new Congress had convened, this important pledge that Father had himself written for the Democratic platform had been fulfilled in so far as Congressional action was concerned. Before the new amendment could be effective, thirty-six states had to approve it, and in the past there had sometimes been long delays before such action had been taken. Now Father's belief that most of the people were opposed to prohibition was promptly borne out, for though the amendment was not forwarded to the Governors of the various states until February 21, thirty-six of the forty-eight states ratified it, and prohibition came to an end by December 5, 1933.

In New York State 150 delegates were elected to take part in a special "repeal convention," of which Father was made president. The convention met in Albany on June 27, and Father, having arrived the day before, was met at the station by an enthusiastic crowd of welcomers.

"Former Governor Alfred E. Smith," said the New York *Herald Tribune,* "marched up Capitol Hill once more this afternoon to the latest and one of the greatest of his many triumphs in thirty years in Albany.

"The veteran foe of prohibition and champion of repeal will be elected president of the ratification convention which meets in the Assembly Chamber at 11 o'clock tomorrow morning . . . Mr. Smith went up Broadway and State Street afoot. Ten thousand persons cheered him on the way . . . Four thousand . . . gathered on the State House Lawn . . . Governor Lehman, welcoming Mr. Smith, gave him full credit for the prospective repeal of the prohibition amendment.

" 'If it were not for him,' said the Governor, 'we would still face prohibition for years to come. To him more than anyone is due the credit for repeal."

I was a visitor in the Assembly Chamber on the morning of June 27, and heard Father as he addressed the convention. I knew better than most how much this action of his native state meant to him. But I also knew that even at this moment of triumph he was deeply troubled by a newer problem that seemed to him much greater than any that had come from prohibition. And knowing that, I detected in his statement a meaning others may have missed.

The convention for the repeal of prohibition, of which they all were members, he said in concluding his remarks, "is a clear vindication of the . . . fundamental theory of democratic government. All the ills of democracy can be cured by *more* democracy. Let the people speak."

Throughout 1933 Father watched doubtfully as Congress, often with little apparent concern for what was being done, passed bill after bill for the purpose of carrying out ideas which, in many cases, were the very opposite of those the Democratic party and the President himself had promised to support. It is true that Congress promptly voted to legalize 3.2 per cent beer and authorized the creation of the widely supported Civilian Conservation Corps. But little more than a month after Roosevelt's inauguration Congress passed and the President signed an act which, in effect, took the United States off the gold standard. Following this the National Industrial Recovery Act, which was passed by Congress in June, opened the way for governmental interference in almost every business in the land, and the President also seemed determined to go ahead with plans for a "managed currency."

Troubled by developments such as these, Father attacked the currency experiment as a plan that would lead to "baloney dollars," saying that "in the absence of anything definitely known to be better" he favored a return to the gold standard. In an editorial in the *New Outlook* he said that he did not believe that "the Democratic party is fated to be always the party of greenbackers, paper-money printers, free silverites, currency managers, rubber-dollar manufacturers and crackpots."

Clearly and repeatedly he expressed his opposition to the New Deal's policy of currency manipulation, but he was fully as worried by other developments. The *New Outlook* reflected his concern by asking questions in many of the titles of its articles and editorials: "Is the Constitution Still There?"—"Where Are We Going?"—"Does the Star-Spangled Banner Still Wave?"

The Administration's rapid creation of many new governmental agencies which were supposed to further New Deal ideas of one kind or another drew some of Father's sharpest criticisms. The names of these new agencies were usually long, and from the first they came to be referred to merely by their initials. They grew very rapidly in number, and before long the newspapers were filled with initials—so filled, in fact, that even well-informed readers often found it impossible to interpret their meaning, especially as new agencies, with new initials, appeared so frequently in the news from Washington.

In an editorial in the *New Outlook* for December 1933 Father let loose a blast of ridicule.

"It looks as if one of the absent-minded professors had played anagrams with the alphabet soup. The soup got cold while he was unconsciously inventing a new game for the nation, a game which beats the crossword puzzle—the game of identifying new departments by their initials."

From the moment that editorial appeared, "alphabet soup" came to be a very widely used expression where these agencies were concerned, but Father's criticisms in this field were often much more specific. Even in this "alphabet soup" editorial his attention was primarily on a more important matter.

"Halfway between a lemon and an orange," he wrote, "is a grapefruit; halfway between a 'public work' and a 'relief work' is a 'civil work.' Up to now the Federal establishments . . . have been increased to include an AAA, an FCA, a PWA, an FERA, an NRA, a CCC, a TVA, an HOLC, an RFC—and now we have a CWA. . . .

"The reason for the new CWA is, however, crystal-clear. It was created to hide the failure of another existing agency. It was set up because the PWA, or Public Works Administration, had broken down. Instead of acknowledging the failure of the Public Works Administration and reorganizing it along sensible lines to insure action . . . this crazy, topheavy structure, choked with red tape and bureaucracy, is being left as it is and out of it is being created the new Civil Works Administration . . ."

"No one," he added, "has yet described just what a civil works project is except that it is some sort of minor construction or repair work . . .

which can be finished before February 15, when the money gives out."

Though Father came to be sharply critical of many New Deal policies and practices before President Roosevelt had completed his first term in the White House, he had had no such attitude at the time of the inauguration.

"I said last month," he had pointed out in the April 1933 issue of the *New Outlook*—the first to be published after the inauguration—"that the Democratic party was at the crossroads. I will say now that it has taken the right turn and that everyone in the country, irrespective of party or other affiliations, should support the new administration loyally and patriotically in the path on which it is now moving."

This editorial, it is necessary to explain, had been written very shortly after President Roosevelt's inauguration, and it was based, almost entirely, on the plans and the policies that had been outlined in the President's inaugural address. Even in this editorial Father made it clear that he had "grave doubts" about the wisdom of certain "regional" plans the new President had in mind, but the promises, both explicit and implicit, in the inaugural address had convinced him that the dangers he had feared would not materialize. Thus he had urged "everyone in the country" to support the new administration "in the path on which it is now moving, because I am satisfied that it is the path back to economic health and happiness."

The inaugural promises, added to the President's campaign advocacy of "sound money" and a balanced budget, had been enough to convince Father that active support of the Administration was warranted. But as the weeks passed and the "brain trust" went into action, he realized he had been deluded. And when, by way of NRA—the National Recovery Administration—and twenty-five other alphabetical agencies that were established in 1933 alone, he saw the New Deal expand until it had invaded almost every activity in the nation, he made it clear that he was in the opposition.

The year 1933 marked the beginning of a long period during which Father was progressively more discouraged for the future of the country. By a most unfortunate coincidence Mrs. Henry Moskowitz—Belle Moskowitz—who, Father said, "had the greatest brain of anyone I ever knew"—died early in January of that year while Father was attending Governor Lehman's inauguration. Bob Moses, having been told of her death at once, called us in Albany to give us that sad news. Long an associate of many of the leaders in New York State, Mrs. Moskowitz had been of great help to Father while he had been in office, and had been convinced, as she herself had said, that he was "the greatest leader of his time." But even after Father left Albany, she had remained close to our whole family, and her death deprived not only Father, but the rest of us as well, of an intimate and very valued friend.

In the months following President Roosevelt's inauguration the New Deal adopted endless plans and policies which, in Father's opinion, directly contradicted not only the party's platform pledges, but also the fundamental principles upon which Thomas Jefferson had created the party more than a hundred years before. He disapproved of many of the new policies, but the NRA had especially troubled him from the time of its authorization, some three months after Roosevelt had taken office. "The National Recovery program," he wrote in the *New Outlook* for November 1933, "has raised a number of extraordinary constitutional questions.

"It is all very puzzling," he added, "and the bewildered observer, hoping ultimately for an honest test of these issues in the courts, is further confounded by the . . . suggestion . . . that the President could ask Congress to create a few more Supreme Court judgeships and fill them with men sympathetic with the aims of the National Recovery Act. That would indeed be a new deal."

Here, if anywhere, is proof of Father's almost prophetic understanding of coming events. In this single editorial he pointedly referred to two enormously important problems that still lay in the future. The first of these—a court test of the NRA—was not to be decided until May 1935. Then the Supreme Court, having considered the "extraordinary constitutional questions" to which Father referred in his editorial, unanimously held the NRA to be unconstitutional, and in doing so brought to an end this particular New Deal threat to the country's free economy. This decision of the Supreme Court then played an important part in encouraging President Roosevelt—though not for another two years—to "ask Congress to create a few more Supreme Court judgeships" so that he could "fill them with men sympathetic with the aims" of the New Deal generally.

Throughout the latter half of 1932 and all of 1933 New York City politics had been in a most unhappy state. Jimmy Walker, who had been re-elected Mayor in 1929, had resigned on September 1, 1932, thus bringing to an end an inquiry into corruption in the conduct of his office, but bringing his career to an end as well. It had long been apparent to Father that some such unfortunate outcome was to be expected, but the events that followed were less obvious in advance.

During a short interval while Joseph V. McKee, President of the Board of Aldermen, served as Acting Mayor, John P. O'Brien was elected to fill out Jimmy Walker's term, but within a few months of his election Father was being suggested as a possible Fusion candidate to succeed him. Both Dr. Nicholas Murray Butler, President of Columbia University, and Fiorello H. La Guardia, who had been the Fusion candidate four years earlier, favored the idea, but Father refused to let his name be used, and finally, in 1933, La Guardia himself was elected on the Fusion ticket in a three-sided contest in which he was opposed by Mayor O'Brien, the Tammany candidate, and Joseph V. McKee, the candidate of the so-called Recovery party.

Late in 1932 a move to revise the charter of the city of New York and to reorganize its government had given Father an opportunity to offer a plan which, in his words, was intended "to bring the city government up to date." Appearing before the Hofstadter Legislative Committee, he outlined in meticulous detail a plan that would have given the city a "legislature" of two houses with the Mayor, as supreme executive officer, assisted by ten "cabinet members" and an elective "assistant mayor." Practically all of the county and borough offices would have been eliminated, the ballot would have been shortened, and the proposed plan included many changes providing for greater efficiency and economy.

Father was later chosen to act as chairman of a commission empowered to draft a new city charter to further these plans. But in the end opposition prevented the submission of the plan to the people within the time that had been specified and Father felt compelled to resign. Further efforts came to nothing, and New York City, handicapped by the outmoded and cumbersome government Father had hoped to see replaced, was forced to continue to operate very much as it had from the time the city of Greater New York first came into existence shortly before the beginning of the twentieth century.

In 1929 Mother and Father had taken an apartment at 51 Fifth Avenue, not far from Washington Square. Later they moved to another at 820 Fifth Avenue, and found themselves across the street from the old Central Park "arsenal," behind which lies the Central Park Zoo. By this time Robert Moses, in addition to his various other positions, had been appointed Park Commissioner of the city of New York.

It is difficult for me to imagine a much busier executive than Robert Moses, but despite the amount of work he is able to do he always seems to have time for other things. And his sense of humor often finds expression in unexpected ways, as when he learned that Father and the animals of the Central Park Zoo were near neighbors. A "private zoo" being quite impossible in a New York City apartment, Father had been unable to replace the collection of animals he had so thoroughly enjoyed in Albany. Bob Moses, therefore, with his sense of humor uppermost, now arranged, with much attendant publicity, to have Father "officially" and impressively appointed "honorary night superintendent" of the Central Park Zoo. I have always understood that the salary for this new and important public office was one dollar a year, which may or may not actually have been paid. In addition Father was really supplied with the necessary keys to the various animal houses, for how otherwise could a "night superintendent" attend to his duties when the daytime superintendent and his assistants had gone home?

Father was delighted with his new position, and sometimes when he had guests in the evening he would take them across the street and around the end of the arsenal to where the animal buildings stand. There, having opened a building in the zoo and turned on the lights to the surprise of the caged inhabitants, he would take his guests on a personally conducted tour.

I especially recall an evening when Father took seven or eight of us, including Mr. and Mrs. Daniel Mooney and Mr. and Mrs. W. F. Kenny, into the building that houses the lions and tigers.

We made our way up to the door in a group, and had to wait while Father got out his key, turned the lock, and found the light switch. Then we trooped in together while lions, tigers, and some of the lesser animals eyed us suspiciously from behind their bars.

It must be remembered that Mayor La Guardia, as head of the Fusion ticket, had very soundly beaten Tammany in the previous election, and it is to be supposed that Tammany was still smarting from the defeat—even that the Tammany tiger of the cartoons might still be licking its only half-healed wounds. Our conversation that evening had mentioned nothing of the kind. Still, the idea must have occurred to Father as we made our way between the facing rows of cages, for he went ahead to where the zoo's biggest and handsomest tiger—with whose reactions he was well acquainted—sat staring silently between the bars. As we came up behind him, he thrust his head threateningly toward the tiger's cage and in his very deepest and harshest voice growled, "La Guardia!"

The tiger, which had been both motionless and silent up to that moment, drew back suddenly, with every muscle tense. Then to our startled amusement it snarled, showed its teeth, and leaped forward as far as the bars would permit, growling in unmistakable disapproval.

It was early in 1934 that Mayor La Guardia appointed Robert Moses a member of the Triborough Bridge Authority. This important agency had the responsibility for the huge construction program that was connected with the Triborough Bridge and related projects. But the depression had interfered seriously with these plans, and unless help could be obtained from Washington—by way of the Public Works Administration in this instance—the work could not be completed. Word of Robert Moses' appointment had no sooner been made public than Harold L. Ickes, who was Secretary of the Interior, and therefore in charge of the Public Works Administration, called Mayor La Guardia to Washington.

"The matter I had to discuss," the Secretary confided to his diary, "was with reference to the naming of Robert Moses as a member of the Triborough Bridge Authority."

I can add little to the story of the feud between Secretary Ickes and Robert Moses, for the publication of the Ickes diary has told it in much detail. Suffice it to say that, "at the instance of the President," Secretary Ickes, hoping to force Mayor La Guardia to get rid of Robert Moses as a member of the Triborough Bridge Authority, refused to approve the PWA projects that were submitted for New York City. Secretary Ickes frankly stated the reasons for this. "Moses is a bitter personal enemy of the President's. The President and such friends as Jim Farley and Louis Howe think that Moses would leave nothing undone to hurt the President and we don't want to do any business with Moses. He is a very close friend of Al Smith." And much more to the same effect.

Mayor La Guardia, confronted with a dilemma, did his best to hold Secretary Ickes off, and because Bob Moses was the 1934 Republican candidate for Governor against Governor Lehman, Ickes "had to declare a truce during that period in order to avoid a charge that I was playing politics." But once the election was over and Governor Lehman was victorious, Secretary Ickes returned to the attack, actually striking off the list all PWA projects for New York City in order to force La Guardia to "get rid of Robert Moses."

The New York papers were highly critical, "and I don't much blame them," said the Secretary. Badly needed funds vital not only to important construction projects but also to great relief pay rolls were being refused because of Roosevelt's opposition to Moses. It is really no wonder that the papers in New York, as Ickes put it, were "raising all kinds of hell" or that the affair had become "almost a national issue." And when, late in February 1935, Father added to the furor by issuing what Secretary Ickes called "a violent statement," both the President and the Secretary "came to the conclusion that a retreat" on their part "was in order." This retreat was carried out by way of a series of prearranged letters, one of which was "predated" by Secretary Ickes "so as to antedate by one day" the statement Father had issued.

Thus PWA funds again came to be available in New York, and Robert Moses remained as a member of the Triborough Bridge Authority. He even presided on July 11, 1936, at the ceremonial opening of the bridge, where he introduced Secretary Ickes and all the other speakers but one. That one speaker was President Roosevelt, who, so Ickes reports in his diary, had "insisted that he would not be introduced by Moses."

While this particular development was under way, the New Deal was also being attacked on other grounds. By now its purposes and methods had become clear enough to bring about at least the beginning of an organized opposition. Late in the summer of 1934 the American Liberty League was organized for the express purpose of recruiting a large number of members who would take part in a national campaign "to judge the New Deal," as an Associated Press dispatch from Washington put it.

For a year or more after the Liberty League was formed, its activities were not especially dramatic. Reference to it appeared frequently in the news, however, and during the final months of 1935 its activities and plans began to attract much more attention. During the year a dozen or fifteen speeches critical of the New Deal had been given under the League's auspices by Jouett Shouse, its president, as well as by Nicholas Roosevelt, James P. Warburg, Dr. Neil Carothers, and others. Governor Albert C. Ritchie of Maryland spoke on "The American Form of Government—Let Us Preserve It," and as the New Year arrived, widespread interest was aroused in two forthcoming speeches—one that was to be given at the Waldorf-Astoria Hotel by John W. Davis before the New York State Bar Association on January 24, 1936, and another that Father had agreed to give the next evening, when the annual dinner of the Liberty League was to be given at the Mayflower Hotel in Washington.

No one believed it was merely by coincidence that these two former Presidential candidates of the Democratic party had arranged to speak so prominently and in such rapid sequence. Both were known to be opponents of the New Deal. Both were known to be members of the Liberty League. And no one could fail to realize that in expressing their points of view these two leaders of Democratic thought could hardly escape stating the reasons for their opposition to the Roosevelt administration.

This much was obvious even in advance, and on Saturday, January 25, 1936, the day the Liberty League dinner was to be given, and the day after Mr. Davis had spoken, the New York *Sun*, in a single front-page story, combined two headlines:

DAVIS ASSAILS DESPOTISM. CALLS VIOLATION OF PUBLIC OATH
"THE MORTAL SIN" IN ADDRESS BEFORE LAWYERS HERE

CAPITAL WAITS SMITH ATTACK ON THE NEW DEAL
EX-GOVERNOR LEAVES FOR WASHINGTON TO ADDRESS LIBERTY LEAGUE

This Liberty League dinner had been very widely publicized, and the fact that Father was to speak had been announced more than a month before the scheduled date. This news appeared prominently in the papers, and shortly afterward a letter from Mrs. Roosevelt courteously invited Father to be an overnight guest at the White House on the occasion of his expected visit to Washington.

When the news of this invitation appeared in the papers, it resulted in widespread expressions of surprise, for though no one knew just what Father planned to say, it had already been surmised that his speech would be critical of the New Deal. When Father wrote to thank Mrs. Roosevelt for the invitation, which he declined because he was to be accompanied to Washington by a large party of friends, the papers seized upon his reply as additional evidence that he planned to criticize the Administration.

For days before the dinner headlines in many papers plainly suggested how widely the news of Father's coming speech had caught the public interest.

MANY GUESSES AS TO SMITH'S SPEECH POLICY, read one headline.

COMING SMITH SPEECH STIRS PARTY LEADERS, read another.

A little over two weeks before the scheduled date of the Liberty League dinner at the Mayflower Hotel in Washington the Democratic party's annual Jackson Day dinner had been given in the same hotel and the same ballroom. President Roosevelt himself had been the principal speaker, and among the guests were most of the figures who were prominent in the Roosevelt administration. "But almost as conspicuous as the list of guests," said the Associated Press dispatch that was written only a few hours before the dinner, "will be the names of the absentees."

But if the Jackson Day dinner failed to attract many of those who were critical of the New Deal—Father among the rest—the Liberty League dinner seemed almost to repel the President's supporters. The dinner was well attended, although I have to rely on hearsay evidence concerning it for I was not well at the time and had to remain in Albany.

Never had I waited more impatiently for a radio broadcast. Father had told me his speech would be an attack on the New Deal and on the record of the Administration, but I knew few of the details in advance. I knew that he had decided to speak only after long and very careful thought, and I also realized that he had spent much time in considering the ground he would cover. As usual, the speech was to be extemporaneous, with only his customary envelopes containing items for direct quotation, and no one could know in advance just what his speech would be. And, as always, no one could know just how his immediate audience—and much less the country at large—would receive it.

John and I, in our living room in Albany, were waiting at the radio long before the clock in the hall struck ten, the hour at which the speech was to go on the air.

Advance reports had told us that the Mayflower ballroom would be filled to capacity—that almost two thousand guests were expected. As we waited we did not know that Father had been greeted by a great cheer when he had entered the crowded ballroom, or that the guests had sung "The Sidewalks of New York." But soon the radio announced that the Liberty League dinner at the Mayflower Hotel in Washington was about to go on the air—that the next voice would be that of the president of the league, Mr. Jouett Shouse, who would introduce the speaker of the evening—the former Democratic Presidential nominee and former Governor of New York, the Honorable Alfred E. Smith.

Mr. Shouse followed, but his introduction was short, and presently Father's familiar voice—deep and always just on the edge, it seemed, of being a little hoarse—was audible once more there in our living room.

"Mr. Chairman," he began, "members of the American Liberty League, and my friends listening in, as I've been told by the newspapers, from all parts of the United States."

He paused for just a fraction of a moment before going on.

"At the outset of my remarks," he continued, "let me make one thing perfectly clear. I am not a candidate for any nomination by any party at any time . . . I have no ax to grind. There is nothing personal in this so far as I am concerned . . . I am in possession of supreme happiness and comfort . . . I speak for no man or no group, but I do speak for what I believe to be the best interests of the great rank and file of the American people, in which class I belong."

I had heard Father speak scores—perhaps hundreds—of times, and hardly more than a sentence of this new speech had reached our ears before I knew that he had never spoken better than he was speaking now.

He told of his great love for our country—of its deep meaning to him, and to the world. He told of the gateway it had opened up for him—a gateway that "showed me how it was possible to go from a newsboy on the sidewalks of New York to the governorship of the greatest state in the Union."

He spoke of his children and his grandchildren, and tears came to my eyes as I thought of Mary and Emily in their beds upstairs. "And I want that gate left open," he went on, "not alone for mine . . . but for every boy and girl in the country."

"Now I am here for another reason," he said presently. "I am here because I am a Democrat. I was born in the Democratic party and I expect to die in it . . . It is not easy for me to stand up here tonight and talk to the American people against the Democratic administration . . . It hurts me. But . . . during my whole public life I put patriotism above partisanship. And when I see danger . . . it is difficult for me to refrain from speaking up.

"Now what are the dangers that I see? The first is the arraignment of class against class. It has been freely predicted that if we were ever to have civil strife again in this country it would come from the appeal to passion and prejudice that comes from the demagogue who would incite one class of our people against the other . . .

"The next thing that I view as being dangerous to our national well-being is government by bureaucracy instead of . . . government by law.

"Just let me quote something from the President's message to Congress: 'In thirty-four months we have built up new instruments of public power. In the hands of a people's government this power is wholesome and proper. But in the hands of political puppets of an economic autocracy such power would provide shackles for the liberties of the people.'

"Now I interpret that to mean: If you are going to have an autocrat, take me, but be very careful about the other fellow. There is a complete answer to that . . . and that answer is . . . We don't want any autocrats . . . We wouldn't even take a good one.

"The next danger that is apparent to me is the vast building up of new bureaus of government, draining the resources of our people into a common pool and redistributing them, not by any process of law, but by the whim of a bureaucratic autocracy.

"Well now, what am I here for? . . . What would I have my party do?

"I would have them reestablish and redeclare the principles that they put forth in that 1932 platform . . . the most compact, the most direct, and the most intelligent platform that was ever put forth by any political party in this country . . . and no administration in the history of the country came into power with . . . a more inescapable mandate than did the party that was inaugurated on the fourth of March in 1933.

"And listen! No candidate in the history of the country ever pledged himself more unequivocally to his party platform than did the President who was inaugurated on that day . . . But what happened to it?"

Father then took the platform up bit by bit—a plank at a time. Over and over again he showed that these solemn promises had not been carried out. He even showed that the administration had sometimes moved in a direction opposite to that which had been promised.

"Now I could go on indefinitely with some of the other planks . . ." he said. "But just let me sum up this way.

"Regulation of the Stock Exchange and the repeal of the Eighteenth Amendment, plus one or two minor planks of the platform . . . have been carried out, but the balance . . . was thrown in the wastebasket. About that there can be no question . . .

"How do you suppose all this happened? Here is the way it happened: The young brain trusters caught the Socialists in swimming and they ran away with their clothes . . .

"It's all right with me if they want to disguise themselves as Norman Thomas, or Karl Marx, or Lenin, or any of the rest of that bunch, but what I won't stand for is allowing them to march under the banner of Jefferson, Jackson, or Cleveland.

"What is worrying me is where does that leave us millions of Democrats? My mind . . . is upon the convention in June . . . The committee on resolutions is about to report, and the preamble of the platform is: 'We, the representatives of the Democratic party in convention assembled, heartily endorse the Democratic administration.'

"What happens to the disciples of Jefferson . . . when that resolution is read? . . . There is only one of two things we can do. We can either take on the mantle of hypocrisy or we can take a walk, and we will probably do the latter . . .

"Now this is pretty tough for me to have to go at my own party this way, but I submit that there is a limit to blind loyalty . . . Why, the fact of this whole thing is (I speak now not only of the executive but of the legislature at the same time) that they promised one set of things, they repudiated that promise, and they launched off on a program of action totally different . . . Well . . . I have known both parties to fail to carry out some of the planks of their platforms, but this is the first time that I have known a party, upon such a huge scale, to not only fail to carry out the planks, but to do the directly opposite thing to what they promised . . .

"Now, suggestions . . . and I make them in good faith:

"Number 1: I suggest to the members of my party on Capitol Hill that they . . . do the right thing and not the expedient thing.

"Next, I suggest . . . that they dig up the 1932 platform . . . and study it, breathe life into it, and follow it . . . In short, make good.

"Third . . . stop compromising with the fundamental principles laid down by Jackson, Jefferson, and Cleveland.

"Fourth, stop attempting to alter the form and structure of our government without recourse to the people as provided in their own Constitution . . .

"Next, I suggest that they read their oath of office to support the Constitution of the United States. And I ask them to remember that they took the oath with their hands on the Holy Bible, thereby calling on God Almighty himself to witness their solemn promise. It is bad enough to disappoint *us*.

"Sixth, I suggest that from this moment on they resolve to make the Constitution again the civil bible of the United States and pay it the same civil respect and reverence that they would religiously pay the Holy Scripture, and I ask them to read from the Holy Scripture the parable of the prodigal son and to follow his example. 'Stop! Stop wasting your substance in a foreign land and come back to your father's house.' "

He paused, and John and I, sitting tensely by the radio, waited impatiently for his final words. They carried a serious message when he spoke them, but many failed to understand the depth of their meaning. Now, after the passage of a score of very troubled years, it is easier to understand what he saw then.

"Now, in conclusion," he said, "let me give this solemn warning.

"There can be only one Capital—Washington or Moscow.

"There can be only one atmosphere of government—the clear, pure, fresh air of free America, or the foul breath of Communistic Russia.

"There can be only one flag—the Stars and Stripes, or the red flag of the godless union of the Soviet.

"There can be only one national anthem—'The Star-Spangled Banner,' or the 'Internationale.'

"There can be only one victor. If the Constitution wins, we win. But if the Constitution——

"Stop! Stop there!

"The Constitution cannot lose! The fact is, it has already won, but the news has not reached certain ears."

It is probable that no other speech by an American not in high public office ever attracted such widespread attention as this startling pronouncement by Father. Carried from coast to coast by radio, it was also extensively reprinted at full length, and reports of it were prominently headlined not only throughout the country, but also abroad. Editorial comment ranged all the way from delighted and enthusiastic acceptance of his point of view to the bitterest kind of denunciation.

"In his masterly summary of the case against the New Deal," said the New York *Herald Tribune*, ". . . he fulfilled all expectations. His aim was deadly as he dealt, plank by plank, with [the] platform, pointing out its violated promises. . . . One must conclude . . . that deep feeling alone impelled him to this unprecedented step and . . . that this same deep feeling will find an echo in countless hearts."

Many other papers expressed comparable views, but opposite opinions were often sharply expressed. Now and again, in fact, acrimonious attacks labeled Father a MOUTHPIECE FOR "DOUGHBAGS," insisting that "The concentrated wealth of the nation," wanting Roosevelt stopped, had "told Al Smith to do the job." Secretary Ickes called Father's speech "the gospel of reaction." John L. Lewis told a meeting of the United Mine Workers that Father had "performed for his masters."

Senator Robinson, who had been Father's running mate in 1928, and who, on the day after the Liberty League dinner, was chosen by administration advisers to give an "official" reply, said that "the brown derby has been discarded for a high hat." "But President Roosevelt himself remained silent on the Smith speech," said an Associated Press dispatch, "telling reporters with a smile . . . that he had nothing to say."

A few days after the Liberty League dinner Father and Mother left New York for Palm Beach, where, for the better part of a month, they were guests of their old friends, Mr. and Mrs. William F. Kenny. For weeks Father had been under even more pressure than usual, and during this Florida vacation he declared a moratorium on political discussion. And in Albany, though for a very different reason, I, too, found myself out of touch with political developments.

I had failed to attend the Liberty League dinner because we were expecting the arrival of our third child. The date was not imminent, but Father and Mother, when they left for Florida, had made plans to return before the expected event. Unfortunately the birth was premature, the baby did not live, and complications confined me to the hospital for an extended period. Father and Mother kept the wires busy between Palm Beach and Albany, but there was nothing they could do, so they did not return until early in March, when I reached home again.

During this time my interest in politics was at a low ebb. Even throughout that spring and summer I gave much less attention to such matters than I usually did.

The Republicans announced very early that their convention would be held in Cleveland, and the Democrats chose Philadelphia. Who the Republican nominee might be was far too difficult to guess in advance, but President Roosevelt's renomination was a foregone conclusion. However, from time to time stories of growing opposition appeared in the papers. Reporters, editorial writers, columnists, and commentators were constantly discussing "new angles" having to do with Father's position, and other signs of opposition were also visible. One New Deal opponent who attracted his full share of attention was Father Coughlin, the so-called "radio priest," who came out as the principal supporter of a new "third party," which, with much fanfare and publicity, chose Representative William Lemke as its candidate for the Presidency. This choice, incidentally, was promptly approved by a number of special pleaders, each of whom, it seemed, had plans for impractical old age pension systems or other utopian ideas.

The Republican Convention, meeting in Cleveland two weeks before the Democrats were scheduled to convene in Philadelphia, nominated Alfred M. Landon of Kansas for President and Colonel Frank Knox of Illinois for Vice-President. What their chances of success were could not be estimated accurately until the Democratic Convention had adjourned. Still, something might be guessed if Father's plan of action could be determined, and reporters never missed an opportunity to question him.

I was spending the summer at Southampton, Long Island, and I saw Father frequently but I had no inkling of his plans.

"I haven't made up my mind yet," he told a group of reporters on June 15. "I have heard and read in the papers that I'm not going to the convention, but none of those reports have come from me."

He was equally uncertain, he said, about "taking a walk" if he did go. Even with the opening of the convention only two days distant he had made no statement about his plans, though the New York *Times* published a story saying he was not expected to be there. Under prominent headlines on the morning of June 22, however, the action he had chosen to take was made public. The headline in the New York *Times* read:

SMITH HEADS GROUP CALLING ON DEMOCRATS TO

REPUDIATE ROOSEVELT AND THE NEW DEAL

The group in question included Father; Bainbridge Colby, Secretary of State in Woodrow Wilson's Cabinet; ex-Senator James A. Reed of Missouri; ex-Governor Joseph B. Ely of Massachusetts; and Judge Daniel F. Cohalan, a former justice of the Supreme Court of New York. Together they had written a letter which was addressed "To the delegates of the Democratic National Convention of 1936," and in it they asked that a "genuine" Democrat be chosen as the Democratic nominee for President. The letter made it clear that those whose names were signed to it differentiated sharply between the principles that had heretofore guided the party and those that were now being furthered by the New Deal, and the letter concluded by saying that if a candidate who accepted the party's established principles was not named, "patriots will know to what standard they must rally."

Papers all across the country made front-page stories of the pronouncement.

DRAMATIC BOMBSHELL, said a headline in the Philadelphia *Inquirer*. The New York *Herald Tribune* called it "unprecedented," and other headlines used other superlatives.

Coming, as it did, just as the delegates were assembling and the convention was about to open, the letter aroused a storm of speculation. It was discussed everywhere, though there was no unanimity of opinion as to its effects.

BOLT ON ROOSEVELT LONG THREATENED, read a headline in the New York *Times*. FIGHT ON NOMINATION IS CLIMAX OF ATTACK BEGUN BY SMITH IN "WALKOUT" WARNINGS.

LOYALTY TO PRESIDENT INTENSIFIED BY REVOLTS, another *Times* headline read on June 23. CONVENTION OPENS TODAY, DELEGATES UNSHAKEN BY SMITH OR COUGHLIN-LEMKE OPPOSITION.

Another headline in the same paper even read, TAMMANY REMAINS "ALL ROOSEVELT."

The fact is that from the first the Roosevelt forces had the convention completely in hand. There was opposition here and there, as when

Senator Carter Glass of Virginia refused to accept a place on the Resolutions Committee. "A mental walkout" was seen by the *Times* in this connection, and other evidences of dissatisfaction were present. By June 26, however, a platform continuing the New Deal had been adopted, the two-thirds rule which had been effective in Democratic conventions for a century had been abrogated, and the opposition that had here and there been apparent was overcome.

During the evening session on June 25 a group of "Al Smith" banners appeared suddenly in the upper balcony, and a free-for-all fight broke out. "Al Smith," the crowd shouted. "We want Al Smith!" But the police broke up the demonstration, and the following day, "after eight hours of eulogistic oratory and demonstration," Franklin Roosevelt was nominated for re-election by acclamation. That session adjourned long after midnight, and the New York *Times* accurately reported in their next morning's paper that "Vice-President Garner will be similarly honored this afternoon."

The convention adjourned on Saturday, June 27, and in the following day's New York *Times Magazine,* James Kieran, in an article about Father and Franklin Roosevelt, pointed out that "again the paths of the two men crossed and the nation wondered what effect the clash would have on the party's fortunes, and the campaign now beginning."

Father's "revolt" had little effect on the election of 1936. By September 20 it was known that he planned to campaign in opposition to the New Deal, and in the end he spoke five times—in New York, Boston, Chicago, Pittsburgh, and Albany. I was with him for all these speeches except the one in Boston, and never had I seen his audiences greet him or cheer his words with greater depth of feeling. But the people of America were preponderantly blind to dangers Father clearly saw, and Franklin Roosevelt carried every state in the Union but Maine and Vermont, and was re-elected with the greatest plurality in the history of American politics.

John and I, with Mary and Emily, our daughters, went to New York to be with Father and Mother on the evening of Election Day. We received the returns by radio in the living room of their apartment, and Father, whom the two children had always called "Umpa," helped them fill in the figures on their blanks.

To his experienced eye the outcome was obvious long before the returns were complete, but the children still kept adding to their record. Their bedtime came, and still they put down figures. Presently Father mildly suggested it was growing late for little girls.

"But, Umpa," Emily objected, "we can't go to bed yet. We haven't heard from Arizona."

I knew how greatly he had been aroused by the contest that had now ended. I understood that his concern was far less for the results of this particular election than for deeper dangers that he very clearly sensed.

"Now we are hearing a whole lot about Communism," he had told a large audience in Albany on the evening of October 31 in his last address of the campaign. "Let me deal with that for a minute, and let me start off by saying . . . don't let anyone tell you that President Roosevelt is a Communist. That is not so. Or don't let anyone tell you that he is a Socialist. That is not so.

"He is neither a Communist nor a Socialist—any more than I am— but something has taken place in this country—there is some certain kind of foreign 'ism' crawling over this country. What it is I don't know. What its first name will be when it is christened I haven't the slightest idea. But I know that it is here, and the sin about it is that he doesn't seem to know it."

Hundreds of thousands of words had been spoken in opposition to the New Deal. Father himself had contributed many of them. Scores of economic, governmental, and constitutional questions had been argued heatedly from coast to coast. On many of these Father himself held strong opinions. But far deeper and more troubling to him than any of these specific problems lay the "foreign 'ism'" that he saw but could not name—the "foreign 'ism' crawling over this country"—the insidious and half-hidden enemy of the American idea that Roosevelt did not seem to know about.

It was clear to me, in the face of my own disappointment, that Father was accepting the outcome of the election better than the rest of us. I even spoke to him about it.

"Well," he replied with a half-smoked cigar still in the corner of his mouth, "I sometimes think that people get just about the government they deserve."

It was in this way that he accepted the outcome of the 1936 election, which, according to the rules of politics, had been decided by the voice of the people. But the "crawling" thing still troubled him, for he understood that it was not only the President who did not seem to know about it. Most of the people of America did not seem to know about it either.

CHAPTER FIFTEEN

The Last Days of the Happy Warrior

IN THE SPRING OF 1937 Mother and Father sailed from New York on Father's first voyage to Europe. Mother and I had gone abroad with our friends the Kennys in 1925, but Father had never been outside the United States before, except for a short visit to Havana in 1928, and he looked forward eagerly to the experience.

He and Mother did not make the trip alone, but were accompanied throughout by Mr. and Mrs. Eugene L. Garey, Justice and Mrs. Edward J. McGoldrick, and Mr. and Mrs. Daniel J. Mooney. Sailing directly for Naples, they were also accompanied for the duration of their visit to Italy by Mr. and Mrs. Richard A. Carroon and by the Reverend Dr. Fulton J. Sheen, who, as a professor at the Catholic University in Washington, had not yet become either a bishop or a television celebrity.

When Father was asked by reporters why he was going, he replied merely that he wanted to see Europe. "What does anybody go for?" he asked. Word of his proposed journey had no sooner become known than a newspaper syndicate asked him to write a series of articles on his experiences and observations, and when sailing time came, he was under contract to write five articles, for each of which he was to receive a thousand dollars.

My husband had to be in Albany when Mother and Father sailed, but all the other members of the family were at the dock, and, as the New York *Sun* put it, "a host of notables" saw them off as well. So many friends came to the ship, and so many remembrances arrived that their rooms were almost literally packed with flowers, packages, and visitors, while halfway across Manhattan Island a huge American

Major John A. Warner appears on Major Bowes' "Amateur Hour" in the 1930s, and is greeted by Colonel Theodore Roosevelt, Jr., who was his classmate at Harvard, as well as by Major Bowes, Walter P. Chrysler (sponsor of the program), and his father-in-law, the former Governor of New York.

Governor and Mrs. Smith, accompanied by Bishop Ralph L. Hayes, and Monsignor Fulton J. Sheen of the Catholic University in Washington, on May 26, 1937, when the Governor and his wife were received by His Holiness, Pope Pius XI.

Republican candidate and Democratic supporter. Governor Smith boards Wendell Willkie's campaign train at Harmon, New York, during the 1940 Presidential campaign.

Governor and Mrs. Smith, having attended Pontifical Mass at St. Patrick's Cathedral, take part in the Easter parade on Fifth Avenue in New York City on April 13, 1941.

flag, waving from the topmost terrace of the Empire State Building, signaled bon voyage from Father's associates there.

"Al Smith at 64 is taking his first trip to Europe," wrote Benjamin DeCasseres in his newspaper column. "Aside from President Roosevelt himself, it is doubtful whether any other American could excite more interest in Europe than our own modern *Innocent Abroad* . . . He brings them no discourses on Homer or Dante or Emerson. What he brings them is an administrative and organizing brain that is the equal of any in Europe or America."

Arriving in Naples late in May and sailing from Ireland only six weeks later, the party had none too much time in which to see even those portions of Europe they visited. Still, between the ruins of Pompeii, which they saw the day after they reached Naples, and the Lakes of Killarney, which they saw the day before they sailed for home, they found time for more than the average tourist's experiences.

When they arrived in Rome they were received in private audience by Pope Pius XI at the papal summer palace at Castel Gandolfo, and called on the papal secretary of state, Eugenio Cardinal Pacelli, who, two years later, was to become Pope Pius XII. Meanwhile the people of Castel Gandolfo, inaccurately informed about Father's position, were immensely interested in seeing this much publicized visitor from America.

"The little town that lies below the papal summer palace here," said a dispatch from Castel Gandolfo to the New York *Herald Tribune,* "buzzed with excitement today as word spread among the peasants that 'the President of the United States is coming to see the Holy Father!' It was impossible to convince the townsfolk that Alfred E. Smith was not the President, and when he arrived they greeted him with shouts of *'Viva il Presidente!'* "

An audience with Mussolini came a few days later, and it was clear that the Italian dictator labored under no delusions as to Father's place in the American scheme of things.

"The Premier asked me twice," Father wrote in one of his newspaper articles, "if there was anything in the Constitution of the United States to prevent a President from having a third term, and . . . with a pronounced smile, he said 'How is the New Deal?' and I promptly replied that, in my opinion, it was 'not so hot.' "

After three weeks in Italy and southern France, Father's party arrived in Paris. Received there by both President Lebrun and Premier

Leon Blum, Father gave his first public address in Europe on June 14 before the American Club of Paris.

"In spite of the present tendency among nations to discard democracy and turn to dictatorship for security," he said, with recent European developments in mind, "I still believe that the form of government in the United States is the best in the world . . . Too many people today seem to have the idea that the government is the master rather than the servant of the people. They give up liberty in the hope of gaining security, but I am afraid that someday they are going to wake up and find that they have lost both."

Exactly three years later—to the day—the Germans entered the capital of defeated France.

To Father, the high lights of the time he spent in England were his visits to the House of Commons while it was in session, and the afternoon he visited with Winston Churchill in the country.

From London the party made their way to Ireland, and the day after their arrival in Dublin they drove to the little village of Moate, where Father's grandmother had been born. He even met some people there who claimed to be relatives, but time was growing short, and after a motor trip to the Lakes of Killarney the group drove to Queenstown, where they went aboard the S.S. *Manhattan,* bound for New York.

"I thanked God," Father wrote in referring to the last day of the voyage home, "for permitting me to be born in His country, the United States of America."

In the years since Father had left Albany he had firmly established himself as a businessman, but at no time had he ever succeeded in withdrawing wholly from public affairs. It was not that he had any wish to return to public office. Even when he had entered the contest for the Presidential nomination in 1932 he had not done so with any personal political ambitions in mind, and this was just as true and much more obvious in 1936. However, public problems often seemed to point to him, and when, in 1938, a new state Constitutional Convention was called, Father, from the very first, was counted upon to play an important part in it.

Elected a member of this new Constitutional Convention in November 1937, he was chosen honorary president despite the fact that there were ninety-two Republicans in the convention to only seventy-five Democrats. But this did not tell the whole story, for the Democratic members themselves were divided into a New Deal faction that was headed by Senator Robert F. Wagner and an anti-New Deal faction that looked to Father for leadership, and the fact that 1938 was an election year seemed to encourage many of the Republicans to consider their political needs ahead of the constitutional needs of the state. I remember how disappointed Father was because the convention was lacking in the outstanding leadership that had been so plainly evident in the Constitutional Convention of 1915.

The convention met in Albany in April, but it was only well under way when, on Monday, May 16, Father and two men with whom he had long worked closely in support of the Catholic Charities of New York, were honored at the Waldorf-Astoria Hotel in a solemn ceremony at which all three were made "Privy Chamberlains of the Cape and Sword"—officers of the Pope's official household. The three honored were Father, John S. Burke, and John Thomas Smith, and the investiture was held under the direction of Cardinal Hayes on behalf of His Holiness Pope Pius XI.

Chamberlains of the Cape and Sword have existed at the papal court since the sixteenth century. Originally chosen only from among the nobility, they are now selected from "those of all nations who are outstanding in their devotion to the Church."

At this investiture Father was honored as being "internationally known for liberal and constructive leadership in statecraft, business, and private charitable work." Mr. Burke, who had succeeded Father's old friend, Michael Friedsam, as the president of B. Altman & Company, was honored as "an outstanding leader in business and art, who has ever contributed generously of his time, thought and means to Catholic Charities." And Mr. John Thomas Smith, counsel to General Motors Corporation, was honored for his "unflagging zeal in support of Catholic action" and for charities covering "a wide field of varied endeavors for the welfare of human kind."

In Albany the work of the Constitutional Convention continued through the summer. So far as really constructive proposals were concerned, however, little was accomplished. Despite Father's insistence that the revised constitution should be put into so few words that a copy of it might be carried in one's pocket, the final draft contained about fifty thousand words and it accomplished far less in weeding out weaknesses than had been accomplished by the amendments that had been passed at Father's urging while he had been Governor.

During part of the time the Constitutional Convention was in session, John and I, with our two daughters, were at Southampton, Long Island, where Father came to see us on occasional weekends. And here, as the month of July approached its end, we arranged to have a party for Mary on her eleventh birthday. We asked her to make out a list of guests she would like to invite, and in doing so she not only included her grandfather, but also spoke to him about it on one of his weekend visits.

"Well, I'd like very much to come," he assured her, "but you see, I'm a delegate at the convention and I will have to be in Albany on that day."

"Isn't there anybody who can let you off?" she asked.

"Judge Frederick E. Crane is the 'boss,'" he explained. "If anyone could let me off I should think he would be the man."

That was enough explanation for Mary, and having obtained the judge's address, she wrote him as follows:

Dear Judge Crane:

Monday, July 25, is my birthday. My grandfather says you are the boss of the convention. So would you allow my grandfather to stay down here and be with me on my birthday? Hoping this will not be too much trouble for you,

Love,
Mary Warner.

Judge Crane was prompt in his reply, but he said that Mary's grandfather was very much needed at the convention. "If you can spare him on Monday for our sakes," he continued, "I am sure he will feel so ashamed to have been away from you on your birthday that he will see that you celebrate it all over again. So you will have two birthdays. The Constitutional Convention, through me, wishes you a very happy and joyous time."

The convention adjourned in September and the results of its work were offered to the people of the state in nine proposed amendments which were voted on in the November election. Three of the amendments were defeated, and others might have been with very little loss to the state. Much of what was accepted, as Father had already pointed out, had to do with subjects that are not properly a part of a state constitution—grade crossings, slum clearance, wages and hours, for example—and there is little doubt that Father was right in believing that the constitution of the state of New York was in as much need of revision after the convention had adjourned as before it met.

More than the people of the United States realized at the time, events abroad during the late 1930s were making themselves felt in our affairs. Hitler invaded Austria early in 1938. A few months later Prime Minister Chamberlain of Great Britain, too intent on "peace in our time," yielded in the face of Hitler's demands at Munich, and Czechoslovakia was tragically partitioned. Developments in 1939 were even more threatening and tragic. Czechoslovakia disappeared as an independent nation. Italy invaded Albania and joined Germany in a military alliance. Nazi Germany and the Soviet Union signed a ten-year nonaggression treaty. And on September 1 Hitler invaded Poland and World War II began.

Two years earlier, when preliminary warnings of war had already been apparent, a "Neutrality Act" had been passed by Congress. It forbade the export of arms and ammunition to belligerents, the sale in this country of belligerents' securities, or the use of American ships for carrying munitions. Furthermore, under the so-called "cash and carry" clause, it required belligerents to pay for munitions upon purchase and to carry all such purchases in their own ships.

The weaknesses of this law became glaringly evident in the light of the struggle that had now broken out in Europe, and President Roosevelt was quick to ask that the act be amended. In Congress, however, a strong bloc formed in opposition to the proposed change, and Father, speaking over the radio on the evening of October 1, 1939, made it clear that his opposition to the New Deal did not prevent his support of the President in this instance.

"Mr. Roosevelt is so clearly right, so obviously on the side of common sense and of sound judgment and of patriotism," he said in reference to the suggested changes in the Neutrality Act, "that only those who lack an understanding of the issue will oppose him."

He characterized the distinction between types of cargoes as "essentially the bunk," and opposed the arms embargo because it proscribed only one kind of trade.

"The best speech so far made on the so-called 'Neutrality' issue was made Sunday night by Al Smith," said the Des Moines *Register* in an editorial, and other newspaper comments in the Middle West, where isolationism was strongest, reflected much the same point of view.

Father was never one to keep a diary or otherwise to record his day-to-day activities, but he had long since found a kind of little pocket notebook that ideally suited his needs—a little leather covered affair about two and a half inches wide and four inches long. The year's calendar occupied the notebook's first page, and the rest of the book was given over to the days of the year—three days to a page and six ruled lines for each day.

Each year Mary Carr, Father's secretary, prepared one of these notebooks in advance of January 1, noting the various birthdays and other anniversaries he especially wished to remember. These varied a little from year to year, and once, having gone through one of the notebooks, I counted seventy-three recorded birthdays and other anniversaries, all of which—by gift, letter, telegram, or telephone call—he wished to remember.

In addition all his appointments were carefully listed—board meetings, business engagements, luncheons, speeches, dinners—and at the very end of the book were the addresses and telephone numbers of every member of the family and forty or fifty personal friends.

In effect these notebooks were Father's guidebooks. They reminded him of his engagements and his duties. In use each day throughout the year, and often referred to almost every hour, they were infinitely useful, but they were mere engagement books, utterly devoid of comment or description. Neither here nor elsewhere was he inclined to keep any record of his daily doings or observations. Now and then some clipping or cartoon, some program or letter or telegram he had received would strike him as being worthy of special attention, but only occasionally did he save one, and even then he would call Mary Carr into his office from time to time and clear away the collected items usually with no thought whatever of keeping anything "for the record." And unfortunately the other members of our family have also been little inclined to record what went on before our eyes during so many active years. Thus many details of Father's life, some of which must have been of more than ordinary interest, have been lost, and this is doubly true of the years that followed his retirement from public office. Prior to that time his activities had been constantly in the news. Thereafter he saw reporters only now and then, and much less of what he did appeared in print.

As 1939 approached its end and the country's interest in the Presidential year of 1940 grew, it was evident that President Roosevelt was not likely to be guided by the precedent that a President should limit his stay in office to a maximum of two terms.

Ever since Father had left Albany, the reporters had made his birthday the occasion for a detailed press conference, and on December 30, 1939, a group of them came by appointment to his office in the Empire State Building. Naturally their questions were political from the first, and Father was entirely willing to reply.

"What would you like to see in the 1940 Democratic platform?" one reporter asked.

"It's what I *don't* want to see that is more important," Father replied. "Here and there the New Deal has accomplished something worth while, but the fundamental policy throughout the New Deal has been to challenge the American form of government.

"Now the way to do that, if it is desirable, is to change the Constitution. It just won't do to ignore the Constitution, or to circumvent it after 150 years."

"What about a third term for Roosevelt?" he was asked.

"I think, and always have thought," he replied, "that two terms are enough for any man. That has been an unwritten part of our Constitution since the days of Washington."

He was asked to express his opinion about the New Deal.

"It has been frankly admitted by them," he replied, "that 50 per cent of the whole thing is experimentation ... If the platform comes out in fulsome praise of the New Deal, it will be time to get the walking shoes out again."

This was material for headlines.

TWO TERMS ENOUGH SAYS EX-GOV. SMITH, read one in the New York *World-Telegram*.

Some six weeks after the news of this interview had been published, Father was the guest of honor at the annual dinner of the New York Academy of Public Education. Here, before a gathering of leading educators, he was awarded the Academy's medal for distinguished service to education, and Dr. John H. Finley, in reviewing Father's contributions, especially cited the part he had played as Governor in increasing the salaries of teachers and expanding the educational facilities of the state.

Unable to be present, Dr. Frank P. Graves, Commissioner of Education and president of the University of the State of New York, wrote to the chairman and, in reference to Father, expressed the opinion that "In my judgment, no one has ever been a better friend to public education in New York, and it is most appropriate that the ... Academy ... should make this recognition of his devotion to the field which they represent. He has repeatedly aided education even when his advocacy conflicted with his own political interest."

This event, gratifying though it was to Father, was almost lost in a world in which war had once again become the vital occupation of many nations. World War II had been under way since the first of September, 1939, and now, as the spring of 1940 arrived, Scandinavia, the Netherlands, and Belgium were swept into the struggle. In rapid succession Winston Churchill became Prime Minister of Great Britain, German bombers blasted surprised and defenseless Rotterdam, and President Roosevelt asked for a huge defense appropriation. The German Army overran France. The British miraculously succeeded in withdrawing their outnumbered army from Dunkerque. Italy declared war on France. And in the United States, where many people imagined themselves to be more remote than they really were from the European struggle, both Democrats and Republicans made ready for their quadrennial Presidential conventions.

The overwhelming New Deal victories of the preceding eight years had severely weakened the Republican party and led to divided councils when unity of action was of prime importance. Even six months before the convention met, when Father had been interviewed on his birthday, he had commented on the lack of widely accepted Republican leadership. Senator Taft of Ohio and Senator Vandenberg of Michigan were both potential Presidential candidates, but neither seemed to have more than limited support, and there were no others of importance. Thomas E. Dewey, the District Attorney of New York, was sometimes mentioned, but his position was not strong at that time for only two years earlier, when he had been the Republican candidate for Governor of New York, he had been defeated by Herbert H. Lehman.

Between December 1939 and June 1940 a remarkable development had taken place. In December, Father had included Wendell Willkie in a list of seven Democratic Presidential possibilities and had expressed a willingness to support him, but by June this newcomer to American politics, who had been properly included among the Democrats only six months earlier, was being prominently mentioned for the Republican nomination. Furthermore, when the Republicans met in June, he swept the convention delegates from their feet and, on the sixth ballot, was nominated by them for President.

Three weeks later the Democratic Convention was held in Chicago. Father had no wish to attend, for even before it met he was certain of its outcome. Nevertheless, its action in nominating Roosevelt for a third term greatly troubled him, and he was horrified when, over the radio, he heard Senator Carter Glass hissed and booed because, in offering Jim Farley's name to the convention, the venerable Senator from Virginia referred to the fact that Thomas Jefferson, the author of the Declaration of Independence and the founder of the Democratic party, had warned against a third term for any President.

It could hardly have been a surprise to anyone when Father, as a result of these developments, announced that he would support Wendell Willkie, but the story made the headlines, nevertheless.

In the New York *Times* of July 31, 1940, a prominent front-page story began as follows:

SMITH AGAIN BOLTS

TO FIGHT NEW DEAL;

SUPPORTS WILLKIE

SAYS DEFEAT IS NEEDED TO RID

DEMOCRATIC PARTY OF BLOC

NOW IN CONTROL OF IT

CONDEMNS THIRD TERM

This account outlined Father's whole record of opposition to the New Deal, and included a quotation from Thomas Jefferson that Father's statement had contained.

" 'Should a President consent to be a candidate for a third term,' " Father quoted Jefferson as having written, " 'I trust he would be rejected on this demonstration of ambitious views.' "

When Father offered to campaign in support of Wendell Willkie he was promptly given a part in the Republican program, and I was with him each time he spoke. Mr. Willkie naturally carried the greatest campaign burden, and his campaign train, equipped and manned much as Father's had been twelve years before, covered far more ground than we did. Nevertheless, as we made our way back and forth in the private car that served as Father's traveling headquarters we found ourselves once more surrounded by the pressure and excitement that are always a part of campaign activities. In Brooklyn and New York, in Chicago, Boston, Philadelphia, and elsewhere the halls were just as packed, the crowds just as enthusiastic, and the various versions of "The Sidewalks of New York" were just as familiar. Everyone's hours were just as irregular as they had ever been. Interruptions were just as numerous. And Father, always at his best under such conditions, was just as sharp in comment, just as quick in repartee, and just as telling and pointed in attack as I had ever seen him.

Speaking at the Brooklyn Academy of Music on the evening of October 23, he gave his conception of a speech Franklin D. Roosevelt might have made eight years before if he had promised only what he was actually going to perform.

"If I am elected President," Father quoted Mr. Roosevelt as saying in this imaginary speech, all the while imitating the President's method of delivery, "I am going to double the national debt . . . reduce the value of the dollar . . . [and] create class hatred as it has never been known in this country before.

"If I am elected President, I will sign more unconstitutional bills than any other President in the history of the country. Needless for me to say, I am going to ignore the party platform and I am going to increase the cost of government from five billion in 1932 to nine billion, one hundred million in 1940."

Father paused at that point and returned to his usual manner.

"Strange as it seems," he said very seriously, "that's exactly what happened. That is the record of eight years—and the hero of that record is referred to as the indispensable man."

Frequently during the campaign he brought his sharpest humor into play. In Philadelphia he aroused his audience to gales of laughter when he referred to President Roosevelt's "nonpolitical" inspection trips, one of which had taken the President to the Revolutionary battlefield of Saratoga.

"All they have there," he explained, "is a lot of grass, some monuments, a few insignia to mark historic spots, and——"

He hesitated.

"—one comfort station," he added.

However, these bits of barbed humor were only high lights. His speeches were basically serious, especially when he was answering the argument that the country needed Roosevelt for a third term because of his experience.

"Experience," Father insisted, "can't *possibly* be an argument for breaking the third-term tradition, because if you offer that argument now you have to admit that at the end of the third term he has four more years of experience, and at the end of a fourth term you might just as well elect him for life."

Father's speeches, filled with biting criticism and cogent arguments, were given in rapid sequence in the latter part of October. His final address was over a national radio hookup on the evening before election. The sharpness of his attacks, and notably the caustic humor with which his speeches had been punctuated, had attracted much attention, and the listening audience he had for that final radio address must have been a large one. But now he cast aside all thought of wit and humor, and when he went on the air he was in deadly earnest.

His appeal was to the people of America, each one of whom, he made clear, was a "stockholder" in America itself. And no one, when Father had finished speaking, could have failed to understand how immeasurably great he believed America was as an enterprise for furthering the freedom, the happiness and the welfare of mankind.

More voters went to the polls on November 5, 1940, than ever before in the history of the United States, and the air was tense with excitement over the outcome. In 1932 Roosevelt's victory had been obvious in advance, and that had been even truer in 1936. But now, for the first time in American history, the tradition against a third term for any President was being challenged, and the outcome was in doubt.

Mother and Father were surrounded on the evening of Election Day by every member of our family. A few friends were there also, and all of us were supporters of Wendell Willkie. But from the first the returns ran heavily against him. Maine and Vermont, as always, remained in the Republican column, but no other state of the eastern seaboard did, and Roosevelt's third victory was soon obvious.

Despite the disappointing outcome of the election Father once again was able to accept the result more philosophically than the rest of us. He was troubled, I know, but he accepted the verdict as the voice of the people, perhaps contenting himself with the fact that the opposition had made enormous gains, and with the thought that the time would surely come when the country would return to the basic principles by which he himself was guided.

President Roosevelt was inaugurated for the third time on January 20, 1941, but ten days before that event, in a radio speech over a national hookup, Father, with all thought of the election already relegated to the past, and with his mind intent upon the country's great international problem, came out in firm support of a proposal the President had just made for the enactment of "Lend-Lease" legislation designed to aid the nations that were fighting Hitler.

"The President," he pointed out as he addressed his national radio audience in reference to the proposed bill, "spoke for the overwhelming majority on Sunday . . . There is no political difference on the stand we must take in opposition to the dictators in the defense of our own country."

For fifteen minutes he spoke on the need for aiding Great Britain against Germany and in support of the plan President Roosevelt had advanced.

"Every red-blooded American," he insisted in his conclusion, "will support the President in his purpose to give full aid to Britain."

ROOSEVELT POLICY BACKED BY SMITH was a common headline as papers from coast to coast carried the story.

I was in Florida at the time, and though I heard the speech over the air and read the newspaper stories that reported it, I heard nothing directly from Father for about ten days. It was only then that I received a letter which read, in part, as follows:

Dear Emily:

I called Albany last night to find out how the children were and I talked to both of them on the telephone—also to John.

Mary tells me in a letter that she had her examination in English but does not know yet what her marks are. The following is an extract from her letter.

"It has been very cold up here and we are going skating in school."

That reminded me . . . of a letter . . . sent by a young man . . . in the First World War. It was . . . to his mother . . . and he said: "I am in the Y.M.C.A. with a piano playing in my uniform."

The letter was signed "Pop" and a postscript was appended.

P. S. I am enclosing . . . a cablegram I received from Winston Churchill . . . It is a rather remarkable thing . . . that a man with the worries . . . that must be Churchill's would take time to read a speech and send a cable.

The cablegram read as follows:

THE HONORABLE ALFRED SMITH

EMPIRE STATE BUILDING NYC

DELIGHTED TO READ YOUR STIRRING SPEECH ALL KIND REGARDS

WINSTON CHURCHILL

War had not yet come to the United States, but throughout 1941 war was in the air. The Lend-Lease bill was pushed through Congress over the opposition of the isolationists, and a flood of American equipment and supplies began to move across the Atlantic. German and Italian ships in American ports were seized. President Roosevelt proclaimed an unlimited emergency and ordered the closing of German and Italian consulates in the United States by July 10. By mid-August the President and the Prime Minister of Great Britain had announced an agreement on war aims in the Atlantic Charter.

In July, American troops occupied bases in Iceland. In September an American destroyer was attacked by a German submarine in the Atlantic, and in October one was sunk with the loss of a hundred lives. Within another month a victorious German Army stood at the gates of Moscow, and on December 7 the Japanese attacked Pearl Harbor.

Throughout the whole of this uneasy period Father had been busying himself with new responsibilities. The tasks he had already assumed were numerous, and he was meticulous in attending to them all. He continued his regular attendance at the many board meetings that were on his schedule, and somehow found the time to join still other boards. For years he had been chairman of the Archbishop's Committee of the Laity, through which, along with John S. Burke and John A. Coleman, he continued to play a very important part in raising funds for Catholic Charities. Now he was also a member of the board of directors of St. Vincent's Hospital, of the Beekman Street Hospital, and of the New York Foundling Hospital. Two years before, he had been made a trustee of the Catholic University of America in Washington. He took part in the "March of Dimes" campaigns, and with the outbreak of the war he never failed to play an active part in War Bond drives, in Red Cross campaigns, and in United Hospital campaigns. Furthermore, when the United Service Organization—the USO—was formed, he became a director, busying himself from then on in its behalf.

His mail was always very heavy. Endless letters asked for autographs, for photographs, and even for autographed brown derbies. Letters, telegrams, and telephone calls were forever arriving from people who were looking for jobs or who needed money, and requests for him to speak in almost every corner of the country made up a considerable part of his correspondence.

Even Mary Carr, who was his secretary from the time he left public life, would undoubtedly find it impossible to estimate the number of autographed photographs he signed. Usually he wrote "To——, with best wishes of Alfred E. Smith," though photographs for personal friends were ordinarily signed "with affectionate regards." The photographs that went to members of the family were almost always signed "with love," but that expression went to others very, very rarely, though Mary Carr possesses one.

He never learned to drive a car but he had two, and when ration cards for gasoline were issued in 1942, he was urged, because of the war work to which he gave so much of his time, to ask for more than an "A" card—that minimum allowance permitted any owner of a car. He refused, however, though he soon learned that with only an "A" card the cars could not be driven very far. For instance, he could no longer drive to Southhampton, where John and I and the children were to spend the summer. In fact, he could very rarely make the shorter trips to Arthur's home or Catherine's in Rye.

"I think I'd better sell the cars," he decided, and he sold one at once. But he had the second one laid up in Catherine's garage in Rye, having offered her a commission if she could find a buyer for it.

It was at about this time that a new War Bond campaign began, and as a part of it arrangements were made with the telephone company for Father, during certain hours, to accept personally all telephone calls from those who would purchase a bond through him. The idea caught the attention of the public, and for hours he sat at the telephone while a corps of telephone operators, stenographers, and clerks scheduled the calls to his telephone, made detailed records of names and addresses, and recorded the orders that were received. It was a heavy task but he kept at it without letup. And in the midst of this my sister Catherine, wishing to play her part in adding to the total of Father's bond sales, put in her own call. When Father answered, she did not give her name.

"I would like to buy a seventy-five-dollar bond," was all she said when she heard his familiar voice.

Scores and scores of calls from strangers had reached him by that time, and his task must have come to be almost automatic, but he recognized Catherine's voice at once.

"Where did *you* get seventy-five bucks?" he asked.

"From you," she replied. "I have just sold your car, and you owe me that much commission."

With both cars gone Father obviously no longer needed John, his chauffeur. But with gasoline so strictly rationed an out-of-work chauffeur might not find a new position easily, and Father felt some responsibility in the matter. He remembered that Vincent Astor was a commander in the Navy and that he was on duty at the Brooklyn Navy Yard, where, conceivably, a good chauffeur might find work. So a call was put in for Commander Astor.

"Send him over to see me," the commander suggested when Father had explained the situation. And John, having gone to the Navy Yard, was given a job at once, and he has been Mr. Astor's chauffeur ever since.

Now Father found it necessary to make his way about the city in taxicabs. When he started his first trip home, however, it was in the midst of a heavy downpour and, as so often seems to be the case at such times, every taxicab was occupied. It was only with some difficulty that he managed to find standing room in a crowded bus. But New York's Fifth Avenue buses do not stop at every block, and Father, whose destination was near the corner of 63rd Street, was uncertain whether to get off at 62nd or at 64th, though this was important in view of the way the rain was coming down. When the bus had passed 59th Street, therefore, he pushed his way through the crowded aisle up beside the driver.

"Which is your closest stop to 63rd Street?" he asked.

The driver glanced up and recognized his questioning passenger at once.

"O.K., Al," he replied, and presently the bus halted directly before the sidewalk awning at 820 Fifth Avenue.

Father thanked the driver for his thoughtfulness, but as he alighted he also found it necessary to lift his hat in acknowledgment of the friendly cheers and applause of his fellow passengers.

During these war years Father used taxicabs very frequently and always had a friendly word for the drivers. When he tipped them, for instance, he was almost certain to say something like "Here. Buy yourself a cigar."

Coming home with him one day, I heard him say exactly that when we left the cab, though this time his suggestion was hardly appropriate.

"You evidently didn't notice," I remarked as we made our way to the elevator, "that our driver was a woman."

During the first year of the war John and I continued to live in Albany, though we visited New York now and then. As the strength of the Allies grew and as more and more conquered or reconquered territory fell into their hands, the task of policing and administering it grew immensely. Large numbers of officers and men were required for duty in regions in which no government existed or where the government that remained was weak, and John, with years of experience as superintendent of the state police, was offered a commission as a lieutenant colonel. He accepted at once, and in 1943, after a short period of instruction and indoctrination, first at the University of Virginia and then in London, he was sent to Italy.

With his departure I found myself uncomfortably alone in our house in Albany, for both our daughters were in boarding school. Father and Mother were alone too, so I closed the Albany house and joined them in New York.

More and more, as the war progressed, New York had come to be a veritable mecca for the great and near great of the world. Endless foreign missions in America on endless errands always spent some part of their time in New York City, and rarely did any of those who headed these missions fail to visit the observation stations on the 86th and the 102nd floors of the Empire State Building. For ordinary visitors, and even for mildly out-of-the-ordinary ones, the usual facilities offered by the building served well enough. Many "very important people," however—VIPs, as they came to be known during the war—called for special handling, and Father, who was known at least by reputation to most of them, often found himself serving as a sort of reception committee and guide when they visited the Empire State Building tower.

Under the date of November 30, 1942, for example, I find, in one of his engagement books, the following notations:

"Mrs. Raskob's birthday

"Patsy Raskob's

"10:30—John R. Todd

"12:00—TOWER—President of Ecuador

"1:00—Thos. J. Watson—lunch"

And there were other engagements in the afternoon.

Now and again these visitors to the tower were not only VIPs, but friends as well, as had been the case before the war began when Winston Churchill came. For the most part, however, they were strangers of more or less importance for whom protocol and our country's interest suggested careful and courteous treatment.

Incidentally, during one of Winston Churchill's pre-war visits to New York, Father invited him to lunch, and John and I were included. A few days later we were shocked to hear that the British statesman had been knocked down by a taxicab and was in a hospital. Father went at once to see him. As soon as he entered the room he asked if Mr. Churchill was well enough for them to be left alone for a little while.

This was a signal for the nurse to leave.

"I suppose," Father began when the door closed, "that you think of me as a politician, though I naturally hope that you may also think of me as a statesman. But just now I am a diagnostician, and I have brought you a little medicine."

With that, he produced a bottle of scotch.

Busy though Father was throughout this critical period, I found it possible to spend much time with him. We had breakfast together every morning, and I often delayed his departure for the office—or tried to —in order to prolong some discussion we had begun. Much of his time was given over to war work—to hospital drives and the USO, to public dinners and radio addresses—but no matter how busy he was during the week he usually managed, at least during the winter, to lunch on Saturdays with a most unusual group. Known as the "Occasional Thinkers," and made up of a dozen or fifteen members, this unique organization no doubt had its serious moments, but it had a well-developed sense of humor too. Headed by the "Sage," who was Dr. Nicholas Murray Butler, President of Columbia University, the members, whatever the subject of their discussions might be, never permitted themselves to grow pompous or didactic. They even prepared a special songbook for use at their luncheons, and the "Thinkers' Chorus," which they sang to the tune of the "Tinkers' Chorus" from *Robin Hood,* was as follows:

> Oh merry, merry, very merry gentlemen are we,
>   Meeting for lunch together
> On Saturdays in winter when the frost is on the tee
>   And it isn't golfing weather.
> We eat, eat, eat and we talk, talk, talk
>   And we do a deal of drinking.
> We're men of mettle and in fine old fettle
>   And only occasional thinking.

This association with men who were wise enough to know that life should not be forever serious meant a great deal to Father, who had his own well-developed sense of proportion. Often on quiet evenings at home when only Mother and I were with him, he retold many humorous stories of his days in Albany and gave me a new understanding of political values as he recounted anecdotes of political supporters and opponents. Sometimes he even sang old political songs, some of which were parodies. One of these, I remember, was "The Sharing of the Green," a title which plainly suggests the kind of doubtful political activity it pretended to recount. He often explained the political methods he had developed, too. I remember what he said, for example, when he told me how he went about preparing a speech.

"Talk to the man on the street in language he can really understand," he advised, "not in Court of Appeals language."

Occasionally when we were talking of events I personally had seen, I attempted to draw him out. His autobiography, *Up to Now*, had been written in 1929, and because it recounted nothing beyond his 1928 campaign for the Presidency, I suggested that he add to what he had written.

"Why don't you write a sequel to *Up to Now?*" I asked. "There are so many more things that you could say."

He shook his head.

"We are at war," he replied. "Everyone must support the government. I will never write a word in criticism of the Administration until Germany and Japan have both been beaten. They come first."

And he held to that determination so far as his public statements were concerned, but he still opposed most of the concepts of the New Deal and in private he never permitted that fact to remain in any doubt.

Early in December 1943 it began to be apparent that many others besides the members of our family were aware that Father's seventieth birthday would soon arrive. Ten years before, he had accepted the responsibility of forming a committee then known as the Cardinal's Committee of the Laity, but renamed the Archbishop's Committee after the death of Cardinal Hayes. In the ten years of its existence this committee had raised almost two and a half million dollars for Catholic Charities, of which Father had personally raised $285,000. The work of the committee, incidentally, was carried on from offices in the Empire State Building which had been provided by the owners of the building at Father's instigation, and as his birthday approached, his associates on the committee decided to celebrate that anniversary with more than ordinary enthusiasm. But other plans were also under way, and when he arrived at his office on the morning of December 30, a very busy day awaited him.

It seems to be a common tendency to accept most birthdays readily enough. The person who is forty-eight is unlikely to be troubled when he turns forty-nine. But the next step is apt to be more difficult, as most of those who have taken it will agree. And Father, having awakened on the morning of December 30, 1943, found himself confronted with the fact that he was seventy.

I recall no particular difference in his attitude as we had breakfast together, and if there was any change in his manner when he left for the office, I was not conscious of it. But Mary Carr recalls that when he reached his office on the thirty-second floor of the Empire State Building his manner was unusually sober, as if, in reaching seventy, he had been struck by the fact that another decade, and not merely another year, had slipped into the past.

More than the usual accumulation of mail was waiting for him, and many gifts had arrived. The office was filled with flowers and packages, and Billy Roy, who had been Father's bodyguard since early in his first term as Governor, and who was still employed in that capacity in Father's office, had been busy arranging everything. Loyal for so many years and always close to Father, he was much impressed by the importance of this anniversary. And Mary Carr, who always opened Father's letters and placed them in a pile upon his desk, had topped the pile, on this particular morning, with a short note that was typed on heavy light blue stationery.

It read as follows:

THE WHITE HOUSE
   WASHINGTON

December 27, 1943

Dear Al:

Our friends tell me that you are about to attain to the dignity of three score years and ten.

That has been known from time immemorial as the Scriptural age. It is a noble age by every manner of reckoning. On that account a man's friends like to make it the occasion of a testimonial in his behalf. I wish it were possible for me to join those who are honoring you next Thursday evening. But I shall be thinking of you on that happy occasion, and I send you hearty congratulations and warmest personal greetings.

With every good wish,
Very sincerely yours,
Franklin D. Roosevelt.

Honorable Alfred E. Smith,
New York, N.Y.

Letters from ex-Chief Justice of the United States Charles E. Hughes, from Nathan L. Miller, and from Herbert H. Lehman, all former Governors of New York, were there also, and accompanying a letter from Governor Thomas E. Dewey was a present.

"From the paneling in the office in which you rendered eight years of great service to the State of New York," Governor Dewey wrote, "I have had made a little paper weight which you might like to have upon your desk, not for itself, but as a continuing reminder that thirteen million people have not forgotten your loyalty to them and that they will love and respect you for so long as men revere great qualities in other men."

Other letters waited to be opened, or were soon to arrive, from John W. Davis, Alf M. Landon, and Wendell Willkie, three former Presidential candidates—from John D. Rockefeller, Jr.—from Mrs. Thomas A. Edison—from Walter Lippmann. Letters came from justices and judges, from members of the Cabinet, from Senators and Representatives in Congress. Still more were received from friends and acquaintances—from former political supporters and opponents. But most of all, perhaps, were the letters from utter strangers, with here and there a few that were very ungrammatical and misspelled, but that nevertheless bore witness to their belief in Father as a man of the people.

Father had not reached the office until almost ten-thirty, and he was able only hurriedly to read his mail before the newspapermen arrived at eleven for his "traditional birthday interview."

Of course their questions began with politics, but he brushed the subject aside.

"The great big interest in the minds of the people today," he remarked, "is the war. Let's polish off Adolph and Hirohito first. Then we can go back to politics."

Typically he had a cigar in his mouth as he talked, and of the many gifts stacked on and about his desk, a large percentage were boxes of cigars. For years, as reporters knew, he had smoked a dozen or more a day, but had recently cut down the number.

"The doctor said three a day," he replied in answer to a question, "but I amended that and made it four. And then I always sneak one, so that's five."

Asked about a possible fourth term for the President, he shook his head.

"I don't know anything about it," he replied, "and I think it's not well to talk about it now."

He was asked about the hundreds of birthday greetings, and especially about two birthday cakes he had received—one from the employees of the Beekman Street Hospital and one from the Empire State Club.

"I'll take the cakes home tonight," he said. "There will be thirteen grandchildren there, and two cakes won't be too much. There is a fourteenth grandchild," he added, "but he's only nine months old and can't eat cake."

"Retire?" he asked in answer to a question. "From what? As a matter of fact, I haven't given it a thought. Anyway, a man is better off working than loafing around."

But these were mere preliminaries. The event of the day was the reception that had been arranged by the Archbishop's Committee of the Laity.

Held late in the afternoon at the Empire State Club, it was attended by hundreds of members of the committee. Dignitaries of the Church were there, along with scores of leaders in finance, business, education, and public life.

John A. Coleman, chairman of the board of governors of the New York Stock Exchange and executive chairman of the Archbishop's Committee, presided. A special apostolic benediction from His Holiness Pope Pius XII was imparted to Father in a letter from the Most Reverend Amleto G. Cicognani, apostolic delegate to the United States.

"I am pleased to inform you," the letter read, "that on this happy occasion . . . our Most Holy Father, Pope Pius XII, has very graciously deigned to impart to you his special Apostolic Benediction. As a particular mark of paternal benevolence, it is the express wish of His Holiness that this Blessing should be shared in by Mrs. Smith and by all members of your family who will join you in observing this joyous anniversary. In thus imparting this Blessing, His Holiness wishes to afford you an expression of his profound appreciation of the outstanding example of Catholicity which you have never failed to give in all your appearances in public life, while he prays that his Apostolic Benediction will be but a pledge of the rich and lasting graces with which Almighty God will reward the unswerving loyalty to Faith and Church which have so characterized your private and public life."

Archbishop Spellman (now Cardinal Spellman) first read this letter, and then referred to Father as one "who has served his country well, and in serving his country he has also nobly served his God."

Then the Archbishop added, "Alfred E. Smith, the man, the American, the patriot, and the Catholic, has been an exemplification in one person of all that is noblest in man, in an American, in a patriot, and in a Catholic."

My brother Alfred, who was a captain in the Army, had telephoned from Texas three or four evenings before. It had been impossible for him to be in New York for Christmas, but now, having talked to Father and Mother, he asked for me.

"Listen," he said when I had answered, "don't let Mother and Pop know what I'm telling you."

"What do you mean?" I asked.

"Well, I couldn't get leave to be away over Christmas," he replied, "but I'm due for a three-day pass on the twenty-ninth and I'll be there and surprise him on his birthday."

Here was news that would delight both Mother and Father. Still, they were within six feet of the telephone, and this was to be a surprise, so I was forced to reply in my most doleful tones.

"Oh, Alfred, I'm so sorry," I told him, hoping that he, at least, would not misunderstand.

"I can't get there," he went on, "until sometime in the evening——"

"Isn't that too bad?" I interrupted.

"—but I'll make it," he continued. "Only don't let them know I'm coming."

The early-winter evening had fallen by the time Father returned to his office and prepared to leave for home. The soberness that Mary Carr had noted in his manner that morning had disappeared, but his usual blunt simplicity had apparently not replaced it. Perhaps, in that strangely naïve way he sometimes had, he was marveling at the friendliness with which he was surrounded and at the turn of fortune that had brought him where he was. His life had certainly not been without its disappointments, but I cannot believe that any of them were in his mind just then. And thirty minutes later, when friends had set him down at 820 Fifth Avenue along with two very large and well-boxed birthday cakes and a considerable assortment of other packages, he was all but inundated by a veritable horde of grandchildren, and by eleven other members of the family as well.

With only two exceptions the entire immediate family was there, and Aunt Mamie, along with our cousins Mr. and Mrs. William Frey and their two children, were present also. Only my husband, who was in Naples, and my brother Alfred, who had not yet arrived, were missing. And such a gathering, as anyone will realize, is enough to place certain strains on a New York City apartment.

Before dinner a group of photographers came in, and with much effort and expenditure of time we were arranged more or less to their satisfaction. But just as the photographer in chief was about to press the button, we heard a sound in the hall and turned to see Alfred, Jr., standing in the doorway.

"Hello, everybody," he shouted with his uniform cap in the air, and it was all of half an hour before the photographers were able to complete their work and leave.

Dinner was something of a problem, for in addition to twenty-six members of the family, a few intimate friends were included. Even Father's task of cutting two birthday cakes was far from simple. Ultimately, though with the dining room something of a shambles, it was over, and Father, who had apparently begun that day a little troubled by having reached the age of three score years and ten, ended it, I am sure, in the belief that no one could ever have had a happier birthday.

"I cannot think," he had said at the reception that afternoon, "of any birthday presents more welcome than the words of the Holy Father, of Archbishop Spellman, and Mr. Burke."

But there were many more that touched him just as deeply. In a thousand ways, and from strangers even more often than from friends, the affection in which he was held came to him from all across the nation. As the New York *Herald-Tribune* put it in an editorial:

"We join the President, the Pontiff, the Governors who preceded him at Albany and innumerable friends in best wishes for a happy continuance of a long and useful life."

But that "long and useful life" was almost over.

A little more than four months from the time of that very happy birthday Mother died after an illness of five weeks, and five months later Father died.

"He was a simple man," said his friend John Burke in an address the following spring. "There was nothing complex about him. He seems to have been one of those rare beings blessed by God with an instinctive sense of the eternal verities."

"He was the most devoutly pious man I ever knew," Judge Proskauer said in a memorial address over the radio. "He gave no mere mouth service to the great Catholic religion which he professed, but utter, complete, and unswerving devotion. That was the path on which he chose to walk humbly with his God, and he gave of himself unstintingly to advance this spiritual cause in which he so devoutly believed. But he knew full well that other men trod on other paths, and I often heard him say how much he wished that every man would yield allegiance to some creed of worship and make this world a common brotherhood of man under a common fatherhood of God."

I know that where Father is concerned I cannot hope to be either analytical or objective. His virtues are not for me to measure. His faults—for, being human, he must have had them—I never was able to see. Even after all these years William Wordsworth's words seem to me to fit him.

> This is the Happy Warrior; this is he
> Whom every Man in arms should wish to be.

INDEX